WHAT PRIZE AWAITS US

WHAT PRIZE AWAITS US

Letters from Guatemala

BERNICE KITA

ORBIS BOOKS

Maryknoll, New York 10545

Third Printing, March 1990

The Catholic Foreign Mission Society of America (Maryknoll) recruits and trains people for overseas missionary service. Through Orbis Books Maryknoll aims to foster the international dialogue that is essential to mission. The books published, however, reflect the opinions of their authors and are not meant to represent the official position of the society.

Published by Orbis Books, Maryknoll, NY 10545
Manufactured in the United States of America

Manuscript editor: Joyce Rappaport

LIBRARY OF CONGRESS
Library of Congress Cataloging-in-Publication Data

Kita, Bernice.
    What prize awaits us: letters from Guatemala/Bernice Kita:
foreword by Penny Lernoux.
        p.   cm.
    ISBN 0-88344-273-6 (pbk.)
    1. Kita, Bernice—Correspondence.   2. Maryknoll Sisters—
Guatemala—Correspondence.   3. Maryknoll Sisters—Missions—
Guatemala—History—20th century.   4. Cakchikel Indians—Missions—
History—20th century.   5. Indians of Central America—Guatemala—
Missions—History—20th century.   6. Persecution—Guatemala—
History—20th century.   7. Guatemala—Church history—20th century.
8. Guatemala—Politics and government—1945-1985.   I. Title.
BV2843.G9K585 1988
266′.27281—dc19
[B]
                                                                88-17842
                                                                      CIP

*I lovingly dedicate this work
to my parents, Helen and John,
from whom I learned justice and compassion,
and
to my friend, Gerry,
with whom I shared a longing
for a just and compassionate world.*

Pescador de Gente
("Fisher of People")

You have come to the water's edge,
Seeking not the wise or rich,
But only that I follow you.

Lord, you have looked in my eyes.
Smiling, you have spoken my name.
On the sand I have left my boat
To seek with you another sea.

You know well what I have,
In my little boat, neither gold nor sword,
But this net, and the work of my hands.

You need my hands,
My weariness, that others might rest,
My love, that wants to go on loving.

You, Fisher of other waters,
Eternal Desire of souls who seek you,
Good Friend, for thus you call me.

Lord, you have looked in my eyes.
Smiling, you have spoken my name.
On the sand I have left my boat
To seek with you another sea.

Contents

Foreword

by Penny Lernoux

It's said that one picture is worth ten thousand words, and that is especially so, I think, of events in the Third World. We read about the carnage and starvation, about the statistics of death, but often the words are meaningless because we cannot feel the pain and desperation. Yet even the photos often seem otherworldly—the pictures of children with swollen bellies who are dying of hunger; the piles of corpses of men and women massacred by the local military—because they are so far removed from our own reality.

That is why this book is so remarkable: It gives us a picture that is more illuminating than any photo, by enabling us to smell, hear, and touch that other world despite our vastly different realities. It does so not through statistical tables or long descriptions of political and economic systems but through the most intimate form of communication—the personal letter. These letters, written by an American nun to her parents and another Sister, describe life in a remote Guatemalan village in the late 1970's and early 1980's when the Catholic Church suffered such severe persecution that it literally became a church of the catacombs. Although the book provides a brief historical overview, it is primarily a story of the "little and unknown" Indian peasants, the *campesinos* who comprise a majority of the population, and the small details that make up their daily lives—the grindings of cornmeal for tortillas, the weaving of cloth, the awakening of faith, and the acceptance of martyrdom. Sometimes the letters are amusing; often, they are indignant. But the principal theme is a deepening of faith as the writer learns to appreciate the peasants' religious insights and wisdom. Like many other U.S. missionaries, she went to Latin America to share her faith with the poor, only to find herself converted by the poor to a deeper understanding of the gospel.

Despite the poverty and repression suffered by the Indians, these stories glow with love, courage, and faith. Here is a community that has preserved values that we, in more materialistic societies, have lost. Though most are illiterate or can barely read, the Indians have a deeper understanding of the Bible than many better-educated Christians because they live the biblical parables. For example, in discussing the story about the rich man whose harvest was so abundant that he lacked sufficient storage space for it, an Indian catechist explains that his people do not have that problem because they never have surplus of corn. Anything extra is shared with widows, the old, and the infirm. "And even if we don't have a surplus," he says, "we look out for those who have none. I think that's what God would want us to do."

What God wants is the subject of many meetings with the parish's fifty catechists, particularly when army persecution makes such work hazardous. Worried that the Indians might be killed for teaching the people about their faith, Sr. Bernice and her coworker tell them the Sisters will stop Bible study classes and cease any contact if they wish. But the catechists vow to continue their work despite the danger to themselves and their families. The Indians' determination not to give up is itself an act of faith. The villagers defy hunger, death, bandits, the military and the guerrillas in order to survive. In such a society a child's first birthday is a time of special celebration—not with cake, ice cream, and presents but with prayers of thanksgiving to God.

In a letter to her parents, the writer tells her mother that, if people ask what her daughter does for a living, she should tell them, "She's present." We are present with her through all the small tribulations and joys—even the frustrating process of growing a vegetable garden—as well as the sorrows caused by the deaths of so many friends. But from death comes life. Just as the vegetable garden eventually flourished, the blood of martyrs has spread Christ's message and the hope of resurrection in Guatemala.

Acknowledgments

A packet of letters doesn't become a book without help. I am grateful to the friends who helped me in the transformation: Dr. Marc Ellis, Director of the Maryknoll Institute for Justice and Peace, who was the first to say, "These letters ought to be published," and who helped me start the process; Phillip Wearne, Anne Nelson, and George Black, talented writers and keen Central American analysts, who convinced me to take this big step and who offered valuable advice along the way; Sandy Galazin, Luise Ahrens, Dolores Rosso, and Jeanne Marie Lyons, my sisters at Maryknoll, New York, who encouraged and advised me in the early, shaky stages; the Maryknoll Sisters in Guatemala, who offered me their trust and support; Robert Gormley, Executive Director of Orbis Books, who guided me in turning a stack of letters into a manuscript, and Robert Ellsberg, Editor-in-Chief, who helped me turn a raw manuscript into a finished book; Lori and the people of San Jerónimo, who shared life with me for many years, and whose stories filled my letters; my mother, Helen, and my friend, Gerry, who saved all my letters, keeping the memories they held from fading, and making this book possible.

Preface

When I was a little girl, my father had a custom that significantly touched my life: he annually made a weekend retreat. We four children looked forward eagerly to his return on Sunday afternoon not only because we missed him, but also because of the surprise we knew he would bring us. In what became a family ritual, we would gather around his suitcase, which lay on the dining room table. As we watched expectantly, he would slowly open the bag, reach in, and pull out a gift for each of us. Once he brought me a medal, another time, a pink rosary. But my very favorite gift of all was a small square booklet on the lives of the saints.

I cannot remember all the saints in that little book, but I know that two of them made a lasting impression and became my special models and friends. They were the Roman martyrs Tarcicius and Sebastian, ordinary people who lived in extraordinary times. Tarcicius was a young boy who risked his life carrying the Eucharist to Christians in hiding until he was caught and killed. Sebastian was a soldier who encouraged persecuted Christians to remain steadfast in following Jesus. He, too, was finally caught and killed. Their stories were simple tales of courage and faith in the face of persecution and death; their lives of discipleship were crowned with martyrdom. I prayed to these friends each night, asking them to give me the courage to follow Jesus as faithfully, regardless of the consequences. It was a fairly safe prayer to make in the United States of America when I was growing up.

As I matured and the demands and challenges of the real world absorbed my attention, I put my martyr friends away with the toys of childhood. I believed that the age of persecution and martyrdom had long since passed. I couldn't know then that one day, in a distant land, people like Tarcicius and Sebastian would be my friends; that I would walk behind many a martyr's coffin; and that *I* would live through a persecution rivaling those of Ancient Rome.

Many years later, as a missioner, I went to live in a remote Mayan Indian town in the Guatemalan highlands. Those native people had been baptized as infants but knew little of their Catholic faith. They requested that missionary Sisters live in their town and teach them. They wanted to know what God had to say to them in the Bible, and they wanted to live that message. They had a deep hunger for God.

It was a good time for me to begin such a work of pastoral presence and sharing of faith. I already had many years of mission experience in that Central American country and felt ready to accept this new challenge. I was eager to share life and faith with this community, a people who were strikingly similar to the rural folk whom Jesus himself addressed 2000 years ago. With another Maryknoll Sister, I moved into the isolated setting, started to learn the Indian language, and began growing in my understanding and appreciation of the people and their culture.

As I came to share in the life of that small community, I wrote about it to my family. In the beginning, my letters were filled with descriptions as I explored the town, visited neighbors, watched people work, and witnessed with wonder the customs and rituals of the community. As I came to know the people as neighbors and friends, I wrote about them and repeated the stories they told me. Some of the stories were funny and others were sad; they described celebrations and tragedies; they recounted the unusual and the ordinary events of daily life.

When I started living in the town, Guatemala was experiencing a period of relative peace. But peace in that troubled country is rare. The powerful few have always controlled the vast majority through the selective use of violence. Periodically, when the oppression has become too much to bear, resistance or open rebellion has erupted, only to be met by increased violence. A new cycle of oppression and repression began soon after we initiated Bible study classes with local teachers of religion, called catechists. We could feel death and destruction seeping into our lives as daily newscasts reported the growing violence. Eventually, some of the victims' names were familiar in the town. They were labor leaders, political figures, student volunteers, schoolteachers, other catechists, and priests.

We studied the Word of God in this unique and frightening moment in our lives and understood God's message in new, soul-scorching ways. While exploring the story of creation, we learned of the dignity of each person; we also learned of the first murder. We acted out little plays on the life of Moses at a time when popular leaders in Guatemala were, like Moses, singled out for slaughter. We read about the kings and prophets of Israel while all around us the powerful in the nation were abusing their power and killing many prophets who had cried out for justice in the land. We studied the life and message of Jesus, knowing that the choice to follow as his disciples could well be a life-or-death decision; we all knew of Church people who had recently lost their lives. The reason for the kidnapping and killing of church workers, from rural catechists to parish priests, was stated quite simply by one of my catechist friends: "They are killing you missioners because you are teaching us. And they are killing us because we teach what we have learned. When the missioners came we didn't even know how to read. You taught us to read and we studied the Word of God in the Bible. You taught us that God gave us human dignity, and we learned to defend our rights. You taught us to organize, and we began to work together for a better life. These new ideas frighten the powerful. They don't want the poor to learn any more, so they kill *us*." And so, by the time we came to study about the early Church with its martyrs like Tarcicius and Sebastian, we ourselves had become a persecuted Church of the Catacombs.

In late 1980, I began writing to Gerry McGinn, a Dominican Sister, who had come to the town as a summer volunteer. She arrived a complete stranger and left a dedicated friend. During this period, my letters reflected the confusion, fear, and anger as well as the faith, love, and courage arising in us all because of the virulent persecution that was unleashed like a raging storm by forces beyond our ken or control. I had to write those letters because the story had to be told: for the people, that their courage and suffering not be ignored; for my family and friends, that they might be moved to awareness and action on behalf of the persecuted people; for myself, to enable me to continue with the people through this time of testing by speaking what was in my mind and heart, thus releasing my psychic energy, and preserving my sanity.

People grow through trial or they are crushed by it. Hope is engendered or it is lost forever; faith either deepens or it dissolves. I witnessed among the townspeople much human weakness during the persecution. But I also witnessed an incredible increase in their faith, their hope, and their love of neighbor.

This, then, is the story of a people in time of persecution. It is not a tale with an end, because the persecution continues today in subtler forms. It is mainly the story of my friends and neighbors in that isolated town in the Guatemalan highlands between 1977 and 1983 as recorded in my letters. And because I shared with them for many years their food, their homes, their joys and sorrows, their hopes and fears and pain, it is also my story. It is a story of a dominated people with indomitable faith, a faith rooted in a fertile soil watered by the blood of martyrs. It is a story that needs to be told to give us all hope.

Maryknoll, New York
March 1987

Introduction

"In fourteen hundred ninety-two, Columbus sailed the ocean blue . . ." and irrevocably changed life for the native peoples whose land he claimed for Spain. In the wake of the Niña, the Pinta, and the Santa Maria, came sailing ships loaded with horses, cannons, gunpowder and armored soldiers who were experts in the art of war. Traveling the Central American isthmus, the Spaniards encountered almost everything nature had to offer: lush jungles and barren deserts; cool highlands and steamy lowlands; majestic volcanoes and black, sandy beaches; exotic animals and luscious fruits. But these men were not tourists; they were conquerors who accomplished their threefold task with brutal efficiency. They subdued the native population, imposed on them the rule of Spain, and claimed a share of wealth as payment for their service to the king.

The wealth the invaders sought was gold and silver, a scarce commodity in Central America. The disappointed conquerors had to content themselves with exploiting the area's main resources, the land and the people. They forcibly settled the natives in Spanish-style towns on enormous estates carved out of the fertile land. Each town was responsible for supplying free labor for a portion of the estate, producing whatever Spain's economy dictated. The natives, called "Indians" by their Spanish masters, were permitted to cultivate their traditional crops of corn and beans on the land surrounding their towns. From that time on, the Indians would constitute a reliable labor pool producing enormous wealth for Spain.

In addition to Spanish government, language, and economy, the conquerors brought the Spanish religion, Roman Catholicism. Catholic missionaries from Spain instructed and baptized whole populations. Some missionaries came to recognize the cruel exploitation of the natives by the Spaniards and urged the king to pass laws to protect them. Meanwhile, landlords lobbied for ever more control of the labor force. Landowners and clergy occasionally clashed over the proper role of the Church in the colony, and some missionaries lost their lives for defending the rights of the Indian people.

The five provinces of the Central American Colony declared their independence from Spain in 1821, and each eventually proclaimed itself a Republic. Guatemala had the largest native Indian population, but nothing changed for them but their masters. Guatemalans of Spanish ancestry held the power tightly in their hands.

In the late 1870's, in order to move the country into the modern capitalist economy of the West, President Justo Rufino Barrios decided that coffee would be the major crop of the country. With the stroke of a pen he initiated a massive "land reform" to benefit the already wealthy plantation owners and European coffee growers: he simply declared that all communal lands of the Indian towns had to be privately owned. Because the Indians were too poor to buy their communal land, it was sold to the coffee planters. Indians now had to work for slave wages on the coffee plantations in order to buy their own corn. The land reform also drastically affected the Church, which lost all its land and buildings to the state. To break the remaining power of the Church, the anticlerical Liberal government expelled all foreign clergy. Fewer than 120 Guatemalan priests, many sick and old, were left to serve the entire population. Most of these priests remained in the cities, leaving the rural population to its own resources. The situation involving anticlerical governments, dependency of the Catholic Church, and abandonment of the rural population remained essentially unchanged for the next seventy years.

With the overthrow of the dictator, Jorge Ubico, in 1944, hope for true democracy swept across the land. Schoolteacher-president Juan José Arévalo abolished forced Indian labor, established a minimum wage, fostered popular organizations like labor unions and student groups, and encouraged political parties to form in a wide spectrum of positions, from extreme right to Communist. His successor, Jacobo Arbenz, intended to carry the modernization even further with a land-reform program aimed at returning idle land to the landless poor. The plan, affecting both local landowners and the U.S.-owned United Fruit Company, proved to be his undoing. The landowners, the Catholic Church, and the United States all feared the specter of Communism in Guatemala. Each contributed to the downfall of the Arbenz government, which finally fell through a CIA-sponsored coup in 1954.

The leader of the coup, Col. Carlos Castillo Armas, was hailed as a savior by many, including the Archbishop of Guatemala City, Mariano Rossell. Church and State buried the anticlerical hatchet and apparent friendship reigned. A new constitution returned to the Church some of its property and privilege, and the government encouraged the influx of missionaries from Europe and the United States, realizing that a strong anti-Communist Church would be a great political ally.

But the Archbishop saw the missionaries' role in a different light. He aligned himself with the stand taken by the South American Bishops in 1955. They had called the elevation of the needy class a moral duty, and urged priests to "strive intensely to form a lively and effective social awareness." They strongly encouraged the creation of centers for the teaching of the Church's social doctrine, and stressed the Church's duty to take the necessary care of indigenous peoples. Foreign missionaries responded to the invitation from Guatemala. Within twelve years of the fall of Arbenz, there were about 531 priests in the country, only ninety-seven of whom were Guatemalans. Even more impressive, of the 805 religious women in the country, all but 100 were foreigners.

Prior to the arrival of this new wave of missionaries, the Indians, who had been pushed for centuries to the fringes of national life and deprived of clergy, had turned their collective back on the outside world. They had developed a life and culture which, while poor in material possessions, was rich in tradition and immersed in religion. They had evolved their own town religion, based on sixteenth-century Spanish Catholicism, obligatory religious service to the town, and pre-Hispanic religious beliefs and practices. They were accustomed to hiring a priest for a fiesta to celebrate Mass and to baptize their children. They would feed him, pay him, and send him on his way until the next year. The town's own religious life would continue throughout the year with rituals, prayers, processions, marriages, funerals, and festivities. The Indians knew they were Catholics, which for many meant being conscientious about following their town's annual cycle of religious activity.

Into this tightly integrated religious world came the missionaries, eager to save the native people from their "pagan" ways, to reconvert them to the Catholic Faith and, incidentally, to usher them into the modern world. Not surprisingly, they were met with some resistance. Not all Indians wanted to be "saved" by these foreigners. But many of the missionaries brought with them a tool uniquely suited to the Indian culture. It was a highly structured lay movement of involvement in the doctrinal teaching and social action of the Church. This movement became the motor force behind much of the organization and empowerment of many Indian communities, who made it their brand of Catholicism: It was called Rural Catholic Action.

The brand of religion brought by the missionaries appealed to many of the Indians. It fit some of their cultural and communal needs while providing new opportunities for personal growth. Because it was brought by the priests, members of Rural Catholic Action felt safely inside the Catholic fold, even though they were ostracized at first by other townsfolk. Catholic Action required very little expenditure and took only a few hours a week, in contrast to the huge expenses and years of service demanded by traditional town religion. The Indians' strong cultural need to serve the community was met in Catholic Action by a parallel system of elected offices and service roles. Many people were attracted to Catholic Action because in it they could avoid obligatory ritual drinking, an important part of town religion and a cause of the alcoholism found in epidemic proportions in the Indian communities. Finally, the missionaries brought education: new ideas and skills, opportunity to learn to read, and a study of the Bible. For those Indian people who felt oppressed by the unquestioning obedience to tradition required by their ancestral religion, Catholic Action was a breath of fresh air. Eventually, the storm of antagonism toward Catholic Action by the followers of the traditional town religion yielded to a truce. Traditionalists continued in their old ways, but Catholic Action continued to grow. Joining Catholic Action signified a conversion for its members that committed them to a Christian response to life, community needs, and religious practice.

On February 4, 1976, a violent earthquake shook almost the entire country of Guatemala. Those areas not touched by the physical destruction were deeply affected by the psychological, economic, and social dimensions of the disaster. Over 30,000 people were killed; almost all of them poor, and the great majority, Indians. In response to the suffering and injustice revealed by the earthquake's discrimination against the poor, the Guatemalan Bishops published an unprecedented document called *United in Hope*. The document offered a serious analysis of the political, economic, and social reality of Guatemala and called for change. It also spoke out against government military oppression in a part of the country where "peasants have died for the 'crime' of defending the land they have possessed for a long time . . . ."

With the Church moving steadily forward in its efforts to promote social justice for the poor, and the government moving to promote the welfare of the powerful at the expense of the poor, the scene was set for confrontation and conflict. The forceful denunciation of *United in Hope* set the entire Catholic Church on a collision course with the centers of power in Guatemala. The poor Indian catechist and the professional missionary shared a common challenge to remain faithful in the face of the ensuing persecution.

Chapter One

The Calm Before the Storm
January 1977–June 1978

THE TOWN

"Don't fall!" That's what the people in San Jerónimo say when they part. "Don't fall!" because everything is either up or down the mountainside from where one happens to be at the moment. The ledges alongside the adobe houses are narrow, and the footpaths are steep and slippery. Walking can be dangerous, even for folks raised here. But, steep or not, San Jerónimo is home for these Guatemalan Indians, and they've learned to make the best of it.

Vicente and Marcela were born here over fifty years ago. They say that things haven't changed much in all that time. Of course, there is now a road into town, with bus service to the capital. There is also a pure water system and electricity for those who choose and can afford to hook up to it. The tiers of roofs one views when climbing the mountainside are almost all of corrugated aluminum, which replaced the traditional thatch because it was more durable and less expensive. But the lives of the people haven't been affected much by modernization, and, living on a mountainside as they do, certain things are done in exactly the same way as they were by their ancestors.

Almost everyone in town wears the traditional native dress, typical of their own town and no other, and woven by the women. The children of the town still go barefoot. It's easier for them to grip the ground with their toes as they scamper up and down and

1

all around, screaming and chasing each other in their games of tag.

When Vicente was just three years old, he was quite confident about going to visit his grandmother who lived several levels up from his house. By the time he was five, he was going with his parents to the religious fiestas of the villages on top of the mountain, walking all the way. Now his grandchildren accompany him on the way to those fiestas. Walking far, uphill and down, will be an integral part of their lives.

By the time boys here reach the age of nine, they are testing their strength, carrying bundles on their backs or hauling soft drinks, at five cents a case, from the delivery truck up the hill to the stores. They vie with each other and brag about how much they can carry. Vicente's youngest grandson, Santos, is at this stage. His fifteen-year-old brother, Diego, has long since graduated from such games. He uses the *mecapal,* a leather head strap that, together with a length of strong rope, will be his constant companion now that he has taken on the duties of a man.

To carry a hundred-pound bag of fertilizer up to his father's fields, Diego first arranges the ropes from his *mecapal* carefully around the sack. Then he squats and pulls the *mecapal* over the crown of his head. With his father lifting the sack, Diego stands and bends over, shifting the sack until it rests firmly on his back. Finally, with his head bent and neck muscles straining, Diego begins the two-hour trek up to the fields. His father follows, carrying a load of 125 pounds. When Diego grows to manhood, both he and his father will carry up to 150 pounds down the mountain, though neither man will ever weigh much more than 100 pounds himself. Although the path is familiar, they walk cautiously. A misstep or a loss of balance near the edge could be fatal.

While Vicente and the other men from town walk great distances to their daily work and wear leather sandals to clamber up the rocky path, Marcela, like the other women in town, goes about her daily chores barefoot. Bringing water from the fountain, taking corn to be ground at the mill, or making purchases at the local market don't take her far from home. A local custom views the wearing of shoes by women as pretentious. And, because the plastic shoes that are available are hot and often painful to wear, most women prefer going barefoot. However, many women do own a pair of shoes. Marcella keeps her black plastic sandals in the family trunk. She pulls them out, along with her best clothes, on special occasions. When she wears them, she feels really "dressed up." But she will still climb the mountain barefoot and only put her shoes on when she gets to the fiesta.

A child sometimes falls over the edge of the family's tiny backyard to the next level. A pregnant woman occasionally falls on leaving the house and loses her baby. A man at times loses his footing while farming the steep mountainside and falls out of his field. But that's part of life, and death, in San Jerónimo. "Don't fall!"

LETTERS

San Jerónimo
February 23, 1977

Dear Mom and Dad,

We've been in our new home for a week, but I am just now able to feel settled in my tiny room with my bed, desk, and chair in place, the bookcase up, and my typewriter open for business. This has been a hectic, wonderful week!

Very early last Wednesday morning Lori and I loaded all our belongings into a rented, open truck, climbed in next to the driver, and took off for San Jerónimo. We had waited so long for this day that, even at five A.M., we were excited. The president of the parish Catholic Action Committee had assured us that the builders would have our house (actually just a few rooms) ready for us to move into the week before, but we gave them five extra days, just in case. We drove about 100 miles that morning with our furniture and belongings loaded high and tied down with lots of rope. Only the major highways are paved, so our trip was a mostly bumpy, dusty, four-hour ride.

A lookout in the church tower spotted our truck long before we arrived, and the bell was ringing a welcome as we pulled in. A crowd of men, women, and children greeted us as we stepped from the truck. They were dressed in their bright native garb, typical of the town. It was a tumultuous welcome. While Victor, the Catholic

Action president, warmly greeted us and asked about our trip, men were scrambling up on the truck and handing our things down to the eager, outstretched hands of women and children. We didn't have much by U.S. standards, but it seemed to me an awful lot to have to carry up that steep, winding hill to our new home. Yet the community worked quickly and, before I could get my camera out to record the big moment, a line of red-bloused, blue-skirted women with boxes on their heads, and barefoot children with luggage on their backs, was winding its way up the hill. The men waited until the heavy furniture was accessible, and then, using ropes tied to leather head straps, they carried the beds, desks, refrigerator, and chairs up that hill. I later learned that they didn't consider our things heavy at all compared with the usual hundred-pound loads they must carry much farther up the mountain to their fields.

I huffed and puffed my way up the hill to the cement block house (the town is over 5000 feet above sea level). I looked in and my heart sank. The house had just been finished—JUST! In fact, a carpenter was still trying to hang the front door. The floor and interior brick walls were covered with a thick coating of fine red dust: the bricklayer had diligently rubbed the mortar off the bricks early that morning. All over the windowpanes were the installers' fingerprints. Through the dust in the air I smelled fresh cement, wood shavings, and soft putty. The house was *finished,* but hardly liveable.

Victor saw my dismay and hastened to tell us that a crew of girls from the parish ''Hijas de María'' (Daughters of Mary) would help us make the house more liveable. Lori can organize any group into a work crew, so we had a good time, sweeping, coughing, laughing, scrubbing, and getting to know each other a little. They spoke practically no Spanish, and we spoke practically no Cakchikel, but somehow we understood each other. In the meantime, all our belongings were stored in the back of the parish hall, guarded by two young men. By nightfall we were grateful to have the house clean enough to set up our beds and prepare a simple meal. We looked forward to getting to bed early after the exhaustion and exhilaration of the day.

What we hadn't counted on, though, was the royal welcome that had been planned for us for weeks in advance. Around six P.M., Lori answered a knock at the door. There stood four men, the whole parish committee. She invited them in but couldn't offer them seats because the chairs were still stacked up in the hall. They had come to invite us to a "Bienvenida," a welcoming program in the hall at seven.

At about six-thirty, a group of young guitarists began to play and sing in church, and their music was broadcast to the whole town through a loudspeaker in the church tower. That advised the towns-folk that everyone had a half hour to finish supper and chores before the program started. Actually, they had about an hour, because nothing here starts on schedule. Just before the program began, the Hijas de María came to escort us to our seats of honor in the hall. These were a few rough wooden benches facing a hastily constructed platform of unmatched boards tied onto sawhorses. Most of the people stood behind the benches, and the little kids sat and squirmed on the floor in front of us.

The program opened with words of welcome from Victor, the president. These were followed by greetings from the vice-president, Antonio, followed by similar words by Marcos, the secretary, and Vicente, the treasurer. That took about twenty minutes. Then the young people took over and put on an entertainment program of songs, poems, music, contests, and jokes (which they thought immensely funny but which I didn't get). It was simple and delightful. The evening ended with Rosario, president of the women's group, giving a little speech in Cakchikel and presenting us with beautiful, hand-woven blouses, just like the ones worn by all the women in town. I had a wonderful, warm feeling of sudden belonging.

The next few days were a blur of meeting and greeting visitors as they came to welcome us. They brought gifts of sweet rolls, squash, black beans, sugar, coffee, oranges, carrots, onions, or eggs. In between the many times a day we sat with visitors drinking coffee and sharing bread, Lori and I managed to settle the rest of our belongings into our "shoebox" house (30×12 feet) and began to feel at home. Lori—the seamstress in our household—whipped up some drapes from old bedspreads, while I tended to the carpentry needs, sanding and varnishing the kitchen cabinets. I really couldn't relax until we had some curtains on our three windows, because they quickly became stopping points for the girls on their way to the corn-grinding mill and for the teenaged church-bell ringers who flirted with them. I didn't mind it much during the day, but at five A.M., it is disconcerting to waken to a smiling face or two peering in at me.

On Sunday, the priest, Fr. Martín, came from a nearby town for Mass and we worshipped for the first time together with our new neighbors, whose yearning to learn about their religion brought us here. For years they had badgered the bishop to send them Sisters who could *live* in their town and teach them their religion, and help them understand God's message in the Bible. And finally, here we are. Our dream and theirs have converged. And now we will all work together on fulfilling the dream of not only knowing what our religion teaches, but also of living it in our lives and sharing our faith and life with others.

March 13, 1977

We now have a kitten we call "Balam," which means *tiger* in Cakchikel. She is at the playful/curious stage, and right now is sitting on the window sill intently watching a fly climb up the window pane. The kitten was Lori's idea, to keep our house rodent-free. From my visits around town, I see that a cat is standard equipment here in San Jerónimo. We already have orders for kittens from her first litter. Little kids come by and ask to play with Balam, and some adult neighbors who drop by ask about her before asking about us! One frequent visitor and fountain of information is a gentle, white-haired old man named Pedro Cumes, who comes by for coffee and reminiscing.

We first met Pedro a few days after we moved in. He came to bring us a gift of five sweet rolls and to welcome us.

"Oh, I am so happy you came to live with us, to teach us. We never had study before. Oh, we had study when the Spanish priests came over twenty years ago. But that was different. They told us that we couldn't be Catholics if we didn't study and get married in the Church. Most people in town were angry with the priests because they tried to change our religious practices. They even got the keys away from the town sacristans who were in charge of the church—imagine! They said it was wrong to have the marimba playing and people dancing and getting drunk in church during the fiesta celebrations. Oh, there were many angry meetings with the town authorities and the priests.'' He shook his head. ''Things are so different now,'' he said with a smile.

Eager to learn more, we invited him to join us for coffee and rolls. I asked Pedro how he had come to be a member of Catholic Action, which is the movement the Spanish priests brought in the '50s to rekindle the Catholic life in the highlands. ''Well, my wife, Micaela, and I talked about what these new priests said. We had a home and children. We have our own traditional ways, and according to them, we thought we were married. Now the priests said we weren't! That troubled us. We wanted to do what was right. We didn't know about the sacrament they called 'matrimony.' We decided that we wanted to be *matrimonied*.'' (I tried not to smile, because he was *so* serious.)

''It was hard,'' he continued. ''Only twelve couples from here went to study with the priests. Many townsfolk said we were betraying our ancestors and being disloyal by accepting the foreigners' teachings. 'We are already Catholics,' many said to us. 'We were baptized as babies, weren't we? We celebrate the patronal fiestas and Holy Week. We pay the priest to come for Mass at those times and for All Souls' Day. That's enough. We don't need them or their teachings for anything else. We have our own religious customs all year long, and the confradías [religious brotherhoods] are in charge. Why do you want to change that?' And you know what they did? They threw us all in jail! It took an order from the governor to release us! But we did not fight back. We tried to live as the priests taught us. We all got married together at Mass in this church, and there were many people from town at that mass. Some had already said they, too, wanted to study to be matrimonied. Others just came to watch. But it was a joyous time for us twelve couples. The priest called us the Twelve Apostles. We each had the task of teaching five other families what we learned. That's how Catholic Action grew here. Now we are more than half the town. And for most of us who accepted the priests' teaching, life is better.''

I looked with new respect at Pedro as he dunked his roll in the coffee. He and Micaela and the other ''Apostles'' had lived, like the early Christians, through a religious persecution.

It's an amazing story, and one we need to know to guide us in our own sensitivity to town life and customs. The old, traditional ways are very much a part of life today and are a definite, integral part of Indian identity. Yet here, Catholic Action, or Acción Católica, as it is called, is also part of the Catholic Indian identity. We will try to learn more and to respect the old way. In fact, we can take our cues from the members of Acción Católica who have had to work out difficulties. These people have agonized over what to keep and what to let go, what to value and what to avoid. They seem to have come to a good balance, and there isn't much trouble between them and the traditional confradías these days. In fact, the Acción Católica leaders go out of their way to communicate with the confradía leaders to plan some religious festivities together.

I'm speaking from the post-Vatican II concept of the missioner who comes to serve and learn with the people, and who discovers, together with the people, the presence of God in their lives. I have much to learn here about being with the people and learning from them, and I've made a good start with the parish committee, the women's group, and Pedro.

March 26, 1977

We've been in San Jerónimo for a month. It has gone by so quickly. Lori and I have tried to establish a simple rhythm to our days, allowing for visits, emergencies, and other interruptions. (The interruptions are as important as the planned part of our work, because we can respond as neighbors to our new neighbors.) We generally have meals together, taking turns with the cooking. Well, not exactly taking turns. Since Lori has twelve years on me in life, she has had a good deal more practice cooking. She offered to cook during the week, leaving me Saturday and Sunday. We also try to pray together before supper every night. I say "try," because we often have visitors all afternoon. Or we may start to pray, and be interrupted by a knock on the door. It could be a little girl asking us to change some foreign coins to Guatemalan ones. (Tourists frequently pass off their useless change to kids.) Or it could be a neighbor with a need to talk. Or it might be someone on parish business. So our prayer, if we're lucky, consists of a few psalms and the reading of the gospel of the day. If we're *really* lucky, we'll have time to think about the psalms and the reading and to share our thoughts. We end with a prayer that takes in the people and events of the day, as well as you, our families. Last night Lori and I were going over the readings for this morning's Mass with some members of the parish committee. I answered a knock on the door and, lo and behold, there stood the mayor! I was surprised, because he had never been to our house before, so I wondered what was wrong. He said that Mario, one of the schoolteachers, had been drunk for a week and was in very bad shape. Mario finally went to the mayor for help, and the mayor came to us. We suggested he go to the local health worker. But Mario had spent all his money, so we gave the mayor the assurance that we'd pay the bill, and he went away relieved.

Mario himself came a bit later to thank us. He looked so bad, as if he hadn't eaten for days, so we invited him to join us today for dinner. When he's sober, they say, he's an excellent teacher, and he makes up for the time lost by working longer school days and Saturdays, and the children and their parents don't seem to mind.

April 1, 1977

The other day Mario and another teacher, José, paid us a call. This seemed to be an official visit, because they were very formal. They welcomed us to the town in the name of the school. We invited them in, offered them coffee and sweet rolls, and sat talking with them for about an hour.

The gist of their conversation was: "Welcome. We are pleased to have you as an 'official' Catholic presence here in town. We would like to collaborate with you and the Church in anything that will benefit the town and especially the children. And we are sure you would like to collaborate with us in the school, too, as we work for the betterment and the civilization of these Indian children. And, as a matter of fact, we were wondering if you might have some materials we could use in the classrooms—posters, newsprint paper, marking pens, typing paper—these are all things we teachers really need. If you have any extra in all those boxes we saw carried up the hill when you came, we would be grateful for any donation to the school. The government doesn't supply the school with such materials. We have to bring everything we use, even blackboard erasers. The children have no textbooks, poor things, but what can we do? We want to do our best for them and we count on your help.''

Of course, all this was said in a roundabout way, over coffee while we exchanged pleasantries, and it took an hour. The reason they came was clear: they saw us as the rich Americans. We are going to have to work very hard not to give that image much substance. We did not come here for that.

The six schoolteachers and the mayor's male secretary are the only non-Indians in town besides us Sisters. The non-Indian Guatemalans, be they fair-skinned or mestizo, are called *ladinos*. While Guatemala's Indians speak many different languages, the ladinos speak Spanish. Even poor, rural ladinos have a great advantage over the Indian people in this, because it makes education easier. Indian children must learn Spanish before learning anything else in school. Some have reached only third grade by the age of twelve. Many drop out at that age to start taking on adult chores at home or in the fields. There are only three sixth graders in school this year.

A few days later José came back. He seemed in a hurry so I dispensed with the preliminaries and asked what I could do for him. He looked at me eagerly and said: ''Could I watch the big game tomorrow on your TV set?'' ''We don't have a TV set,'' I replied. ''What?'' he asked. ''We don't have a TV set,'' I repeated. He looked around the room almost furtively, searching for the missing box. ''Honest,'' I said with some amusement. ''We don't have one.'' He looked at me with disappointment and said: ''You really don't! You are the first Americans I ever knew who didn't have one!'' I laughed at his surprise and said: ''We don't intend ever to get one, either.''

Only a couple of families in town have TV sets. They are mainly status symbols, because the people can't understand the Spanish programs. Almost every family has a battery-powered radio, though. They pick up Cakchikel language programs and Mexical cowboy music on ''La Voz de Atitlán'' (The Voice of Atitlán), a radio school founded years ago by the U.S. missioners in the parish of Santiago Atitlán.

April 10, 1977

Holy Week here was a new and wonderful experience for me. The week was very full, but I can at least give you highlights.

On Holy Thursday we received a stream of visitors from town and were beneficiaries of their custom of sharing bread and honey with each other. I'm sure it came with the early Spanish missionaries, as did all the rest of the Holy Week customs, but when I asked a few of the visitors the meaning of the custom, they just smiled and said, ''It is our custom for today.'' The visitors were mainly children dressed in their finest clothes, carrying baskets of the traditional Holy Thursday sweet rolls and tiny pitchers of honey. Lori and I could never keep up with giving something back to each family who gave to us, and didn't know the protocol of who gives to whom anyway, so we had to be satisfied with giving a very sincere thanks to the bearer of the gift. We were able to share the bread and honey with all the visitors during the Holy Days and still had some left over—too bad I'm allergic to honey, and couldn't share in that part of the gift. It smelled so good!

The parish committee was in charge of the liturgy for Holy Week. They turned to us for guidance through the maze of unfamiliar details. To tell the truth, we were a bit bewildered by it all, too, but together we managed to get through the Holy Thursday evening Eucharist, complete with the washing of the feet of the Twelve Apostles. The Twelve were very restless little boys dressed in purple robes that were obviously just pulled out from a jumble in a box from last year. No one but us seemed to notice they were wrinkled, torn, and stained, and we tried not to notice too much. Fr. Martín, a kind and likeable Spaniard, lent that foot-washing ceremony the dignity that Christ himself might have given. I was pleased that he was serving our town.

On Good Friday there was a lot of activity in the church for the celebration of the crucifixion. I have never seen anything like it and found it very moving. With ritual handed down for centuries, the people's reverence for the suffering Christ spoke eloquently of their own suffering. At noon they solemnly re-enacted the crucifixion, using a life-sized statue of the Dead Christ. Later they re-enacted the lowering of Christ from the cross. They carried the statue, in a wood and glass coffin, all around the town.

For most people in Latin America, Good Friday is the end of Holy Week. The Resurrection gets very little emphasis in popular religious practice. Here though, Father came for the Easter Vigil and that had lots of people excited about the celebration. Although they find the official liturgy unfamiliar, eventually we hope to help them bridge the gap so they will understand and find meaning in the readings from the Bible and the ceremonies of the liturgy. That's part of why Lori and I are here, at their request. We listen closely to what many people say they want, or need, or hope for. When the time is right, we'll try to incorporate those desires into our courses, which someday they will teach each other, without us.

May 6, 1977

Lori and I are happy that we have finally been able to get someone to help us study the Cakchikel language five days a week. He is a young bright married man with a little two-year old daughter. His name is Eduardo and he is one of the tallest men in town, matching me at 5'5". We have known each other from our first days here, when he was president of the youth group. Eduardo has been traveling a lot, buying typical woven goods here in town and peddling them to tourists elsewhere. But he was grateful to find work closer to home, and we are very lucky to have him working with us. Although he has had only four years of schooling and doesn't know much about grammar, he can explain to us the things we need to know in order to learn his language. The real teaching for his class falls on us, as we have to prepare beforehand what we want to learn, then present it to him in such a way in Spanish that he can give it to us in his language, and then we have to learn it. We are both teachers and pupils in this situation. It's going to be hard, but I'll give it my best effort.

When I began this study, Eduardo said, "There is one sound that is almost impossible for you *Gringos* [Americans] to pronounce. If you can do this"—he demonstrated a *Lkuk* in the back of the throat—"you will have no difficulty with this language of ours. Can you try this sound? *Lkuk*." "*Lkuk*," I repeated. He stared at me, then broke into a grin. "You'll do fine," he said.

May 16, 1977

This is the end of the dry season and we expect a big downpour any day. Right now everything is covered with dust. Walking on the road when a gust of wind comes along or a bus passes is dreadful. You are not only immediately covered with dust and end up choking for air, but the dust is so fine and light that it doesn't settle for several minutes, so you can't even run away from it. When the rains come, the dust will settle and everything will be fresh and green again. Here the folks take dust for granted, but they don't take rain for granted. They need it for their livelihood. The men, gathered around in front of the church before Mass, talk about planting and trade predictions as to when the rain will come.

We have a tiny plot of dirt in front of our house. Everybody who comes to church can see our barren yard and many ask what I'm going to plant. I had thought of planting grass on it to keep the dust down, but a lawn seems so useless in this culture of subsistence farming. Any patch of ground not planted in edibles has flowers growing in it, so grass just won't do. Lori, who is very practical, suggested that I try planting a vegetable garden. It will be a long, hard struggle, though, I know. It's not soil; it's just clay and fill dirt, with rocks and bricks and other stuff thrown in during the construction. I'll have to play God, creating earth from nothing! I can get sand easily enough. We've been composting our garbage for a while, but there's so little that I can't count on it for much. I'll have to see if I can buy some compost somewhere. After the first rains moisten and soften the ground I'll start to work on just a small part, digging down a foot or so to see what's there. I'll remove the big stones, sift out the smaller stones, break up the clay, mix it with sand, manure, and compost, and hope it will become soil. Already I'm getting excited about planting the first seeds.

Meanwhile, we've begun planting seeds of another kind. When we first arrived we asked the representatives of various organizations and some individuals of the parish the same question: "What do you want from us?" Almost everybody expressed the hope and desire in one word: *estudio,* study. "What kind of study?" we asked. The answer was equally broad as the first: "Any kind of study that you can give us." The answer was disconcerting. We saw many opportunities but wanted to avoid the pitfall of seeming to have all the answers before we really knew what the questions were. We also knew we had much to learn from these neighbors and friends. The study will have to be mutual. So we plan to invite small groups from the parish to come and spend a bit more time talking and thinking about what kind of study they want, and why. We don't plan to initiate any classes or programs for several months, but we have begun working with a few groups here who have requested our help now.

One of these groups consists of eleven men and one woman who are taking a government-sponsored correspondence course to complete their primary school education. The Ministry of Education is promoting its course through parish-sponsored radio schools. The people come to our house three nights a week and work on their studies together. The booklets provided by the Ministry of Education are very poorly organized; they make Lori and me work almost as hard as the students. For people who speak very little Spanish, studying from a Spanish book makes their task extra hard.

Once a week we meet in our small living room with about ten men for Bible study. Some read Spanish minimally, and just a few can grasp most of the meaning in the Spanish sentences. There is a Bible translation in their own language, but not in their dialect, so they prefer to use the Spanish Bible. I find this part of my work very exciting and challenging, because it means working together to get to the root of the meaning of Scripture for me as well as for them. It is a small beginning that I hope will lead to much greater participation in Bible study, and to the sharing of the new "estudio" with others. Their insights into the gospels are opening my eyes to new ways of understanding old familiar texts. They live very similarly to the people among whom Jesus walked.

A couple of very special seeds were planted for the town's religious study program when two of the four men on the parish committee accepted an invitation to study in Huehuetenango, about 100 miles from here. That diocese offers a series of courses for rural religious leaders called catechists. The program is well known throughout the country. We are lucky to have been invited to send candidates from our parish. Both Victor, who speaks and reads Spanish very well, and Antonio, who speaks Spanish poorly and can hardly read at all, wanted to go to learn what they could about living their Christian faith.

Victor is my age, thirty-five. He is a natural leader who just finished his two-year term as president for the Catholic Action parish committee. He has a marvelous mind for recalling Scripture passages and connecting them to daily life. He and his wife, Juana, have six children and have been members of Acción Católica for many years. Antonio, about Victor's age, is the father of four. He is a natural "pray-er" to whom many people here in town turn in times of illness and difficulty. He is invited to pray in somebody's house at least one night a week. Both men should be back soon. Then we'll see what they have absorbed, what was awakened in them, and what they can do with their experiences. They will have lived, eaten, slept, studied, and prayed with over ninety other men, both Indian and ladino, from other language groups and from various parts of the country. It's a wonderful chance for them to meet people from other places, break down the barriers of distance, language, and race, and come together as a community. And, most important, it will give them a grounding in the basics of the message of Jesus.

June 2, 1977

Last Friday evening, Victor and Antonio came home from their Basic Evangelization course. Even before going home, they came right to our door, eager to tell us all about it. Over coffee and bread, we learned of the new friends they made from other places— even from Mexico—many of whom had made great sacrifices to attend the course. They shared some of their new insights about how to live as followers of Jesus, the reinforcement they received for some of their own ideas, and their real awareness of who Jesus is in their lives. A big hardship for them was sitting longer than a half hour at a time in the classes. They frequently had to get up to stand or walk around in the back of the room during a session. For men who walk long distances and stand all day at work, sitting can be exhausting. And for Antonio, listening to Spanish for three weeks straight and not understanding much in the beginning was a real hardship. But Victor helped him, and they both gained much from the experience. They are eager to share what they have learned with the people of the parish. Lori and I will begin working with them on how to do it.

We have been carrying on with our study of Cakchikel with Eduardo. The progress is slow because there isn't any grammar or easy-to-use textbook to help us learn. And Cakchikel, one of the twenty-three languages in Guatemala, is not related in any way to the European languages we would be more comfortable learning. Hard as it is, we are happy to keep at it, although we are a little too pleased when Friday rolls around and we get a break.

As I learn more vocabulary and grammar, I occasionally get an insight into the root meanings behind some of the words. Those are exciting, though rare, *aha!* moments. For example, the Cakchikel word for the tortilla, their basic food, is *wey*. Their word for bread is *cashlanwey*. Knowing that bread was brought here by the Spanish, I wondered how it got its Cakchikel name. Then it came to me: Cashlan is the Indian pronunciation of Castilian, the Spanish national language. Aha! *Cashlan* (Spanish) *wey* (basic food) is bread. Of course! It's little things like this that can make my day after a struggle with the unfamiliar grammar and sounds!

The rains have come with a vengeance. I'm told they come hard for a few days beginning around noon, and then they taper off a bit. The day of the first rain, I was in the house and heard some children screaming. I ran to see what was happening, afraid that somebody got hurt. Well, I needn't have worried. At the first sound of raindrops pounding on the roof the kids shot out of the classrooms before the teachers could stop them and were jumping and dancing in the rain! A few men on the street smiled as they passed the children. Rain means life to the poor farmers, called ''campesinos.'' I'm anxious to start work on the plot out front.

Since I last wrote I attended my first funeral. It was for a man who died accidentally. Since he was not a member of Catholic Action, no one requested anything from us. But because the dead man's brother Vicente is on the parish committee, we accompanied him. Young men carried the black wooden coffin into church and the family prayed while guitarists played and sang a few church songs. Then I saw a custom I had never witnessed before. Several people came up to the casket and each tapped it with a coin, speaking to the dead man, offering him some money to take with him on his journey to the other side. This was repeated by many people along the way to the cemetery. The money was pocketed by a family representative and later given to the relatives.

The harsh reality of death and burial was quite evident at the cemetery. The grave was about nine feet deep. The gravediggers found some old bones from a previous occupant and raked them under the mound of dirt at the side of the grave. Several men lowered the coffin into the ground with ropes, while someone shouted directions. When it hit bottom, the ropes were retrieved. The diggers shoveled some dirt on top of the coffin, and then lowered a young man in to stamp it down. The process was repeated until there was a nicely rounded mound over the grave. Throughout the burial, the family wailed and staggered around the grave site, clapping their hands in grief, as is the custom. They had already consumed a great deal of the local moonshine, called *cusha,* by the time we reached the cemetery, so they were free to let themselves go. But they didn't begin to wail until the casket was about to be lowered into the grave. Then it started as if on signal. The dead man was a widower. Lacking a wife to mourn him, his brother's wife, Marcela, did the wailing instead.

It is customary for the family of the deceased to provide plenty of cusha to the gravediggers, the pallbearers, and the mourners. But they also bring along soft drinks. The people of Acción Católica who were at the funeral, including the deceased's son and brother, all refused the alcohol and took the soft drinks instead. I was struck by the obvious accommodation to both the old ways and the new. I was also very touched by the naturalness of it all. The funeral procession went to the cemetery, up a hill, on foot. It was a fifteen-minute walk, and the pallbearers had to change off frequently. The event was REAL—not dressed up and covered over to look like something else. Everything is done by family and neighbors, from digging the grave and saying the prayers to the novena of prayer at the home of the deceased for nine nights. Death is a community affair here, very much so.

June 16, 1977

Mom, you asked what a radio school is. Sorry I never explained before. I am so used to them here, that I forgot you don't have them back home. A radio school is a radio station set up originally as part of an adult educational program. Many parishes started radio schools to reach people who never went to school, or who dropped out after a year or two. I know of several that broadcast to the people who speak Cakchikel, Tzutuhil, Mam, Quiché, and Kekchí. I'm sure there are others. They are recognized and licensed by the government, and they perform a valuable service, broadcasting literacy classes, civics studies, agricultural tips, nutritional and child-care programs, and entertainment to the hundreds of thousands of people in Guatemala who do not speak Spanish. The radio school that serves our area, broadcasting in Tzutuhil and Cakchikel is "La Voz de Atitlán," "The Voice of Atitlán." It originally belonged to the parish of Santiago Atitlán, but now is independent. It has a native board of directors, staff, and volunteer teachers.

We have just finished planning with Victor and Antonio for the week of evening classes they will give to the community, based on what they learned in their Basic Evangelization course. Together, we picked five themes and went over them several times so they could determine the best way to present the material to the people in their own language, using examples from their own life experience. They also have large pictures that go with their theme book, and a simple outline and summary to help them give the lessons. Neither of these men has ever taught anything like this before. They will have to use Spanish materials while teaching in Cakchikel but they are undaunted; in fact, they are eager and excited. The themes are not the usual, old-style catechism lessons. Instead, they deal with topics like the relations between men and women as equal human beings, and God's plan for humanity.

June 22, 1977

I had a strange experience yesterday. A woman, about forty years old with a baby on her back, came to the door. I invited her in, but she shook her head and said in Cakchikel, which I struggled to understand but doubted that I did: "I can't. I am in jail." I asked her to repeat what she had said, and she gave the same response. Convinced that I had heard wrong, I tried to engage her in a game of Twenty Questions in her language to discover what she wanted. But all I could get in answer to my questions was this story: "I am in jail. My husband put me in jail. My baby is sick. It is cold in the jail. I want to go home. Will you pay my fine for me?"

I was really puzzled. Obviously she wasn't in jail; she was at my front door. And apparently she couldn't come into the house because she was in jail. If I paid her fine, what would happen next? Lori was away for the day, so I decided to ask Alejandro, who was building an addition onto the parish hall.

"Yes, she is in jail," he explained. "But the jail door is open. She can go to friends or townsfolk to ask for food, because the town authorities are not obliged to provide food for the people in jail. If the family doesn't bring food, the prisoner has to go look for it. This jail is only for a day or at most a week, for petty problems. The woman and her husband are always fighting. They frequently bring each other to the Justice of the Peace, who is also the mayor, to hear their arguments. After hearing the accusations and counteraccusations, he makes a decision. Sometimes he fines them both and sends them home. Sometimes one is put in jail for a day or two, and sometimes the other is. Sometimes they both go to jail. This time she was fined, but didn't have the money to pay, so she went to jail. But she has put her husband in jail many times, too. If I were you, I wouldn't get mixed up in that family quarrel."

So, armed with this enlightening explanation of the local judicial system, I went back and told the woman that I was very sorry (which I truly was), but that I could not pay her fine to get her out of jail. However, I could offer her food and a blanket. She said that she was already getting food from a friend but accepted the blanket, and then went back to jail. I believe I did the right thing within this culture. When I went to visit her the next day, she was out of jail and back home. I wondered if she and her husband were fighting yet.

June 28, 1977

Last night we had a visit from the men of the parish committee. They are responsible for the religious services and other church-related activities in town, and we work closely with them. They arrived at about eight forty-five P.M., but it wasn't until ten P.M. that they told us why they had come. Poor Lori; she's wide awake at five A.M. and usually asleep by ten. We just sat and talked about all sorts of things, knowing all the time that this was not a social call—this was a visit from a delegation. They finally got around to the purpose of the visit, which was to talk over the ceremony for the transfer of leadership to the newly elected parish committee. That business was taken care of in ten minutes, whereupon they got up, shook hands all around, as is the custom, and left. I admit that I had begun to yawn a bit. But that's the way things are done here: nothing too abrupt, nothing too hurried, nothing too direct, everything with tact and respect. Sometimes we can guess the motive of the visit, but at times like this we just have to wait it out.

In our Bible study group we are finding that, even with the help of Eduardo, some words we take for granted can't be directly translated. Words like *glory, Kingdom of God,* and *faith,* have no equivalent word in this language. So we have to do a lot of discussion of the text, going around and around, using examples, until the idea becomes clear. It is very challenging!

The other day a couple of little boys came to the door. I'm used to children coming on errands for their parents, but these boys had an errand of their own. They had bought a huge orange for five cents but couldn't peel it, and came to ask me if I had a knife. So I peeled it for them, and they thanked me and ran happily off. A minute later they were back. "What's the matter?" I asked, in my best Cakchikel. The bigger boy held out half the orange, which was ragged and blackened by his efforts to part it. Smiling shyly, he said in his best Spanish, "For you."

One lesson I keep learning over and over here in town is that the poor always have something to share. We have received gifts of eggs and bread and vegetables from many visitors who are poor, and they aren't asking for anything in return. I wonder why it's so hard for us, who have so much more, to part with any of what we have.

July 5, 1977

The Fourth of July passed unnoticed yesterday—just another work day for Lori and me. We have had a chance to look back on the town course given by Antonio and Victor over these past two weeks. I mentioned in an earlier letter that we planned a five-evening course for the townspeople. I had wondered whether there would be enough interest to sustain five sessions. Well, when we talked to the leaders of the parish organizations about it, they asked us to repeat each class twice so that those who couldn't come one day would be able to get to the repeat. I was amazed! Victor and Antonio said they were willing to do it, so that's what we did.

About two days before the course was to begin, we received the startling news that Victor had fallen out of his field! Now, you may wonder how someone could fall from a field. Well, for the men who farm the steep slopes of these mountainsides it isn't hard to do. Some tie themselves to trees as they work their way down the slopes with their hoes. Victor's land was so steep that it was terraced. As he worked backing toward the edge, he miscalculated and fell over to the next level. Fortunately, he didn't break any bones, although he suffered a bruised wrist and some battered ribs. The night of the course, he arrived at our door, moving a bit stiffly, yet ready to take his part as scheduled.

Each of the five sessions began with simple dramatizations from their own daily experiences. For the first act, Lori invited her friend Vicenta to bring her seven-year-old daughter to demonstrate the woman's work of food preparation. They stepped in front of the more than 100 onlookers and, like seasoned actors, performed before the group. Vicenta arranged the firewood, her daughter placed the *comal* (clay griddle) over the wood and then lit and blew on the imaginary fire. Kneeling before the *comal,* they formed, baked, and served invisible tortillas. They were so serious that I had to suppress a smile.

The acts focused the group's attention and got them involved in discussions that revolved about God's plan for humanity and our response. Many people came for all ten sessions. The women were especially pleased with the course because it was presented in their own language and in a way in which they could easily participate.

At the end of the course we had a special Celebration of the Word. The hall was packed. We drew together the five themes, emphasizing the Gospel message that "You are the light of the world." Lori explained that everyone has a gift from God to share with others. To symbolize our gifts, we all lit candles, filling the darkened hall with warm light. I then asked, "Who among you would like to learn more about your religion, so that you can share it with others?" Over fifty hands went up!

With such explosive response, it's hard to keep our fingers on all the buttons. We'll have to prepare courses for translators, Bible teachers, and presacramental teachers or catechists. And we haven't even touched working with women yet. We have to take it one step at a time. Most women in town can't read or even *speak* Spanish, so we are starting with the men who can. We hope eventually to give a role to all who want to participate in this program of religious study.

Remember the twelve people who were studying for their elementary school certificate in the government-sponsored program? They are very discouraged. After they finished the first level of lessons they took the tests and sent them to the Ministry of Education through the Atitlán radio school. They waited very long for the results and the second-level material. Finally, Victor and Pedro went to the radio school to find out about the delay. They learned that no group in the program had yet received a response. The radio school director promised to send a representative to the Ministry of Education to ask about the delay.

After a few weeks, the men went back to Atitlán and learned that nothing had arrived. The radio school director was also discouraged. He said, "We did everything required by the government to foster this education program and got a great response. The hopes of Indian men and women throughout the area were raised. The students did all they were supposed to do, but the government is dragging its feet. I'll go myself to the Ministry of Education."

In the end, nothing ever came back from the Ministry of Educa-

tion, not even an explanation. We were left to draw our own con-
clusions, and mine were hardly kind toward the government. These
people spent weeks studying by candlelight, struggling with the
material, hoping that they would have a chance to receive the education they missed as children. They felt disappointed and cheated.

July 12, 1977

It was good to hear from you. I went over to the post office to
pick up the mail around supper time and decided to wait until things
quieted down before I took the time to read it all. Here, from supper time until about ten P.M., we can never predict what will happen or who might drop by. Our house is right on the beaten path
where lots of people walk by at seven P.M. to go to church for
evening prayer. Some decide to drop in here rather than go to church;
some stop in before and some come afterwards. We never expect
to be alone during that time. We have encouraged people to stop
by and decided not to attend the evening prayers so we could be
available for visitors. Sometimes people come with a problem. For
example, a man came last night asking if we had any medicine for
the relief of his pregnant wife's swollen feet. Sometimes people
like Antonio come, bearing gifts. He brought us green squash for
our next meal.

Sometimes they come on business, or for meetings. Recently,
representatives for the newly forming weaving cooperative asked us
to help them understand the official bylaws, required of all co-ops
by the government. They meet with us on Monday nights, and it is
very hard going! Spanish legal documents can be as hard to deci-
pher as English legal documents. Then try to put it into Cakchikel!
If this co-op can get off the ground it will mean a better income for
the women for their native weavings. It could also mean work for
some men who want to learn to weave bolts of cloth. I never realized so much of a missioner's life would be spent in sitting and
listening at meetings!

We are enjoying lovely weather these days. Although July is in
the middle of the rainy season, right now it is a rather dry time
around here. The season has stages and there are times when there
is no rain for weeks. Then, in August, the rainfall becomes stea-

dier, and in September and October it comes daily and is very heavy. So we are enjoying a respite from rain without the plague of dust that we have in the dry season.

We took advantage of the dry spell to hire a man to build us a simple cane fence around our front yard. As soon as the fence went up, indicating that the yard will no longer serve the town as a freeway past our windows, folks began asking what we intended to plant. So far, I have been offered onion sets, tomato seedlings, lily tubers, and geraniums.

Our town school was damaged last year by the earthquake. It has finally been repaired by the Department of Public Works. For weeks, the teachers worked with the school children to prepare for the reopening. Yesterday Lori and I represented the Church at the inauguration.

There is no school hall, so the ceremony was held in front of the school, near the town water fountain. Luckily it didn't rain. The visiting dignitaries sat on a bench on the school steps, and the teachers took charge of the program. All the children were there, standing, fidgeting, and being mischievous. After many speeches by government officials and teachers, songs and poems by children, and a flag-raising, we were invited to the town hall for lunch. The hall was just big enough for the two long tables, that were covered with big sheets of white newsprint paper.

As we took our places at the tables, the mayor's helpers, young men called *alguaciles* brought in cases of soft drinks, opened the bottles, and put one before each guest. Another group of *alguaciles* came with armloads of liquor, or *aguardiente,* in hip flasks, and put those on the tables. Large baskets of hot tortillas came next, followed by the main course, a steaming bowl of soup, served by the children. The bowls were deep. A fish stared balefully up at me from the broth. The soup also contained a hunk of tough soup meat, a small potato, half a carrot, and stringy herbs. A big bowl of rice worked its way down the table, and I scooped a large portion into my bowl. The aroma of the combination set my mouth watering. But, as custom dictates that no one eats until all have been served, and since we had not yet received spoons, I waited impatiently to begin.

Suddenly I became aware that Lori and I were alone in waiting for spoons. Everyone else was already drinking from the bowls, using tortillas to spoon out the food. I looked at my bowl with panic: if only I had not been so greedy in serving myself that rice! It floated throughout the broth, too thick to drink down. I tried using tortillas, but in my hands they became soggy and fell into the soup. I glanced at Lori and saw she was not faring much better.

Well, I finally finished my meal, but I made such a mess that I was embarrassed. Most of the guests left their places quite clean. To make matters worse, there were handshakes all round immediately after the meal, and I had no chance to wash my sticky fingers. I noticed, as I shook hand after hand, that no one else but Lori and I had greasy, sticky hands!

August 7, 1977

This morning we had Mass at ten-thirty. At eight A.M. I answered an insistent knock at the door to find two men from the parish who wanted to translate the readings from Spanish to Cakchikel for Mass. They plunked themselves down and spent the next hour discussing the readings. I was glad to see their keen interest. Today, a priest from a seminary high school was coming to talk to the people about sending their sons to the school. The priests encourage boys to study there, hoping that something might rub off so that they will serve their communities and the church even if they don't become priests. But in our town, with so few students even reaching the sixth grade, it's hard to think of any boy going on to the seminary. I know of only two young people from here, a man and a woman, who have as much as a high school education. They are both rural schoolteachers. Language problems, cultural differences, economic hardships, and the parents' fear that the children will become alienated from their own people are very strong deterrents to further schooling.

With the rain moistening the earth again, I finally took a pick to my plot out front and tried getting down deep to work the soil. I hit some bricks and debris from construction, which I removed. I also found some chips of obsidian, which is black volcanic glass. Such chips were used by the Ancient Mayans as arrowheads, knives, and razors. They are relics of a past civilization, and I will treasure them. I sifted some dirt to get out big stones and break up clods of clay, and then I mixed some sand and manure with it and threw in some earthworms for good measure. The worms will speed up the soil-making process.

September 9, 1977

We are still supposed to be in the rainy season, but it's quite dry. Lots of the corn crop, the basic staple for the Indian people, is drying up. This same story has been told for the last five years. Each year they planted, hoping that the season would be better than the last, and each year there was not enough rain. The water supply here in town is being rationed because the spring on the mountaintop that feeds the water system is running slowly. We must be very careful in our use of water these days, so I water my seedlings with the laundry rinse water.

I took three men, including our language teacher, Eduardo, to the Basic Evangelization course in Huehuetenango on Monday. Our parishioners donated 100 pounds of corn, 100 pounds of beans, and lots of onions and squash for them to take to the course. Each community is encouraged, though not required, to send a contribution of food with their candidates for the course. In addition to showing the community's backing, the contributions give the men a sense of obligation to give back to the community some of what they learned. I stayed with them for a few days until they felt comfortable in that strange place. I'm sure they'll be fine.

I went up the hill this afternoon to visit Juana, Victor's wife. I found her and her eight-year old daughter, Rosario, weaving. I am always enthralled by the backstrap-weaving technique of the Mayan women. I believe that Guatemalan Indian women do some of the finest weaving in the world, and they do it with deceptively little equipment: a few sticks, some rope, a leather strap, and the thread. A woman in our town can take her weaving with her and set it up anywhere in a few minutes. She simply attaches the rope from one end of the rolled-up weaving to a hook on a roof beam or to the branch of a tree. She unrolls the weaving, loops the leather strap from the other end around her back, and sits on her heels, pulling the weaving taut. She can then weave as long as she wants. It's an ingenious system, simple yet amazingly intricate, and it was obviously invented by a busy woman! With this loom, a woman can weave strips of cloth about one and a half feet wide in her town's own pattern and colors.

To a casual observer, all the women's blouses, called *huipils* (pronounced wee peéls) in Cakchikel, look the same. But upon close examination, there are no two alike. Each woman weaves the basic colors of red and white, adding touches of other colors in the design, in such patterns and colors as please her. In fact, most weavers don't repeat the same pattern twice.

Juana was sitting on a reed mat on the floor as I entered the house. She welcomed me with a hearty handshake, and I hastened to say that I didn't want her to get up. She smiled and pointed to a chair by the wall, but I said I would prefer to watch her work. She was unraveling the red thread from hanks and spinning it into a big loop on a carousel made of bamboo. As this carousel spins freely, she will prepare the warp, the length of the piece she is weaving. She also winds her different-colored threads on old juice cans so that each color will be handy for the pattern that she will weave into the fabric. She'll sit down and line up the cans at her side, reaching for one or another color as the need arises. Nothing is wasted here; juice cans make great spools.

While Juana prepared to set up the loom for her own weaving, Rosario was sitting quietly across the room on her little mat; she was weaving a sash for her father. She had graduated from simple weaving with just one color for practice, to weaving with several colors to make an item she was sure would be worn. I went over to watch her; she was very serious about her work. Juana told me that Rosario wove very well for a beginner. Little girls start at age eight to learn the skills they will need as adults—not only weaving, but also preparing tortillas and other cornmeal foods basic to the family's diet. When I complimented her on her weaving, Rosario smiled shyly and thanked me in Spanish. She is in first grade, and both of her parents encourage her to speak Spanish, even at home. Most Indian women can't speak more than a few words of Spanish, but Juana learned it on her own. She is the only woman in the group of twelve taking the radio school basic education course.

September 18, 1977

The three young men we sent to the two-week course came back on Friday all excited about the experience. We have lined up Vicente, the former parish committee treasurer, and Alejandro, the new president of the parish committee, to go to the next one. That will make seven who have had the same course and whose experiences can be shared with the community. It's great to see the enthusiasm and commitment in these men after a course. They have a new sense of their own dignity as children of God. Eduardo told me that he views his wife in a new way, with more respect as an equal partner in the work of participating in God's creation. He now looks on his wife as a friend, and will spend more time with her at home, talking and sharing thoughts about things he used to discuss only with other men. I hope his wife can handle it—she's used to having him out of the house most evenings. It will be a new idea for her, too.

October 25, 1977

Our garden continues to draw comments from well-wishers. I don't know how our pepper plants will be able to sustain the peppers that might come, because the plants themselves haven't grown in a month. Maybe that's a sign that I shouldn't *expect* any peppers. The problem, of course, is the dirt—it's not soil but plain (almost), lifeless dirt that needs a lot of help. I just harvested all the turnips. The leaves were a good size but the turnips themselves were about the size of marbles, though we did have a giant one the size of a golf ball. It's all relative.

We are having a very special, intensive course to explain the meaning of the Mass. Most people have no understanding of what it all means. No one ever taught them. But I guess we could say the same for many American Catholics, too. We will continue the course for three Sundays. The parish committee, with our help, wrote short letters of invitation to each family in Acción Católica in town. Almost no one gets mail here, so a hand-delivered invitation is very special. The young men's group was delivering them all over town today. In addition, some of the leaders in town gave talks encouraging the people to attend, and to become apostles themselves by inviting others to join in this study.

The effort was so successful that we had a packed house. There were people standing three- and four-deep outside the doors! When I say ''packed,'' you can't imagine what I mean. The heat from the bodies was enough to heat a five-room house if we could have piped it out! But we couldn't, so everyone sweltered. Men customarily stand on one side of the hall, while women sit on their heels on the floor on the other side. Children fill in the front on the floor, fidgeting and squirming most of the time. Well, from the back of the hall to the altar there was not room to put one foot in front of the other. Let's hope that the fervor continues.

November 18, 1977

In a few days we will celebrate the first anniversary of the death of Father Bill Woods. Do you remember him? You met him when you visited Guatemala. He worked in an area called The Ixcan, where he helped people homesteading jungle land at the invitation of the government. He had worked insistently for the people's right to own title to the land. Because of that, he had many enemies in high places. Last year, just before Thanksgiving, his little plane crashed under circumstances that were never clear. Many think he was murdered, and consider him the first modern martyred priest of Guatemala.

There has been a new development in our town among some of the men. They had heard about a course in raising bees, and so they got together a group interested in learning this new agricultural skill. It makes sense for them. They can't grow much on their small plots of land. But if they have bees, the bees can range all over to gather the pollen and nectar to make honey in the hives on tiny pieces of land. Honey is something they can sell easily around Holy Week when it is customarily exchanged as a gift among relatives and neighbors. They may even be able to sell their honey as a group to an outside buyer.

There must be about fifteen men including our friends Antonio, Victor, and Alejandro, who are interested in at least discussing the possibility of forming a bee-keepers association. If they can agree, they must choose one man to send him to a course in a distant town. While he is there, the group must support his family. He, in turn, must teach them what he learns.

It will be a challenge to work together in this new way, but it will be to their advantage. Honey sells for a good price. Its value doesn't fluctuate as wildly as that of other cash crops. In the market the other day I heard a woman haggling over the cost of a bunch of ten onions. "Three cents for that bunch?" she asked. "It's a sin to charge so much for such little onions. I'll give you a penny." But the vendor was not *that* desperate. He replied: "It takes me four months to sow the seeds and harvest them, and I have to water the plants by hand and transplant them several times. For all that work you think three cents is a sin? And you don't think it's a sin for me not even to break even?"

December 27, 1977

Christmas is over and there is a bit of a lull in our work, so I have some time to think about my first Christmas here and tell you about one incident that taught me a good deal about being a Christian.

After midnight Mass, the community of Acción Católica served a sweet, spiced pineapple drink and bread to everyone who came to the parish hall. Lori and I were escorted to special places at a table with the parish committee. Everyone else was standing or squatting or kneeling around the hall, waiting to be served.

As we sat chatting, drinking our beverage, and eating the bread (we were served first), Marcos, the young secretary of the group, got up to go across the hall to give somebody a message. Almost immediately, his seat was taken by a young man named Carlos, who is retarded. He looked at me with a big grin and a sparkle in his eye and began eating Marcos' bread and drinking his beverage. I looked around the table, expecting someone to tell him it was Marcos' food and seat, but no one bothered to do so. I wondered what would happen when Marcos got back, and felt a bit embarrassed for the poor fellow sitting in his place.

Well, that's when I had an important lesson in Christianity as it is lived here in town. When Marcos came and saw Carlos, he turned around and went off again, and came back with another hot bun and a steaming cup for the occupant of his seat. He gave him a pat on the shoulder and wished him a Happy Christmas. Marcos turned to me and said: ''Carlos is the best Christian here! He helps everyone. He never misses Mass, and plays the gourd rattle to accompany the guitars at all church services. He runs errands for us on the parish council. He attends all parties, funerals, and fiestas. He helps clean the church, and he takes up the collection at Mass. What would this town be without Carlos?''

February 5, 1978

Lori and I alternate in taking Communion to sick people in town. This evening I took Communion to Micaela, old Pedro Cumes' wife, who is dying of tuberculosis. She is confined to her bed now, and is losing ground fast. Their home is a poor one, even as these homes of mud brick go. It is very small, and her bed, made of small canes of bamboo laid across a simple bed frame, is softened with just a few blankets—no mattress. When I enter the house, it takes me a while to adjust to the dark, because there is only a tiny window. However, when I go in the evening there is always a candle lit for me on a table, so I can read the prayers for the visit to the sick. Pedro is so attentive; he makes sure I have what I need. I don't need anything, really, but he wants to do something in return for the visit, and usually has some sweet rolls and a Pepsi waiting for me when I finish. Even though Micaela is in such poor health, she is alert and looks forward to the Communion call every Sunday. I must admit that I like going on the call, too. I feel something of God's presence in that poor house with those two old folks.

February 19, 1978

Holy Week will soon be upon us, and Lori and I are giving classes to prepare the people for a better understanding of this season. Meanwhile, the catechists are planning a course with us for all the parents and godparents of the children being baptized in the

Easter Vigil service. Finally, we are preparing a four-talk Peniten-
tial Service for Wednesday of Holy Week. We want to show that
the whole sacrament is one of Reconciliation with God and with
those people we have offended, as well as with those who have
offended us. The catechists are really enthused about these courses;
it is a "first" for many of them and their hopes are high.

I hate to bore you with my garden woes, but here is an update:
Last week, the strong winds took the only tomato plant I had left;
our cat continued playing "swat the ball" with the tiny peppers,
knocking them off all the struggling plants; a little duck nibbled the
tops off the carrots; and caterpillars ate the celery! I have come to
respect and appreciate the trials of the poor farmers of this town,
the campesinos of all of rural Guatemala, and indeed, of all the
world! So much hard work goes into preparing the soil with just a
hoe and a machete. Then comes the hopeful planting time. Seeds
that were saved from last year's harvest are planted, with the people praying and following rituals, because the farmers know they
depend on the spirits of the earth and the rain and the sun to produce the corn crop they need to feed their families. Since last year's
crop was poor, many families made a hard choice in saving corn
for planting, rather than eating it. I now understand better the lines
from Psalm 126 which I've read many times over the years:

> Those that sow in tears shall reap rejoicing.
> Although they go forth weeping,
> carrying the seed to be sown,
> they shall come back rejoicing,
> carrying their sheaves.

Then come the months of working in the hot sun and in the
pouring rain. The campesinos buy 100-pound sacks of fertilizer with
hard-earned money and haul them up the mountain, on bent backs,
to feed the young plants. But a campesino can never predict the
outcome. A drought may dry up the plants, as has happened here
several years in a row. Or there may be too much rain, or hail, or
strong winds, destroying the full ears as they wait to dry on the
stalk. In fact, when I talked with our catechists about the meaning
of *hope,* a word not found in the Cakchikel language, the men

quickly turned to the example of planting the seeds of corn and looking forward, working all the time, to a good harvest. As Vicente said, "We never can be *sure*. We hope for a good harvest, but we may not get one. Hope means having trust and confidence in God, without being able to control our future or God." Hope is not something you give up easily, they concluded, because even after five bad years, they still look forward to the first rains this year and are planning how they will plant their corn. "Hope in God is like that."

On Sunday we had a Celebration of the Word, since no priest could come for Mass. I love the Celebration because it allows many people to participate. Lori and I alternate giving the homily in Spanish, and the catechists translate it into Cakchikel. They don't feel ready to tackle the job of giving homilies themselves, but they're getting there gradually. In fact, I believe that their homilies will be much better than ours, since they are closer to the kind of life portrayed in the parables.

The Gospel reading was about the rich man whose harvest was so abundant he didn't have storage space for it. He decided to tear down his barns and build bigger ones. But God said: "You fool! This very night I will demand your life from you. And this hoard of yours, whose will it be then?"

In my talk, I tried to make a sympathetic case for the wealthy man, with his grain stacked up outside rotting in the rain, eaten by rats or stolen by thieves. Then I asked the congregation what they would do in his place.

Alejandro raised his hand. "I would like to speak," he said. I was delighted, since he is one of the catechists I've been trying to coax into giving a homily. "That man should have done what we do here," he said. "What do you do?" I asked. "Well, if we are lucky enough to have more than we can use, we share the surplus with those less fortunate. We all know of families where the husband has died, or is sick, and who don't have their own harvest. So, we take a few ears, or a sackful, to the home of the needy neighbor. Little by little, the store of corn builds up in the house of the widow or the sick one or the old man. That way, they don't starve and we don't have to worry about storing excess. And even if we don't have a surplus, we look out for those who have none. I think that's what God would want us to do."

March 14, 1978

A few days ago, Micaela succumbed to the tuberculosis that was eating away at her frail frame. For several months, Lori and I had been taking Communion to her on Sundays. The visits and the Communion were an obvious consolation to her. We knew that the end was near, and we had expected the news when it came. Her husband, Pedro, sent word asking us to come to the house just after her death. We found him and his family grief-stricken, and contradicting the stereotype of the stolid Indian, this family had no desire to hide its sorrow.

Stooping slightly to enter the tiny, one-room adobe house, we found Micaela's body laid out on the bed, covered with a blanket; her face was hidden by a red cloth. Pedro insisted on uncovering her face so that we could bid her farewell. Afterwards, we prayed with the family, and they asked us to return in the evening for the wake.

That night we found that the furnishings had been rearranged to accommodate the simple black pine coffin and the visitors. The coffin rested on a small table in the middle of the room, surrounded by candles that were set on boards on the dirt floor. In the open coffin, Micaela's body was shrouded in a white cloth. Men sat shoulder to shoulder on the rough wood benches lining the walls. Lori and I were the only women in the room! Women here don't mix with men at such functions, but we were different. We were from outside the culture and we represented the Church. The women were busy preparing food in the kitchen.

At nine o'clock, Alejandro, the new president of Acción Católica, signaled us to kneel for the rosary and prayers for the deceased. Afterwards, we all sat again while guitarists played and sang hymns. In a few minutes, Pedro and his son served the traditional coffee and bread. Each guest received two sweet rolls and a cup of coffee, which were placed at our feet. No one reached down until all were served, and old Pedro invited everyone to partake of the food. I saw more than one man eat a roll and pocket the second. I knew they were for the children or the wives waiting at home.

Once again, an intriguing custom caught my eye. As people came in, they gave a handful of candles or some coins to a man who served as the family's official spokesperson. For each caller, he would go to the casket and, in a conversational tone, address Micaela. He would announce the name of the visitor, stating that he or she had come to bid good-bye and wish her well on her journey. He would explain that the money was to be used to buy a soft drink or some bread for the journey. And finally, he would express the visitor's sense of loss at the passing of such a good friend and neighbor.

The next morning the community held a funeral service. Michaela's coffin was opened in the church and remained open throughout the service. Alejandro, a small man with a gentle manner, gave the homily. I was able to catch a good part of his talk even with my limited Cakchikel, because most religion-related words are Spanish.

He began softly, with compassion: "My brothers and sisters, we welcome Micaela into our church. We will pray for her, bless her body with holy water, and take her to the cemetery. We will leave her resting there, with our ancestors. We are sad. We do not understand death.

"As I passed the church yesterday on my way back from my cornfield, I stopped and looked at the high steps, the weatherbeaten doors, and the darkness beyond them. From where I stood I could not see the beauty inside. 'Death is like this,' I thought. We spend our lives working and suffering in the cold and rain and hot sun outside the doors of eternity. This is all we know. Yet by death we go up the steps, through the doors and into a new, wonderful world. Heaven is like the inside of this church. My brothers and sisters, you see the saints on the altarpiece: here we have San Pedro with his keys, over there, San Pablo with his book. Our patron, San Jerónimo, has a place of honor in the corner. Lining both sides of the church are many saints who are our friends. We come often to ask their help. Up high, above the altar, look: we see angels, the Holy Trinity, and the Virgin Mary, who watches over us like a mother. They are our heavenly community."

Alejandro warmed with enthusiasm as he continued. "Here we bring flowers for the altar, and their scent pleases us. We burn incense here every day, and the church smells holy. We light candles and the flickering flames remind us of our ancestors. We listen to the music of the guitarists and we sing praises with them. Some of our happiest moments are spent here.

"I think that, when Micaela died, she went up the stairs and through the weatherbeaten doors of this life and passed through into a New Life. Our patron San Jerónimo welcomed her and escorted her to the heavenly community. Lilies and carnations surrounded her; thousands of candles lit her way; sweet incense filled the air; and hundreds of musicians sang hymns of praise. San Jerónimo introduced her to San Pedro, San Pablo, the other saints, the angels, the Holy Trinity, and oh, she must be very happy, my friends! And I think the Virgin Mary, our mother, took Micaela by the hand and said: 'You must be very tired, Micaela, after your long journey. Come, sit by me and rest a while. Better still, sing with us.' ''

April 8, 1978

I told you that we were going to try an ambitious project in preparation for Lent and Holy Week. It took us and the catechists a lot of time and hard work, and, I must say, it turned out fairly well. We enlisted the aid of the seven men who took the Basic Evangelization course last year. They divided into teams, usually consisting of a young man and an older one, and gave the classes from the guidesheets we helped them prepare. I'm sure they learned more than anyone else! In the beginning, we had a pretty good turnout because we used filmstrips and slides to illustrate the material. But later on, when we had to rely just on the explanation of the message of the prophets and St. Paul (with no pictures), the attendance dwindled. The people are not used to sitting and listening to classes for any length of time. Just listening to words, words, words is very hard if you have never been to school. Lori is a good teacher, and she has ideas for a better way to do something similar next year. We are learning along with them.

A few weeks ago we two had a challenging new experience. A young man we hardly knew came to us for first aid. His machete had slipped and cut him badly on the palm of his hand. The practical nurse who is *the* staff at the government health center was away for the day. (Besides, she had already told us that she couldn't do much because all she had to work with was a pair of tweezers.) Well, neither of us is a nurse, but we tried to act as if we did this sort of thing every day. Lori held his hand steady while I poured water over the wound (producing basins of bloody water). I dabbed it with Mercurochrome (Ouch!), pulled the skin over the wound, and held it in place while Lori closed the wound with Band-Aids and wrapped it up with a gauze bandage. It looked good to us and he seemed relieved. After giving him some coffee and a few aspirins, we advised him to go to the clinic in a nearby parish. Not bad for the first time!

Our cat is a mother! Balam gave birth to two fine, healthy kittens about two weeks ago. We're having a delightful time watching them grow. Here one has no problem in "getting rid" of kittens. They are often sold in the market. We'll give ours away to friends. We already have a waiting list for the next ones.

May 1, 1978

Today is Labor Day in Guatemala. I guess there are celebrations and parades going on in the cities, especially the capital. But here in this Indian town, as in most others, it's just another work day. Our farmer friends here have no union or campesino organization to represent them and fight for their right to land or for better wages on the plantations. Most get one quetzal (= $1) a day, and some get $1.25 if they are lucky. They are at the mercy of the owners. Even though a minimum-wage law exists, very few farmhands ever get what the law designates. And since there are so many of them looking for work one or more months of the year (when their own fields don't need work or when they aren't needed to work for other people in town), the large plantations can pay less if they choose. It's not legal, but it's life.

Lori and I have begun to work with a group of women who want to learn to write. They are excited and attend the classes at our house faithfully. Most have never been to school, and only a few had gone as far as the first or second grade. Add to that the fact that they speak Cakchikel but must learn to write in Spanish since their language is not used for written communication, and you can see the challenge. First they want to learn to write their names, then other words. You should see them, crowded around our small kitchen table, bent over their copy books, carefully penciling their letters, so intently.

I am very happy that these women approached us with their request. It's something *they* want and need, and we are helping. It also gives us a chance to get to know them a bit better. As we establish friendship with them, we will offer other classes and courses and they may well form a core group, inviting family and neighbors to join them.

May 14, 1978

This is Mother's Day in the United States, and I hope my card arrived in time, Mom. Here in Guatemala we celebrate Mother's Day each year on the tenth of May. The night before this Mother's Day, the public school borrowed our parish hall to hold a program for the mothers, and we were invited to attend. The next day, the girls from Acción Católica's Hijas de María had a Mass offered and served a dinner for the mothers (and fathers, and anyone else around). They started preparing for the meal a day ahead and it was the mothers of the girls who did most of the work! They served the usual feast-day fare: chicken soup with some carrots, potatoes, rice, noodles, and tortillas. They served Lori and me hot chocolate, but it looked like the others had coffee.

Now, if you imagine long tables set up in the parish hall, covered with white table cloths, mothers sitting and chatting over coffee while the girls served, erase that picture! First of all, there is only one rickety table, formerly used as an altar. The girls set it up for Lori and me, as the guests (and the only ones who are used to sitting at a table and eating with forks). Everyone else is adept at using tortillas as forks and spoons. The rest of the food was served to the mothers in shallow plastic soup bowls, set neatly on church benches. The women sat on their heels on the floor before the benches. The girls placed the food on the benches only because we suggested this. Otherwise, they would most likely have set the dishes on the floor before each woman, the way they eat at home. Most of the women took the dishes off the benches and set them in front of themselves anyway, because that is their way.

It may seem that we are imposing our cultural values by making such a change, or even simply by suggesting it. However, we know that disease spreads with dust that blows into the food on the floor, and by animals getting too close, or other floor-related events, so we plan to offer some courses in health, nutrition, and child care for the women in town. We'll try to tread softly and respect their cultural ways, learning from them while at the same time introducing new ideas. That's why they brought us here. They said, "We want to learn." The women have expressed a desire for classes in child care, because childhood illness is the bane of every mother's life. Here in rural Indian Guatemala, infant and child mortality is exceptionally high. Of every thousand deaths, sixty-five are of infants under one year of age.

I know that teaching for change is a very slow process. No one will accept a new way or a new idea unless she is convinced it is a better way. The culture is very traditional. The people respect the wisdom and ways of their ancestors, and with good reason. I must admit, our scientific explanations so often seem contradictory as the years go by. All the more reason not to change too hastily what the ancestors have always done.

Speaking of mothers, our mother cat is doing well, as are her kittens. My garden is suffering, though. Balam enjoys digging holes in my newly planted plots. The kittens find it great fun to romp among the seedlings and tender young plants. But the kittens' days here are numbered, because we will give them away next week. Apart from bugs and wind and kittens and cats and ducks and grubs, I guess my garden is doing alright.

May 21, 1978

I had hoped to write a lot of letters last evening, but, as happens with distressing frequency almost every time it rains, the lights went out. In fact they went off and on again four times. There was nothing to do at that point but go to bed and try again today.

This morning we had Mass at 8:30 and then had a meeting with a parish committee until about 11 A.M. After that, a young man asked me to help with a project for the parish boys' group. Then I had to get a room ready for a guest catechist, coming from another town, who will be here for two weeks. He is a natural teacher who lives what he preaches. The people who have studied with him really enjoy themselves as well as learn.

This catechist, Justo, is also a good friend of many people. He has been godfather for innumerable children. I say innumerable, but I believe Justo knows each one and that he visits their families when he is in the town or village. He has counseled many couples whose marriages were in trouble, and, in addition to being a very good religion teacher, he is an Indian campesino who has learned new things about agriculture. He wants to share those ideas, too.

I just looked outside and saw a group of women sitting on the church steps, waiting for a class to begin. I have a few things to do to prepare for another class, but I may get out there at least to say hello. Saying "hello" is an important part of our work here. Mom, if ever anyone asks what your daughter does for a living, tell them "she's present." It may sound crazy, but more and more I see my "work"—that is, the classes, the preparation, and so on—as secondary, even though there is a lot of it. I am growing in the awareness that my presence here is my main contribution to the people. We never know what will happen. Sometimes nothing happens for a few days and we can catch up on work and other obligations. Other days, from morning to late at night we can't do a thing we had planned because we are "being available." Our prayer is even frequently interrupted by visitors. That's our life. I console myself with the knowledge that Jesus, too, spent most of his public life just being available to the people.

June 4, 1978

While here in Guatemala City for a five-day Bible course, I learned something terrible. A newspaper headline shouted: "106 Massacred in Panzós." At first I thought Panzós was in some other country that was involved in a war. But when I read the article, I was shocked to learn that Panzós is a town in Guatemala, in the province of Alta Verapaz. The paper didn't give many details and it left me frustrated. I had to get in touch with some reliable Church sources to get a clearer picture.

It seems the leaders of several rural Indian settlements in the area of Panzós were trying to get legal title to land that they had lived on and worked for many years. They received a summons from the mayor for May 29th to discuss the problem. Many families accompanied them, since they were all affected by the discussion. When they arrived in the town square, they saw armed soldiers surrounding the town hall. The campesino leaders went inside and the crowd remained in the street outside. Suddenly, the soldiers began shooting directly into the crowd. Victims fell all through the crowd as the people ran for their lives. Many women and children were shot in the back.

Afterwards, in the town, the army dispensed with the legalities regarding autopsies and death certificates. They loaded three waiting army trucks with the bodies and dumped them in a huge pit that they had dug *before* the massacre. They prohibited the Red Cross from entering the area, saying the army would take care of survivors. The lucky few who escaped certainly didn't want the *army* to "take care of them," as it had done for their relatives and neighbors. They hid a few days, until the soldiers left, and then sought help from the Church.

I couldn't help thinking of Micaela's funeral, and the reverence and ceremony, prayer and ritual required by the culture of the Indian people in order to part properly from their dead. In Panzós, a double violence was done: to the murdered and to their mourners.

I'm going on a week's retreat tomorrow. Panzós has given me much food for thought as well as for self-examination. The people of Panzós were Indian people with the same love of life, of family, and of community as the people in our town are. What does this slaughter say to me?

Chapter Two

Storm Warnings
July 1978–December 1979

THE TOWN

The homes of the people in San Jerónimo are very different from what we think of as ''home'' in the States, but they are the kinds of homes most rural poor people have lived in since before history was ever recorded. They provide shelter from the cold and wind and rain; they protect the sleepers on their mats from attack by wild animals. They are the center of family activity, the place where food is shared, illness is nursed, babies are born, and family members breathe their last.

An American would be struck by the sameness of style and size and structure of the one-room adobe homes. The size, about four by five meters, is 'imited by the small amount of space available on the tiny lot as well as by the cost of adobe, metal roofing, and beams. The houses made of cane and mud are even smaller, because the material is weaker than adobe. Yet, while the houses are small and poor and dark, they have a freedom that many modern, big-city homes don't have. They can be decorated by whatever the owners find appealing, colorful, interesting, devotional, or all of the above. They aren't limited by requiring the ''right'' color scheme or the ''right'' period furniture, or the ''right'' artistic flavor.

Bernarda, wife of Antonio the prayer leader, always finds time for a guest. She welcomes the visitor graciously, offering the only chair in the house, and placing it near a table against the wall where the light from the open doorway falls. There is only one window in the house, at the far end, so visiting is best done near the doorway.

The table in a typical Indian home is not used for eating. Eating takes place on the floor around the fire, with the family sitting on reed mats. The table serves as the family altar. It is here that the religious motif is explicit. On Bernarda's table stands a large holy picture of the Sacred Heart. Other homes would have other pictures, but the big picture in the center of the table focuses attention on the altar. There are always candles on the altar, serving to illuminate the house at night as well as to honor the figure in the picture. A clay incense burner sits under the table. Incense is burned each night before the altar. And there are always flowers. They may be artificial, dusty plastic flowers, or they may be freshly cut, but flowers are essential for the family altar. Their function in the Indian home is much more than aesthetic; it is religious as well. They are part of a whole complex of articles that make the simple wooden table against the wall a place of family worship. Here the family gathers at night to pray before going to bed. Here prayers are offered by the ''praying person'' for the sick or the dead. And here the ancestors are remembered and honored. Photographs of recently deceased family members are beginning to show up on some family altars, but the ancient ancestors are remembered because their names are written down. The frequently folded, fragile list of names is carefully stored away in a plastic bag and is pulled out for times of anniversary remembrances and All Souls' Day. It is also at the family altar that the religious memory of the people is stimulated by pictures of Jesus, the Virgin Mary, angels, the saints, and lately, the Pope.

On the wall behind the altar-table are hung important family papers and documents, like certificates of courses passed, awards, or certificates of recognition. In Guatemala, these latter are very common and are proudly displayed. A young man can be recognized as a cooperative member of the soccer team at the end of the season even if he rarely played and the team lost every game. That certificate of recognition will be proudly displayed on the wall. Another new addition to the wall of many homes is the official identification photograph of adult family members. These photographs are required for the internal passport that every man and every married woman must carry. So, when they have the photo taken, they buy an extra copy for display.

On the other walls, anything goes. In Bernarda's house, the walls are decorated with three calendars, all of past years, but all with interesting pictures. One is of a blond, blue-eyed little girl, dressed in a short, pink dress, holding a puppy; another is of a bathing beauty in skimpy swimwear; the third is of a herd of cows grazing in a pasture. Each of them has the name, address, and phone number of a fertilizer and insecticide distributor in Guatemala City. None of the pictures comes from or fits the reality of the people in town, but that's what makes them worth putting up as decorations.

The following are also on the walls: a picture of the Swiss Alps, a flashy car from about 1960; a cigarette poster; a church bulletin from a parish in Guatemala City; and a picture of a cat, cut from an old package of thread. The pictures take the family across the miles or across the years. And Antonio and Bernarda can redecorate whenever they find a new calendar or poster that strikes their fancy. Meanwhile, the present display serves as a sort of world encyclopedia of the poor, bringing the world into their home.

LETTERS

San Jerónimo
July 1, 1978

Today in Guatemala the new president, another military man, took over the reins of government. His name is General Romeo Lucas García. In the eight years I've been in Guatemala there has been an orderly turnover of government every four years after elections. But the only presidential candidates that have won all this time have been army men.

Our "fiesta," or patronal feast, has come and gone, so things here in town are a bit quieter now. The juke boxes rented for the week of celebrations have finally been returned to their owners, and the nights are peaceful again. Even before the fiesta week little "cantinas" popped up all over the streets. They were shacks, sparcely furnished as bars. Big blaring juke boxes appeared in several, next to stacks of cases of beer and hard liquor. Many men spent much of their time in and around the cantinas. In the first days, they danced to the music; later they roamed the streets shouting how brave they were, or cursing their enemies; finally they could be heard wailing at night, crying that they were orphans and had no one to care for them! Now things are back to normal, thank God, until next year.

The photographer is still here, though. He came just before the fiesta and set up his hand-painted canvas backdrop against the wall of the health center. In front of the backdrop, which showed a picture of a colonial church, he put a wooden chair. His old-fashioned box camera on a tripod was ready for business from early morning each day. I suppose he didn't have another fiesta nearby to rush off to, so he stayed hoping for more business. I coaxed Lori into getting our picture taken together with us seated in front of the canvas church. The last time I saw a photographer stick his head under a black cloth and peer into a big, box camera, saying: "Hold it . . ." was in a movie about the 1880's. I was delighted with the chance to sit for a portrait like this. And for $1.50, you can't go wrong. After he took the picture, he developed it right there on the street with some solutions he kept handy. He rubbed something over the faces in the picture as it was getting visible. When I asked what that was for, he told me it was to bring out our eyes. Our pale faces and blue eyes would look washed out otherwise. He is geared for dark eyes and brown skin, but with his photo "first aid" we came out fine.

July 5, 1978

There is a cloud hanging over me these days that won't go away. On Sunday, when Fr. Martín came for Mass, he brought the shocking news that a Guatemalan priest had been murdered a few days before. He told us that Father Hermógenes López, a man of about fifty, had been on a parish sick call on Saturday, June 30th. He was ambushed and machine-gunned as he returned in his jeep to his rectory in San José Pinula, a town on the outskirts of Guatemala City. Martín heard that the parishioners carried his body into church and laid it on the altar. They also brought the jeep into church and saved the steering wheel as a relic of his martyrdom.

I wondered what motive there was for the murder. He said he knew of a letter Fr. Hermógenes had published in a newspaper on June 29th, calling for a halt to the repression by the army. The next day, June 30th, was Army Day, a national holiday. That's the day he was killed. And the following day the presidency of Guatemala passed from one army general to another. Could the timing be a coincidence?

Hermógenes could have been killed for another stand he took. The people of his rural parish are mostly subsistence farmers who sell vegetables in Guatemala City's markets. A water company proposed diverting the river that flows through their land to supply the growing water needs of Guatemala City. Hermógenes fought that plan, convinced it would cause the death of the community. Perhaps it caused *his* death.

I asked Martín to meet with the catechists and parish leaders after Mass. I knew this murder was significant for the lay leaders in the Church, as well as for priests and Sisters. After he told them the story, the men sat quietly for a time. Then, one by one, they spoke of the possibility of such a thing happening again. One said, ''If he was helping his people and was killed for that, what about the many other priests we know who are working to help people like us improve our lives? Can they be safe now?''

When I asked about their own future participation in the Church as catechists, parish leaders, and community organizers, Alejandro, the new president of Acción Católica, said, ''Why would anyone want to kill us? We are not able to do anything to threaten the powerful. We are too simple, too uneducated, too tiny. We are simple people. I have no fear. I will continue with my work in the parish.'' Heads nodded in agreement.

I wish I could be as confident as they are. I have an uneasy sense that this murder is not an isolated case, but rather the beginning of something. Once such assassinations begin, where do they end? Will anyone be immune?

July 15, 1978

I'm wrapping up everything I can before taking off for Huehue-tenango and a second-level course in the Basic Evangelization program. I'm going with Victor, Antonio, and Vicente, who took the first course last year. The parish community has been enthusiastically collecting donations of food or money for them to take. It's clear that the folks of Acción Católica are eager to learn more.

No one can go to the second course who has not worked to share the knowledge and experience gained in the first one. Our parish's catechists certainly have worked hard and deserve to go to the second course. This one is only two weeks long and is designed to help them learn to use the Bible. I'll stay with them for the whole course and bring them back. That way I will know what they have learned, and we will be able to refer to the same experiences.

Dad, you asked about my garden. After a year, my efforts to make fertile soil are paying off. Let me tell you that my tomatoes are beginning to ripen and that I have some peppers, Swiss chard, leaf lettuce, celery, string beans, and parsley. My squash plant has produced eight football-sized squashes and there are many more in various stages of development. We have given four away and have just eaten our fourth one ourselves. Now we are having a little dry spell. When the rain returns in force I may lose my garden entirely, so I'll use what I have now. As I get more time to work in the garden I'll add more manure and compost to improve the soil, and prepare more space for planting. I think I'll try carrots again. Maybe I'm getting the hang of it at long last!

July 29, 1978

It's Sunday night, the town is quiet, and I still have energy to write to you before heading for bed. We came back from the course on Friday evening with much more to think about than we had anticipated or could ever have expected. In the course, we learned about the work of St. Paul in spreading the message of Jesus throughout the Roman world, and we looked hard at the difficulties and hardships involved in being a preacher and teacher of God's Word. In the middle of the course, we had a very real experience of that suffering: we attended a martyr's funeral.

On Thursday, July 20, just as we were breaking from class and looking forward to lunch, a man came in looking white and agitated. He announced, "They just shot Guigui!" Immediately, he was surrounded with a crowd asking for more information. Most of them knew the victim, whose formal name was Mario Mujía. I knew him too. We had met occasionally in the diocesan center where he had worked up until recently in literacy and leadership training. He had spent thirty days at a time in many of the remote villages and settlements these men call home. They knew him and loved him as a brother and a friend.

Guigui had accepted a job as a union organizer after the diocesan program was discontinued. He had successfully organized the workers of a small factory in Huehuetenango and was in the process of organizing another. I later learned that he had already received death threats and had a plane ticket ready in order to flee quickly. But he was at his desk when some men entered his office and shot him. Somehow he managed to make his way down the steps and out into the street before he collapsed. It is a busy street, so he was aided immediately and taken to the hospital. There he remained conscious, while people gathered outside in a vigil of hope for this man they loved. Stories about his sense of humor even in pain circulated around town, giving us a new spurt of hope that he would live. But he didn't. Guigui was about twenty-eight years old. He left his young widow to care for their three little daughters.

We who were at the course were quite shaken by the murder. Classes were cut so we could all attend the wake and the funeral. Even though the men from our town did not know Guigui personally, they got to know him through the stories of so many of the participants who did know him. They wanted to join their new friends in mourning and honoring this friend of so many, who lost his life because of his work on behalf of the poor.

When we arrived at the home where the wake was held, it was almost impossible to make our way through the crowds. The walls of the room were hung with wreaths, and long lines of people shuffled slowly past the coffin, each person pausing to look at Guigui for a last time. The men from the course, over fifty of them, lined up to pay their respects. When Victor and Vicente reached the front, each placed a few coins on the coffin, just as they would have done in their own town. I was deeply touched.

The next day at the funeral, I was struck by the women wearing orange miners' helmets who lined up to embrace Guigui's widow. They were there, along with their husbands, in gratitude for Guigui's support in their union struggle. Guigui had walked with them on a march from the tungsten mines to Guatemala City, over 200 miles. Now they were conspicuous by their presence at his funeral, as he had been conspicuous by his presence on their march.

After Mass we joined the funeral procession as it wended its way through town, past the black-draped office where Guigui had been shot. Large banners identified groups of mourners: elementary school girls and college students, miners and campesinos, factory workers and government employees. Four miners carried a banner that read: "If the seed does not die, it will not sprout." At each block a new group stepped forward as pallbearers. They carried Guigui to the university on the outskirts of town. There his body lay in state for well over an hour as students and professors stood honor guard by the coffin. At the foot of the coffin, in this university setting, lay an orange miners' helmet. Above the coffin on the wall hung a large wreath, encircling Guigui's picture. Draped above the wreath was a banner that stated: "Mario Lives."

I walked near the front of the procession and reached the cemetery well before the great majority of mourners. I climbed up so I could look back and was struck by the sight. As far back as I could see, the long, straight, and wide avenue was packed with people. A man standing next to me said in awe: "Not even on Good Friday, in the procession of the Holy Burial of Christ, have I seen such a crowd." A man of simple faith had made a profound connection.

August 15, 1978

Today is the Feast of the Assumption. In the United States it's a day when Catholics try to work a Mass into their busy workday schedule. But here it's a big holy day and the town is in a festive mood. At three A.M. I was awakened by the ringing of church bells, followed by the chugging of the diesel-powered machines that grind the corn for tortillas. Ordinarily the bells don't ring so early, except in preparation for a special fiesta. The custom comes from the time when women had to rise at that hour to grind the corn to have the tortillas prepared by five A.M. Since there are now these motorized grinders, called *molinos,* there is no reason beyond tradition to wake the women and the rest of us so early. And tradition is so strong that no one would dare think of not waking the town for the excitement of the day about to dawn.

On ordinary days, the church bells are rung by the young mayor's aides at six A.M. for the Angelus. But the molinos start their BUBUBUBUBUBUBUBU . . . at five A.M. I am willing to offer it up because I know it lets the women sleep a few more hours. By five they are awake, draining and washing the kernels of corn that have been soaking all night in a solution of lime dissolved in water to soften them. Actually, it is the young girls who take the basins of corn to the molinos. These girls get a chance to see the young men who work for the mayor and who ring the bells. This is an unusual opportunity for both, because talking in public between boys and girls is strongly frowned upon. After the corn is ground for a penny a basin, the girls take the dough back home for a final grinding by hand with traditional grinding stones. The round flat tortillas are then formed from small balls of dough and are toasted on a round ceramic griddle. The tradition is ancient, and the way things are done has changed little, except for the diesel molinos. The people say they are people of corn, and without tortillas and corn they would die. Corn is so much a part of their culture (from planting through cultivating, to harvesting and on to storing, preparing, and eating) that, without it, I think they would also lose their identity. I know of some men who were born here in town but who have lived and worked in Guatemala City for most of their adult lives. When the rains come they return to town to plant their corn in the small patches of land they own. Corn is part of them, and they are a part of the corn. It is sacred to them in a way we secular moderns could never really appreciate or understand.

Last week we held a meeting of all parish men who want to learn more about religion and share it with others. Over sixty men arrived from town and from all over the mountain. Each community sent representatives of its elected Catholic Action Committee as well as its candidates for catechists. Of these sixty, at least thirty were interested in having a monthly Sunday session, after Mass. So, in September, our catechists who studied the Basic Evangelization course will begin to give that course. I believe they'll do well, and hope the monthly sessions will bear much fruit for the parish committees.

August 31, 1978

It's 5:30 in the afternoon and it usually gets dark these days around 6:30. Ordinarily that shouldn't matter, but today the lights went out at 2 P.M. and haven't come back on yet. Who knows if they'll come back on tomorrow, either. So I'm writing this letter by the open door, and I'm hoping that the lights will go on, but am ready to use the lantern as well.

I want to give you a little update about the weaving cooperative that has formed here in town. Lori and I helped a bit with classes to explain the bylaws of cooperatives and the principles of cooperativism. The women are so used to selling to others that they find it hard to see that they, as a group, will *own* the cooperative. They will each weave and sell products to the cooperative and together will set the prices for the products. They are both the owners of the venture *and* the labor force. Before this cooperative became a reality, the women would undercut each other's prices until they actually lost on a sale. To illustrate how joining in a cooperative effort can actually raise income for each weaver, Lori and I proposed a tug of war. We gave one end of a heavy rope to a group of five woman and called them "tourists." We gave the other to one woman and called her "weaver." I put a strip of masking tape on the floor at the middle of the rope, and smaller strips in each direction from the middle. These indicated rising or falling prices. As twenty women watched, the "tourists" easily pulled the "weaver" right across the midline to the very low prices on their side. I looked at the spectators and asked what had happened. I got smiles and shrugs in response. "Of course they pulled her across to their side," Vicenta said. "It was five against one." "Well," I replied, "what can we do about it?" For a few seconds they just looked at me, puzzled. Then Juana, with her eyes twinkling, said, "She needs help," and walked over to the weaver's end of the rope. Together they began to tug, and soon all twenty bystanders had joined the "weaver" and easily pulled the "tourists" over to the higher prices on their side. That exercise convinced those women of the benefits of forming a co-op.

We did a study with them of how much the thread costs, and

how much time they spend on a weaving, figuring on a seven-hour day. We estimated that they were making thirty to thirty-five cents a day, or less when competition was really stiff. I asked how much they would want to earn. One of them blurted out, ''One Quetzal,'' which is equal to our dollar. Everyone laughed at such a preposterous hope, but in trying to set the co-op's prices, judging how much a tourist might be expected to pay, and determining what products they might want to buy, we came up with a price list that could yield a woman between eighty-five and ninety cents a day. They were amazed that by joining together, not lowering their prices, and not lowering the quality of their weaving, they could make almost three times as much as they did. The women are now very pleased with the improvement in payment they receive. And I know that the money they make goes for medicine and food for the family. I wish they could get more, but tourists expect to pay little. The pay raise is an accomplishment that this organization of women recognizes came from *themselves*. They all want to learn to write their names now, so that they can sign for orders and receipt of payment slips!

In June, we began three-day courses (about two and a half hours each afternoon) for women interested in learning something new about child care and nutrition. An average of twenty-five women from the parish attended the first course, and the number remained fairly constant for the following ones. Lori and I had a translator help us. After a few classes, many women began to speak more freely, without covering their mouths with their shawls. They were losing their embarrassment about speaking out in front of others. The translator made it possible for them to speak in their own language; they did not have to struggle with Spanish to please us. *We* were the ones who had to struggle—which is as it should be.

At our last session, we had some lively discussions on what the women had learned, and about the age-old problem of change. When they want to change traditional home practices, even just a single one, or share new ideas, they are subjected to criticism for being different. This criticism is a very important part of the way their culture controls behavior. Either one does what is socially acceptable, or one is criticized. Being criticized by members of the community brings on a great sense of shame, and a desire to fit back in by conforming. As a result, desirable changes often do not take hold. In this tightly knit society, where togetherness far outweighs rugged individualism, to make any change in one's traditional patterns is very difficult. But, with time, I'm sure some of the ideas we share with them will be retained, just as others have taken hold in the town. For example, metal roofs have replaced thatched roofs, radios are common household items, and the women gladly use the diesel-motored molinos to grind their corn. If a change is seen to be of use or of benefit to their lives, it will catch on.

We are not trying to change the basic patterns that are tied to their traditions and their culture. Rather, we want to show them how they can improve health, in simple ways, and how they can better use what they already have. So far, they have responded well. For example, they were amazed to learn that a can of fruit juice, just six ounces, is mostly water and thickener, with little nutritional value. They were under the impression, because of strong advertising on the radio and posters in stores, that canned juice is something you should give your children, especially when they are sick. At twenty cents a can, that is a very expensive practice. For that same twenty cents, they can buy four or five oranges, which have much more nutritional value and which can feed more children. Another dangerous deception advertised on the radio is vanilla-, chocolate-, or strawberry-flavored cornstarch, promoted as being able to give a baby the same nourishment as powdered milk. Since these woman could never afford powdered milk, they will buy the cheaper flavored cornstarch. Our discussions lead them to make their own choices and decisions about what to buy for their families.

Change can come from the most unexpected sources, too. I was delighted to learn that our class on how a fly carries disease and the need for hand-washing before eating had caught the attention of a three-year-old girl who accompanied her mother to the class. That evening, as they sat down around the fire to eat their evening meal of tortillas, she told her mother that she wanted her hands washed! Her father, Marcos, who did translating for us at these classes, was so impressed he told his wife never to refuse their daughter's request for clean hands.

Later, when we offered Marcos three Quetzales for his three afternoons of translating, he returned one Quetzal to us, saying that his wife was attending the classes and that both he and she were learning a great deal. He wanted to repay us a little for what they had learned. Marcos is a man who owns no land, and who has to look for work every day. He can little afford to give up one Quetzal, but he did it willingly. He demonstrates the Indian view that working for the benefit of the community is a good thing, and that money, although necessary, isn't everything.

September 25, 1978

On September 15th, the town celebrated the Independence of Central America from Spain. The schoolteachers borrowed our parish hall for their Independence Day program. The children spent most of the previous day sweeping, decorating, and setting up benches for the program that night. By eight P.M., they had a packed hall. The children put on the usual program of oratory, poetry recital, and songs, with lots of prompting from the teachers and laughter from the audience. Since the performances were in Spanish and most of the audience spoke Cakchikel, the adults were entertained more by the children's actions than by their words.

Lori is still on vacation, so I represented the Church at the performance. When the show was over, the mayor's secretary, a short, balding ladino man in his mid-fifties, invited me to the mayor's office for the traditional coffee and bread. I went across the street with him and found a place on a bench along the wall next to our young translator, Marcos. As is customary, we all sat quietly, speaking only in muted phrases, until the mayor tapped his desk bell twice. At the sound of the bell, two of the mayor's helpers, called *alguaciles,* came in with a bottle of whiskey and a double shot glass. They poured the local moonshine, called *cusha,* into the shot glass and handed it to the man at the beginning of the row of benches. After he downed it in one gulp, an alguacil refilled the glass and handed it to the next man, who did the same. I became alarmed. This was not coffee and bread! I looked at Marcos. He shrugged and smiled. "Where's the coffee?" I whispered. "It comes after we all have a drink," he replied softly. I felt trapped. I have *never* drunk liquor straight! How could I down a double shot of firewater? As the cusha made its way down the line toward me, I made my decision. I got up, walked across the room to the mayor seated at his desk, and said in a low voice: "Señor Mayor, please forgive me. I cannot drink that big glass of cusha. It is not my custom. To drink it I need some Coca Cola."

The mayor smiled solicitously. "Of course, Madre," he said, and whispered to the alguacil standing next to him. The fellow ran off on the errand. I felt relieved, thinking that I would be able to dilute the cusha in a glass of Coke and sip it slowly, while the double shot of whiskey continued to make its rounds. But I was wrong. The alguacil returned in the nick of time with the Coke and the mayor sent it over to me just as the glass brimming with cusha arrived at my place. There was nothing in which to mix the Coke and cusha. What could I do? Holding up the show, I took a long swallow of Coke, followed by a tiny swallow of whiskey, then some more Coke and a sip of whiskey, repeating the process until they were both gone! Marcos barely stifled his laugh as I sat, dazed, watching the others gulp down their whiskey. I was grateful when the coffee and bread at last appeared, and I was so glad to get to bed that night!

October 13, 1978

I am happy to report that our first catechist session went beautifully. The seven teachers who had studied in Huehuetenango were very well prepared because last month they came to study with us for at least three hours every week. Their hard work paid off in the participants' enthusiastic reception of the class. We conducted an evaluation with the teachers afterward, giving everyone a pat on the back. They want to start studying for next month's class, but we haven't begun to prepare it yet!

We planned the session to run from nine A.M. to four P.M., with lunch around noon. The participants were advised in advance that we would provide hot beans and coffee, but that they had to bring their own tortillas. That way we would be sure that there were enough tortillas for everyone. When the men began arriving, we told them to take their tortillas to Vicenta, the cook, in the kitchen. Each man pulled from his tote bag, carefully wrapped in a hand woven napkin, the tortillas his wife had made for him that morning. I estimated that there were between eight and ten tortillas in each bundle. Shortly before lunch, I went to help Vicenta, who was warming the tortillas and placing them in baskets. I put two heaping baskets on each table—plenty for everyone.

When the first men lined up, holding plastic bowls for their beans, they asked for their tortillas. Vicenta told them that they were on the tables. The men looked puzzled. One said: "Those aren't mine. My tortillas were in a white napkin with blue and green birds on it." Another said, "And mine were in a red napkin. I can show you which one it is." That's when I realized that we Sisters and these men had acted on very different assumptions: we understood "pooling" of tortillas to be an efficient way of feeding everyone. But the men fully expected to have received, each in his own napkin, his wife's tortillas! We had quite a bit of explaining to do before they settled down to eating tortillas prepared by everyone else's wife. Some were convinced they knew their wives' tortillas from the others in the basket. Sharing a meal, and sharing tortillas, is a good way to start becoming a community.

All thirty of the men who came to the session are campesinos. They study at night by candlelight, or on Sunday, their only free day. The rest of their time is spent working in their fields, hoping for a good crop. They talk a lot about the weather, the state of the crops, and the chances of a better harvest than last year's. Even if the corn survives the wind and hail of November and December, it could still be stolen in January. Around harvest time, most campesinos sleep in their fields with their sons and their dogs. They can't be sure of a harvest until it's stacked in their homes.

Most families don't have enough corn to last all year. Many men go to the coastal plantations for one or more months each year, to pick cotton, cut sugarcane, or harvest coffee. This is their only source of income, aside from their own crops. Sometimes they return with more money than when they left home, but often they have less. If they are lucky, they will return with their health intact. Recently a man died here in town of malaria contracted on a coastal plantation. The suffering is greater when a whole family has to go to the plantation. Parents and children work in the fields. Mothers carry their infants in shawls on their backs as they work. When crop-dusting planes spray DDT on families in the fields, adults may get sick, but babies can die. If the child survives, it drinks DDT as it suckles, since DDT accumulates in the mother's milk. The average life expectancy of a person in Guatemala's rural area is 49 years.

So, my gardening is child's play compared to the serious business of farming for survival here. Yet I get all sorts of advice and encouragement from the folks in town. They want my tiny garden to succeed as well as their own small patches of corn and beans.

November 25, 1978

We have become very friendly with a woman named Vicenta, who lives on the outskirts of town. She and her husband, Santiago, have only two children, daughters who are spaced ten years apart. When I first asked her how many children she had, she told me, "Ten: two living and eight in the cemetery." Illness and accident are the most natural forms of birth control here.

I like to visit Vicenta because it's a pleasant walk that gets me out of the house, and she enjoys helping me with my Cakchikel. We have a dialogue in Cakchikel when I arrive, and I feel comfortable speaking with her. Vicenta, at 4'11", is a big woman. She learned to speak Spanish as a young woman while working on the coastal plantations during the coffee and cotton harvests. There, people from many language groups gather to work, and Spanish is the only common language. Like most women here, Vicenta can't read. However, she is one of our most enthusiastic and loyal women's course participants. Her daughters, aged eighteen and eight, come with her to study.

Vicenta's husband, Santiago, suffers from a breathing ailment that prevents him from climbing up to the mountaintop and working their fields. They have to hire men to prepare the land for planting and later, to cultivate it. Vicenta and her daughters join in the planting and harvesting. To pay the men and provide for the family's other needs, Vicenta travels several times a week to nearby markets where she buys and sells fish, lime rock (used in preparing tortillas), and a stomachache remedy made of anise and herbs. At home she raises chickens and sells their eggs. In her free time, she weaves for her family and for sale. She reminds me of the Valiant Woman from the book of Wisdom.

I also enjoy visiting Vicenta because she tells me a lot about the people here. Through her and some other good friends, I am slowly coming to understand the intricate web of relationships in town.

For instance, I have learned that old Pedro Cumes, the man who first told us about the history of Acción Católica, is the grandfather of Marcos, our translator and catechist. I never would have associated those two. For those of us from big U.S. cities, whose ancestors were born in another country, it is mind-boggling even to begin to know who is related to whom here. Everybody we know is closely related to everybody else we know! And since everyone in town knows this information as part of everyday life, they never think to mention the relationships, except in passing.

December 10, 1978

Next week Lori and I will meet with fourteen women from town who are interested in starting vegetable gardens for their families. Their interest was sparked by our classes on nutrition. To add some incentive to the idea of planting gardens, we bought a variety of seeds by the ounce, packaged them in little plastic bags, and sold them for a penny apiece. And I am pleased that my own garden is doing fairly well, so they can see what a small plot can yield. I frequently receive compliments on the garden from the women who visit. Now some seem ready to heed the injunction: "Go ye, therefore, and do likewise." While my successes have inspired them to try a garden themselves, my failures, obvious though they have been, have not discouraged them.

December 20, 1978

We are being initiated into still another custom of this town, the Posadas. This is a procession through town each night for the nine nights until Christmas Eve. In the procession, statues of Mary and Joseph, dressed as pilgrims for a journey, are carried to a different house each night. They "ask" for a place to stay—a *posada*. The Posadas are an old Spanish custom that took root in most of the places colonized by Spain. Yet the local cultures have added their own little twists and colors to the custom, so that there is a big difference between even the Posadas celebrated in Guatemala City and those celebrated in the Indian communities of Guatemala.

The people who participate in the Posadas here play a variety of roles. Some are musicians who play guitars and keep time with rattles as the procession moves along; others carry the statues on a thatch-roofed platform, and still others—mostly noisy, playful little boys—light the way with multicolored lanterns. When the procession reaches the designated house, some people enter the house and others stand at the door outside. All of these people sing the traditional carol of the Posadas. Those on the outside sing for Joseph and Mary, asking hospitality for the night; those inside sing for the innkeeper, who says there is no room. Finally, the innkeeper gives in, opens the door, and there is a joyous chorus of "Enter Pilgrims." The statues are carried to the place of honor and the house immediately fills with the people of the procession. Once all are inside, the catechists lead the prayers of the novena of the Posadas, after which they all sing some more and then enjoy the very special Posada food served by the "innkeeper," who is the owner of the home that is that night's stopping place.

For at least a week before the 16th of December, which is the official starting day of the Posada, there is a good deal of activity around the church. Little boys bring bamboo canes and colored cellophane paper to the parish hall where they make lanterns, with a candle placed precariously in the center of each one. Older boys take the platform out of storage, refurbish it, and decorate it with paper flowers. The statues are also dusted off and set up on the platform. The men of the Acción Católica committee are responsible for arranging the hospitality for the nine nights of the Posada, and many householders vie for the privilege of hosting the Posadas for a night. The stops are chosen so that each night the procession will wend its way through town for a good distance between the houses.

Women and girls here do not ordinarily walk in the Posada procession, because it is customary for women to stay at home after dark. Those in the house receiving the Posadas are busy all day preparing the hot pineapple punch or chocolate drink for the guests, and female neighbors and relatives usually come to help out. But since Lori and I are women from outside the culture, representing the Church, we are expected to participate in the Posadas. And since we are participating, some women and girls have decided to break with tradition and join us in the procession each night. There are no street lights, so I go in fear and trepidation, because it's so easy to stumble and fall on these narrow, steep, and rocky paths. Some folks carry flashlights, but that helps only those near the light. And I marvel that more lanterns made of bamboo, cellophane, and candles don't catch fire. But, all in all, it is a happy time, and a good preparation for Christmas. The catechists have studied the Christmas story, and each night they read about the trip from Nazareth to Bethlehem and the birth of Jesus. The talks they give on each night's reading are well prepared and right on target. They use as examples experiences they themselves have had of going to Guatemala City for legal matters or for market, and having to sleep in a patio somewhere, or in a friend's tiny shack. They talk about their common experience of not having enough money to pay, and the shame of having to beg for a place. They know, more than I ever could, the meaning of the journey of Joseph and Mary to Bethlehem.

December 26, 1978

I'm staying with some friends today. It is the day after Christmas. I need a break after the intensity of the pre-Christmas preparations, the Posadas, and the Christmas Eve Mass. I also needed time away from town and my work to reflect on the year. And as I do that, I feel compelled to write you an unusual letter, one in which I must let my thoughts flow. You may not understand everything I say, because we live in two different worlds, but I have a great need to tell you about mine. The situation in Central America is getting worse, and the situation in Guatemala has deteriorated markedly this year.

In all of Latin America there is great social ferment and effort for change. Hope for a better life is rising among the poor, who constitute about eighty-five percent of the population. For the last ten years, the Catholic Church's official stance has been to aid in the efforts for social change. These efforts aim for more justice for all people, but especially for those who have no power over their lives or their livelihoods. Of course there are people, including

Catholics, who oppose any change in the status quo. The fear of losing wealth, power, and prestige through allowing changes that will benefit the majority of the people is just too great.

We have, in recent years, heard about assassinations and political prisoners across our borders in El Salvador and Honduras, and in Nicaragua as well, especially during the current struggle against the dictator, Somoza. Recently, death squads have been reactivated here in Guatemala. This is nothing new in Latin America, but it is becoming more and more blatant and shameless now.

Since July we have had a new president, an army general. Most of his predecessors for over twenty years have also been army officers. That in itself is frightening because they can run the country as they choose, with the whole army and the civilian police force carrying out their wishes and those of their powerful friends. Just before this new president took office, we got a whiff of what we were in for. I wrote you last June about the slaughter of over a hundred peasants—men, women, and children—in a town called Panzós.

Why this slaughter of innocents? I believe the answer has to do with the age-old and thorny problem of land-grabbing and land ownership. In that area, as in many parts of rural Guatemala, the people settled virgin territory generations ago. Now, new "owners" are coming to claim the property as theirs, waving a piece of paper called "title" and demanding that the people leave. It's an old trick that has been used many times in Guatemala's history. It works like this:

First, the government announces a plan to help the poor, landless rural people by opening up government land to colonization. Families accept the invitation and the challenge to carve a home and fields out of forests and jungles. They work energetically and enthusiastically, to clear and plant and make the farms profitable. Maybe they've passed land on to their grandchildren, or maybe they have been on the land just a few years. But for all those years, the government has not been able to give them clear title to the land. Red tape and double talk, empty promises and signatures or thumbprints of illiterate campesinos on false documents finally wear the people down. Some may slacken in their efforts to get title, while others keep at it.

One day, new owners arrive, usually from Guatemala City. These people claim they own all the land. The settlers are ordered, often at gunpoint, to leave homes, roots, ancestral graves, and their beloved cornfields without a word of complaint or resistance. Of course, those who wish are welcome to stay on the land as tenant farmers or live-in fieldhands, working for the new owner at a pittance, so long as they remain docile and grateful. If they aren't, off they must go.

This has been happening for too long, and people in some places who have already moved once or twice simply refuse to move again to accommodate the claims of a new owner. They believe their only defense is to organize to protect whatever shred of rights might still be left to them. I once heard a professor of political science observe that there is not an area of the country's life in which the wealthy and powerful are not organized. There is the national coffee growers' association, an organization for the cotton plantation owners, one for the cattle ranchers, another for the sugar cane growers. There is the chamber of commerce, the bankers' federation, the industrialists' organization, and so on. These groups have formed a larger umbrella organization representing all of them. No one thinks it unusual that they organize. It is their right, and it is expected. But when campesinos and factory laborers try to organize, they are looked upon by those in powerful positions as rebellious, even treasonous, and Communist-inspired.

Here lip service is given to equal rights for all. Rights are even guaranteed in the Constitution of the nation. But when the downtrodden begin to claim those rights there is trouble. Those who side with them, especially priests and Sisters who live and work with the poor, are called Communists, subversives. If that doesn't get the desired result, leaders are threatened anonymously. And if that still doesn't work, some leaders are kidnapped, tortured, and killed, or simply never seen again—they "*disappear*." Mutilated bodies turn up with distressing frequency along the highways these days.

Until recently, priests and religious have been immune from these unpleasant side-effects of supporting the efforts of the poor. But after the Panzós massacre came the murder of Father Hermógenes López. A few weeks later, a Spanish nun was whisked off and thrown out of the country. Those who knew her said she was the last person whom you could accuse of political activity of any sort. But she *was* training catechists and leaders. The bishop of the diocese pressed the government for a reason for the expulsion but nothing convincing was ever produced. Many Catholic church workers believe that her expulsion was part of an effort to scare us into submission and silence.

But the expulsion had the opposite effect. The national Committee for Justice and Peace, an independent ecumenical group, published a statement denouncing the Panzós massacre, and another deploring the expulsion of the Sister. The bishop of her diocese offered a public protest, as did the national association of religious. Rather than frightening them into silence, the government succeeded in provoking their angry response.

Later on in July, Guigui (Mario) Mujía was murdered. He was another Catholic leader, who used his skills and lived his faith in the service of the poor. After his murder, there followed a wave of murders of labor organizers and leaders around the country. Most were simple laborers themselves who felt the economic strangulation of wages that were too low and prices that were too high to support a family. And just a few days ago, a German priest working in a colonization zone in the northern jungle was deported before anyone even knew what was happening. He was just grabbed, thrown into jail, then put in an unmarked car and expelled. Even with the protests of the Committee for Justice and Peace, the bishop, the Apostolic Delegate representing the pope, the Organization of Religious, and the German ambassador, this government won't budge. It has rid itself of one more "troublemaker." There was no trial, no charge. If someone in power finds you a nuisance, you are *gone*.

So, almost every month, we have a murder or expulsion of some significant person aligned with the poor. Those being killed so far have been Guatemalans. They haven't killed foreigners, yet. We are waiting to see what new surprises are in store for us in the coming year. Of course the government publicly deplores the assassinations and kidnappings and claims to be trying to discover who the responsible parties are, but they never get any clues. I wonder why? Rather than feeling secure with so many thousands employed in the secret police, the regular police, the treasury police, and the army, the country is in a state of permanent terror.

I don't expect the end of the year to bring an end to these murders and threats. These acts appear to be the beginning of a new policy under this new president. Resistance is springing up among the people. There are rallies against this brutal policy. Banners proclaim: "For every one killed, one thousand will rise up."

Most of the people being killed aren't "important" enough to make the headlines. The announcements of their deaths are buried obscurely somewhere in the middle of the newspaper with just a line or two saying "campesino kidnapped" or "worker found murdered." But who would want to kill just any old campesino or worker? These are leaders who are being killed. The people trained to be catechists and parish leaders, teachers and organizers, are the ones disappearing. Or they are appearing tortured and dead somewhere far from home. These are folks who have studied the Gospel and the story of creation, and now know the meaning of human dignity and freedom and rights. They know and live the truth that we are all God's children, brothers and sisters in a family following Jesus our Brother. And they dare to teach Jesus' own message, the message of the Beatitudes: "Blessed are the poor in spirit for theirs is the Kingdom of God. Blessed are the meek, for they shall inherit the earth. Blessed are the peacemakers, for they shall be called children of God. Blessed are those who mourn, for they shall be comforted. Blessed are they who suffer persecution in the name of justice, for they shall be called children of God." Jesus didn't preach a religion of "pie in the sky when you die." Rather, he said, "I have come that you might have life and have it in abundance." He wanted people to live as children of God here in this life as well as in the next.

We who work with the poor campesino or in the cities with poor workers and their families are trying to follow in Jesus' footsteps. It is sobering to realize that going all the way means martyrdom. We believe that Father Hermógenes, who was shot after making a sick call, was martyred. We think Guigui, the labor leader, was martyred. And we believe that the hundreds of obscure campesino leaders who have died for their Christian ideals and actions are martyrs. When I think of the atrocities committed against religious and catechists in China when the Communists took over, I see the same things happening here. But there is one terrible difference: In China the missioners knew where they stood. The government was antireligion, any religion. In Latin America, many in the government profess to be devout Catholics. They claim that they are trying to help the Church by preventing its slipping unwittingly into the

Communist camp. Any Church person perceived to be working a little too closely or too effectively with the poor is labeled Communist.

We religious who work here in the rural "boondocks" don't have the concerns and worries that you folks back home may have. You live normal lives and are concerned about your children's welfare and their education. We who have no children of our own worry about the children whose parents are being trained by us to be catechists and leaders. Which of them will become a "threat" to the establishment? Some of them will become martyrs. We worry about the economic deprivation of the people with whom we live. They work from before sunup to past sundown, scratching out a livelihood on a few acres or struggling to weave extra pieces for sale, so that they can feed their children, as they would put it "a few tortillas, and maybe some salt."

And we know there are unscrupulous people scheming to get their land, to add their few acres to the thousands of acres they already possess. We know that the Catholic Church is under great suspicion and will be pressured increasingly to stop its programs of adult education and leadership formation. Yet, rather than slow down, the momentum in the Church is building, as is the momentum in the general population. More and more people are speaking out, putting ads in the newspapers stating the facts (the only way the newspapers can clearly state the facts is by these ads, for which they can claim no responsibility).

I personally am in no way involved in anything that could be considered outrightly political, much less subversive. But as a member of the Catholic Church in Guatemala, I am under as much suspicion as the next priest, Sister, or Brother. If anything happens that gets this government angry enough, maybe all foreign missioners will be expelled. It wouldn't be the first time such a thing has happened in this country.

The rub is that the government says there are no laws against what we Church workers are doing among the poor. They sometimes even praise a program here or there. What all of us do is perfectly legal and guaranteed in the Constitution. But the faceless, nameless "they" who don't like it will do everything they can to stop it. So there will be more murders, kidnappings, and deportations. It's a vicious circle and no one knows where it will stop.

Guatemala is a lovely country. It has wonderful scenery, and the government wants to promote tourism and show off the Indian women in native dress. The red carpet is always out for the foreign tourists and business people. It's only the foreign Catholic missioners who are having increasing difficulty in obtaining permission to stay in the country more than six months. Some can't stay more than thirty days. But life goes on and I do what I can to help prepare the people here in town for the day when they may well be the ones to keep the Church alive, as did their ancestors when the two expulsions in the last century sent most priests and religious packing. Anyway, I just want you to know that, although this is a beautiful country, all is not sunshine and flowers down here. Guatemala is a land of volcanoes and earthquakes, and we are sitting on a political-social-economic-religious volcano right now. And the situation is likely to get worse for the Catholic Church. Yet, after all I've said, I want you to know I love being here, and I plan to stay as long as possible.

January 1, 1979

Lori and I had a pleasant Christmas, complete with midnight Mass and a Christmas-night meal. It is a custom here for families to go home after midnight Mass and eat tamales before retiring. Last year after midnight Mass, our friend Ramon Pérez and a couple of his daughters asked us to wait up so they could bring us tamales from their home before we went to bed. This year, since they didn't say anything, we went to bed at about two A.M. when things had quieted down. Just as I was falling asleep, I heard a light tapping on the door and someone calling very softly. In retrospect, the situation was amusing. Our lights were out and the door was locked, so he must have known we were already in bed. Ramon tapped and called softly, as if he didn't want to wake us if we were asleep. Yet he kept it up until I got out of bed, put on a robe, and went to the door. So he really intended to wake us after all! His three daughters were with him to wish us a very Blessed and Happy Christmas and they left us with four huge, steaming tamales. Rather than waking Lori and offering her a tamal then and there, I decided we'd have them for breakfast. However, in the morning we received many more tamales from several other families. By midday we must have accumulated at least sixteen—and believe me, one tamal is enough for a meal. Since we were invited to a neighboring parish for Christmas dinner, we took some of the tamales to give to friends who lived along the way.

Christmas in this Indian town is not the commercialized event that it is in the States. The merchants don't count on the Indians to buy Christmas presents for the family. For the most part, the Posadas and midnight Mass followed by tamales wrap up the celebration of Christmas here. The only Christmas decorations are twinkling lights around the manger scene near the altar in church.

Being attached to our own Christmas customs, Lori and I cut a branch from a pine tree, stuck it in a bucket of wet sand, and trimmed it with a few Christmas balls and a set of lights. Well, our Christmas tree was the focus of attention of all our visitors for weeks. We left it up so that everyone who wanted could come and see it. No one felt like copying the custom in their own homes, which is just as well, but they were delighted with our "tree."

My garden is coming along slowly because the weather is cool at night and the sun comes up from behind the mountain directly behind the house, which throws its shadow over the garden until about noon each day. Besides, our cat seems to think that red beet seedlings make a lovely bed. My tomatoes didn't make it this time, so that's another disappointment. Why do I even bother to try? I guess because the attitude of my neighbors and friends is rubbing off on me: "We must continue to hope and work for something better. God does not want us to suffer, so if we have bad luck now, maybe things will soon change. Never give up."

That idea that "God does not want us to suffer" may sound hollow to some families in town these days. We're in the middle of an epidemic that is causing grief in many households. Several little children have died already. Would you believe the disease that is killing these little ones is measles?

January 15, 1979

Today is a national fiesta, the feast of El Señor de Esquipulas. Esquipulas is a town in Guatemala way to the east, near the Honduran border. It has been a center for pilgrimage for centuries. It might even have been a holy place for the Mayans before the Spanish came and imposed Christianity. People travel to Esquipulas for pilgrimage daily, but today is the biggest celebration of the year.

The Indian people of Guatemala have a great devotion to the crucifix of El Señor de Esquipulas. The sculptor, Quirio Cataño, carved the corpus out of native wood almost 400 years ago, giving it the face of a suffering Mayan Indian. The image soon acquired a reputation for miraculous powers and became a focus of religious sentiment. After centuries of aging and exposure to the smoke and heat from millions of candles burned before it, the corpus is so dark it is affectionately called "the Black Christ."

Remember my telling you about Ramon Pérez, the man of the Christmas tamales? He is also a devotee of the Black Christ in the basilica at Esquipulas. Each year he organizes a pilgrimage from our town to the shrine and manages to get a busload of people to go. It is a really festive occasion, like going on a picnic. The people have to climb our mountain for an hour with all their things even to reach the bus. The trip takes over seven hours, so they stay in Esquipulas overnight, sleeping out of doors, just wrapped in blankets. The buses returning from Esquipulas can be spotted easily, because they are festooned with multicolored garlands. The people in the buses also wear adornments and hats that can be purchased only in that town. The souvenir merchants do a brisk business on this day, for sure. Ramon says no one goes to Esquipulas to ask for anything—they all go to offer thanks. If that is true, it is a very unusual shrine!

When Ramon gets back he'll be a busy man. He is the local unofficial health worker and more people go to him for curing than go to the practical nurse at the government health center next to church. With this measles epidemic, he frequently doesn't close his clinic door until midnight. In the evening, he comes home from working in his fields, eats a supper of tortillas, some greens, and sweetened coffee, and then goes to his "clinic," the room next to the kitchen. Even while he's eating, mothers line up outside his house rocking and shushing crying babies slung in shawls on their backs. Fathers carry older children, wrapped in blankets. The health center nurse is on vacation all month, and the doctor, who should come every two weeks, hasn't been here in months. So Ramon is the only one available to give them the compassionate concern and treatment they seek.

Measles is a viral disease and, as those of us know who grew up before inoculation was possible, it is highly contagious. It can run through a whole family like wildfire. When I was small we all expected to get it. We'd miss some school, be miserable for awhile, and then recover. Nobody I knew of ever died of measles. But here it is frequently fatal. Either the children's resistance is lower, or it's a different strain of virus, but it seems so much more virulent. I don't think the little ones die of the measles so much as they die of complications: dehydration, secondary infection, respiratory complications. Ramon injects antibiotics to ward off infection. He also puts intravenous solutions into tiny veins that are on the verge of collapsing. He instructs parents in how to bring down fevers and force fluids into the little ones. But for many children, the struggle for life is too great, and they succumb. These days, the church bell tolls almost daily at around four P.M. Usually one, sometimes two or three small white pine boxes pass the church, each on a man's shoulder, on the way to the cemetery. And most nights, a drunken man's voice can be heard wailing in the streets: "Ay! Ay! My child is gone; my child died! Ay! Ay!"

I am angry, but I don't know whom to be angry at. The doctor who comes only every two weeks when he comes at all, and then only for a few hours? The nurse who is on a long vacation? Me, for not being a nurse? The parents, for being too poor to give their children better medical care? Or a system and government for not caring?

January 29, 1979

While you folks are in the throes of winter, here it is harvest time for the corn growing on the mountainsides. The harvest continues for several weeks, because the cornfields are found all over the mountains, from the low valleys to the peaks. The corn ripens in the valleys first, and then in stages up to the mountain tops. It is a joyous time because another cycle of the year is finished with the gathering of the sacred crop and mainstay of life. Here the people stack the ears of corn against a wall in the house, from roof to ceiling, several layers deep.

Nothing of the corn is wasted. To give you only a partial list: The stalks are used for fencing; the leaves are used for tamales or are fed to cattle; the outer husk, when dried, can be used for scrubbing; and the cob can be cooked and ground and fed to the dogs, or dried and used as fuel for the fire.

The corn kernels stay on the cob until the women are ready to start the tortilla process. They begin by vigorously rubbing the kernels from the cob (I tried it and it is *not* as easy as it looks!) and soaking them overnight in a clay pot filled with water in which a lump of lime rock has dissolved. In the morning the softened grains are rinsed and taken to the molino for the first grinding. At home the women grind the mass once more, kneeling on the floor behind a small sloping surface made of heavy black rock, the grindstone. A rolling pin of the same black stone is deftly and quickly rolled back and forth over the corn dough with a rhythmic "click-click." Finally the tortillas are formed between the palms of the hands with another distinctive sound, "slap-slap, slap-slap," and are laid on the ceramic griddle over an open fire. I watch the process with great respect. This is the very same way corn tortillas, the basic and sacred food of the Mayan people, have been prepared since time immemorial. Archeologists have unearthed grinding stones that are thousands of years old, yet just like these. Pictures from Mayan records also show the women kneeling behind the grindstones, just as they do today. A tradition passed on for so long must be very important. When Vicenta offered to teach me how to grind on the stone, I was touched and honored. You can imagine my delight when my work was declared "very good." I can grind, but when I try to form the dough into the perfectly round tortillas, all of equal thickness and size—which even a ten-year-old girl can produce—I am a miserable failure. My tortillas come out square! So I leave that art to the experts.

February 7, 1979

It's over a week since I last wrote to you, because it's over a week since I nearly cut off the tip of my thumb while trying to crack open one of our hard-shelled squashes. I had sharpened the knife especially well so that I could crack the shell with one whack. Of course with my other hand I held the squash still. I am very fortunate that the knife was not a fraction of an inch closer to my thumb. I could have lost a whole joint! I stuck the tip back on with a Band-Aid and hoped for the best.

It makes me wonder how the children who use machetes manage not to injure themselves more than they do. I have seen a little boy peel oranges with a huge machete, as well as whittle a toy top from a stick of firewood. The other day I was visiting Alejandro, one of our catechists, at his house. In horror I watched his little two-year-old son dig in the dirt with a big pen knife. I asked Alejandro if he noticed what the boy was playing with. Smiling, he assured me he did. In fact he had given it to the child to play with. He said the boy was learning to use it, and was being careful! So, if you start that young, I guess you learn how to handle sharp knives pretty well. They use their machetes for digging holes, cutting firewood, killing snakes, and many other chores. I admire the versatility of this tool and their masterful use of it. I would need several tools to accomplish all that they can do with just a machete.

Another daily hazard here is in the kitchen. Every kitchen has an open fire on the floor, and women spend a lot of time tending the fire and heating beans, coffee, and soup. Children hover around mothers, and accidents happen. Several days ago, a teenaged boy came with his eight-year-old brother, Mateo, and asked us to look at a burn on the child's arm. Little Mateo, who looked a bit frightened, stood very quietly while the older boy explained how Mateo spilled a pot of coffee on his arm that morning. The nurse was not in town, and Ramon was in his fields, so we took on the job. With his brother interpreting for us, Lori gently undid the rag on Mateo's arm while I searched in our reference book, Werner's *Where There Is No Doctor,* for burn treatment advice. We were fortunate to have what we needed to dress the burn, which was quite nasty. Lori gave Mateo a piece of candy and smiled. "Will you come back again tomorrow, Mateo?" She asked. Mateo nodded solemnly, and his brother promised to return. I was surprised when he kept that promise the next day, because most people think one treatment is enough. But that afternoon a happier Mateo was at the door with his brother. He was ready for a change of dressing and another piece of candy.

Every day since then, the two boys have come, and by the third day little Mateo was literally dancing into the house. He has a winning smile and is very bouncy. His more serious older brother keeps him out of trouble, though, and gets him settled for the change of dressing. The last time I saw the burn, the skin was healthy and pink while the boy's arm was brown. But there was no scar, and the pink will turn brown with time. Mateo and his brother are very happy, and so are we.

February 24, 1979

I had a long talk with Antonio, one of our catechists today. He is a man of small physical stature, but of great spiritual stature. I want to tell you about him. He is one of the men whom I first met through our work with the Acción Católica parish council. He was vice-president at the time. Antonio is well-liked in town, and is a man gifted in prayer. He is called on several times a week to pray with people who are sick or in trouble. He goes to their homes whenever he is called, even if he is woken out of a sound sleep. He might not come back for hours, so his wife locks the door when he leaves, and when he returns, rather than waking her and the children, he beds down in his clothes, with no blankets (the family has only two blankets, one for the parents and one for the children) on the floor of the lean-to kitchen outside the house.

Antonio is a man of deep faith who has always believed in God and the power of prayer. But he was not a member of Acción Católica until recently. Today, over coffee and bread, he told me his story. I found it fascinating. As a young man, he was a staunch defender of the traditional ways and fought the foreign import called Acción Católica. He even participated in the campaign to have the original members thrown in jail. He did it much as St. Paul did, in defense of his people's religion and their way of life. Obviously, he was threatened by this different way of being Catholic.

As time went on and Acción became a part of the town's life, Antonio accepted the change gradually, though he still didn't want to become a member. He believed in the live-and-let-live approach to community life. As a young husband and father, he worked hard and was faithful to his duties to family and town. But his first child died, bringing grief to Bernarda, his wife, and to himself. When they lost their second child and then their third, even though they had done all they could by taking them to spiritists and local folk doctors, they were beside themselves with grief.

Ramon Pérez, a member of the original twelve couples, had become Antonio's friend over the years and had tried to persuade him to join Acción Católica. He stressed the spiritual benefits that he found in it himself, as well as the communitarian good. But Antonio wasn't interested. Finally, when his fourth and only living child was very ill, he let Ramon convince him to take the child to a nearby parish clinic. There, with the antibiotics of modern medicine and the care of the clinic staff, many of whom were Mayan Indian women, the child recovered. Antonio was deeply affected, and asked Ramon, who was himself a catechist of the old Catechism for First Communion, to teach him so he and Bernarda could marry in the church and become members of Acción Católica.

By the time Lori and I moved into town, Antonio and Bernarda had four healthy children. He had moved into leadership roles in Acción. He was elected to the parish committee and served as catechist and official prayer person for the group. But he couldn't read very well. When we invited him to study in Huehuetenango he hesitated a bit before accepting and plunging wholeheartedly into this new world of studies in Spanish. He comes frequently to talk over the material for the catechist classes. In addition, he arrives an hour before the other men who meet with us weekly to prepare for the monthly catechist sessions. He wants to go over questions or difficulties he has encountered in the study.

Antonio is a very good example of how some people find that this new way of being Catholic, and following Jesus by learning his message from the Gospel, brings a whole new joy to life, and they want to share it with others, at great cost to themselves. When I visit with Antonio, I am struck by his simple wisdom and deep insights into the message of Jesus. I learn a lot from him. More, I think, than he learns from me.

Yesterday I visited a family whose three little children had measles. One looked almost dead. He lay listlessly in his mother's arms, hardly able to cry, totally dehydrated. She was rocking him, rubbing his head and crooning, as if that could put life back into the tiny body. The other two were in bed, but might make it. I prayed with the parents and, at their request, laid my hands on the children's heads. Perhaps some of Jesus' healing power will come to that house. But I'm not Antonio. I believe his prayer could bring healing. And I'm not Ramon, who knows how to cure. I'm just myself, hoping and praying with the family.

March 10, 1979

We are preparing once again for Lent and Easter, with discussions and meetings with catechists and leaders on how to make the message of Holy Week more meaningful. The old customs have meaning for the townspeople, of course. But the original meaning, the meaning stemming from the life of Jesus, his death and his resurrection, needs to be made clearer. This year we will again use the filmstrips on the life of Christ to instruct those who choose to come. Lori and I will participate in the Stations of the Cross every Friday of Lent. This is a very popular custom in town, and the Catholic Action committee is responsible for it. Two weeks before Lent began, the committee was refurbishing the four-foot-high statue of Jesus carrying his cross; the statue is called *Jesus Nazareno*. Volunteers carry it on a platform in procession around town, stopping at fourteen points along the way to pray the stations. This year, the catechists have very simple, understandable booklets that connect the story of Jesus' last hours with the life of the people today. I have heard that many people like coming for the readings. The procession stretches out along the street for such a long distance that the parish committee carries a portable loudspeaker system, and the catechists take turns translating the readings into their own language over the speaker.

The faith of this people always inspires me. They are so clearly in touch with the suffering of Jesus, because they are so clearly in touch with their own suffering, both as individuals and as a community. And the recent measles epidemic provides a good example of that suffering. This plague comes about every five years. The people say they are relieved when it passes, because it won't come again for another five years. But they know it will come. And that children will suffer and die. And that there is nothing they can do.

I visited a family with several small children who were down with the measles. Knowing that the government sponsors periodic vaccination programs and that the government health center fosters participation, I asked the mother why she didn't have the children vaccinated. I told her they would not be suffering so, and nor would she, if they had been vaccinated. I must have looked at her accusingly, because she put her head down and didn't look up for a minute. Then she reached up onto a shelf and took down some papers wrapped in a smoke- and dust-covered plastic bag. She unfolded the plastic, removed the papers, and handed them to me. "We did have the older two vaccinated," she said, "only the baby wasn't vaccinated because it had not been born yet."

I looked at the papers. They were immunization cards, one for each of the two elder children. The immunization boxes for polio, diptheria, typhoid, and measles were all checked off. I was stunned, and very ashamed. I must have blushed, but in that dark, airless room, no one could see. Who was I to accuse a mother of failing to take advantage of a free health program? My criticism turned to the government health program that allowed the use of vaccine that was too old, or that was useless because it was not stored properly. The health program went through the motions and convinced people to vaccinate their children with useless vaccine; the government raised their hopes falsely with the idea that their little ones would be spared the scourge of measles. And I wondered what I would do if I were this mother, the next time the measles vaccine campaign swung into motion. Would I trust those strangers, coming from the faraway capital, with their needles and equipment and government jeeps? Would I let them vaccinate my child? Would I trust them? Why should I?

Today, at four P.M. the bells tolled again. I knew already that the baby I visited yesterday had died. I went to the window to watch the young father carry the tiny coffin past the church on the way to the cemetery. That little coffin on his shoulder suddenly reminded me of the image of *Jesus Nazareno* of the Stations of the Cross. This was his cross, his sharing in the suffering of Jesus. And I knew that his and his wife's suffering shouldn't have happened.

March 27, 1979

I haven't written in a while because Lori and I are so involved in preparing for and giving classes in mountain settlements all over the parish. We are hardly at home long enough to read our mail, much less to answer it. Since Lent began, we have had the Celebration of the Word in church every Wednesday night, and a lot of people come to that. The custom when we first came was to have prayers with the rosary every night, but only a handful of people would come. The Celebration of the Word is a simple prayer service with readings from the Bible, a talk on the readings, prayers by the people and an Our Father. Lori and I take turns giving the talk, but we have to do it in Spanish and ask for a translation. I look forward to the day that our town catechists will do the reflections on the readings themselves, in their own language.

I also have my garden to take care of, since everybody in town expects to see great things coming out of it. You should see the men examining everything after Mass on Sundays. They give advice and admire whatever is worth admiring. Some bring a plant they'd like me to try, or offer some fertilizer to help the soil and plants along. This has become a community concern. And I now have a women's "garden club." In fact, some of the women have already brought me some "first fruits" of their own gardens, mainly radishes and Swiss chard, two vegetables they use a lot. If the club succeeds, others will follow our example. That is the way change comes about here. It can't be imposed. It has to *work* for somebody first; then the others will begin to follow suit.

May 15, 1979

I just had a visit from a little boy who came with an urgent request from his mother for some milk. He told me his whole story in Cakchikel, mind you, and I was able to understand! His mother sent him for milk because their cat which had kittens five weeks ago just died. They wanted to save the kittens. Since they never buy milk themselves, they wondered if we had milk to sell them. I was so pleased with myself for understanding his story, that I gave him quite a lot of powdered milk and even managed to explain how to prepare it—all in his own language!

I want to tell you about a very special "first" that we celebrated a few weeks ago: the first Silver Wedding Anniversaries of the original twelve founding couples of Acción Católica here in town. Twenty-five years ago, as a result of a missionary priest's efforts, the first couples in town were married in a group marriage ceremony in the parish church. Before that, the people here in town married according to ancestral custom, but were not married legally in the eyes of the civil or Church authorities. Actually, their ancestral marriage rites predated the coming of the Spanish with their new laws and new religion. As far as the townspeople were concerned, they *were* married. In fact, the possibility of a Church marriage was probably never even presented to them, since there were practically no priests in the distant rural areas.

But, with the arrival of the missionaries from Spain in the 1950's came Acción Católica to bring those Indians who were interested into the modern Catholic Church. Since they were all baptized as infants, matrimony became the way for them to "join" Acción Católica. The first twelve couples were all parents of families, and some were already grandparents when they were married in the Church. Ever since then, as each fiesta rolls around, several new couples come to the parish council asking to study for matrimony. These, too, are mainly couples who have lived as man and wife for years. But by marriage they take on a responsibility to the Acción Católica community, and must study more about their Catholic faith. The Catholic community has grown this way year after year until today it is of considerable size.

Father Martín joined us in suggesting to the parish council that we invite the surviving couples, as well as the widowed partners, to a special anniversary Mass and celebration. It was a wonderful idea which the parish council wants to make an annual event, celebrating each successive year's Silver Anniversaries. It may just become a new parish custom.

June 5, 1979

It is no news to you that our Central American neighbor, Nicaragua, is embroiled in a civil war in the attempt of the people to shake off their dictator-president, Anastasio Somoza. Here in Guatemala, various groups within the Church have launched a national campaign to aid the civilian population—victims of the war—who are trapped in refugee centers or in their own homes without food, water, or electricity.

A few weeks ago, we announced at Mass that on the following Sunday there would be a special collection for the Nicaraguan people. When the day arrived, the parish council leaders announced the collection over the church loudspeaker system, so the whole town heard about it.

In our town, the men are mostly subsistence farmers, and the women are weavers. If a man works his own land (often just an acre or two) he may grow enough crops to feed his family. With luck he might have a small surplus to sell. If he is a hired hand he could earn up to $1.50 a day, which is not very much, even here. Our Sunday church collection usually averages around four dollars, and is mostly pennies. Ours is really a "penny economy."

At Mass, when the collection for Nicaragua was placed in a basket on the altar, I was amazed to see paper money, bills worth 50 cents or $1.00, sticking out from the quarters and small change. To our great surprise, the collection for the Nicaraguan people totaled $42, ten times the usual Sunday collection! In addition, the leaders announced that they would continue accepting donations all day, and took turns staying in the parish office to receive contributions. They were wise: many more people came to leave a donation who were not even members of the Acción Católica community.

Do you remember the Gospel story of the widow's mite? When Jesus compared the large, noisy donations of the rich people who gave of their surplus to the temple coffers, and the single penny of the poor widow, he said that hers was the greater gift, because she gave all that she had. I think the people in this town are just like that widow.

June 17, 1979

Today is Father's Day, and I remembered you, Dad, at Mass, in gratitude for all you are. I enjoy and appreciate having you as my father.

I woke early this morning, around three A.M., to the crow of a cock. That crowing doesn't wake me every day, and it doesn't keep me awake. I must have been sleeping more lightly than usual. Here in town the crowing of the cocks does not happen just at dawn. It happens every hour or so. And the people who grow up with cock-crowing know what time it is by the *way* the cock crows. It has always amazed me that men going to the capital to sell their vegetables can get up at two A.M. and catch the bus that passes on the road on the mountain top at 3:30. I also couldn't figure out how people can wake up at three A.M. to ring church bells before a big fiesta, or how a woman can wake up every day to make her tortillas so long before dawn. The cock's crowing, I've learned, acts like an alarm clock. It is wonderful the way nature and people here are so in tune.

Our friend Antonio always comes for the weekly seven P.M. catechist meeting at seven on the dot. Since almost no one here goes by "American time," I asked him once if he had a watch or clock. "No, Madre, I don't," he replied. More curious now, I said, "Do you listen to the radio for the time?" "No. Why do you ask?" I admitted to my curiosity about his punctuality. "I just know what time it is, and I come," he said simply. I found that hard to swallow even though he's a friend, so I thought I'd try a little test. After discussing the class material with all five of the catechists for a while, I suggested a coffee break. "Antonio, do you know what time it is?" I asked. He looked up from his Bible, paused, looked out the window at the stars and said, "It's ten minutes to nine." I looked at my watch: eleven minutes to nine. Was I fast, or was he slow?

The news from Nicaragua leads me to wonder not *if* Somoza will be toppled but *when* he will fall. Everyone in the country but his army and National Guard opposes him, so he can't last much longer. His fall might inspire the poor and downtrodden of El Salvador and Guatemala to have hope that they, too, might be able to get out from under their oppressive burdens. His fall might also inspire the governments and powerful of these countries to act strongly to keep any such hope from being fulfilled.

July 6, 1979

We received an invitation to a child's first birthday party the other night. A first birthday party is not one where all the little children in the neighborhood come and eat cake and ice cream and play games and carry home party favors. It is, rather, a solemn time of thanksgiving by the family and the neighbors (who are probably also relatives of the child). They publicly give thanks to God that the child has lived to see its first birthday! So many children die before this first anniversary of birth that people refer to infants as "little chicks." They are so delicate.

This party was to start at seven P.M. in Francisco's home, about a ten-minute walk from here, near the outskirts of town. Lori and I went with the parish council, the guitarists, and a catechist, all of whom were officially invited. When we reached the home, we found that the other guests had already arrived and were sitting on benches lining the walls. Francisco, the father of the child, welcomed us and gave us the seats of honor. He offered a ritual welcome and thanks to the parish council president, while the president expressed his thanks to the father. Both spoke at the same time, without looking at each other. That's the way the beginning ritual is done. Then the young guitarists sang a few songs. Alejandro, the catechist, read from the Bible and commented on the precious gift of life that comes from God and belongs to God and that can be taken back only by God. Then the guitarists played and sang some more, and the prayer-service part of the birthday party was over. It was quickly followed by the food: hot coffee and sweet rolls, the standard party fare.

After we finished eating in silence (the only proper way to eat here) a signal by the president brought the evening to a close. He said goodnight to the parents, and then we all shook hands with everyone in the house and followed him out the door. I have been to other birthday parties, but this one struck me as especially poignant because I realized how many little ones didn't reach their first birthdays this year because of the measles epidemic. I whispered an extra thanks to God for this child's life and good health.

July 20, 1979

It seems incredible, but Somoza has really been defeated and has fled Nicaragua! We are all praying that the new government will be able to do all that needs to be done for the people.

The other day, Lori and I were giving a three-day course to the women from town, as we do every month. Our courses usually treat of nutrition, child care, health, hygiene, and religion. The material all focuses on living a better human and Christian life. The classes usually attract around twenty women, which is a good-sized group. Well, this time we had twenty-five women the first day. I told them we would be giving them a little more in the religion courses and would give them pictures from which we would study together. They are simple line drawings that depict scenes familiar to them from daily life. I told them they could take their pictures home and use them for review, or for teaching their families.

Since most women come at around three P.M. for the two P.M. class (wristwatch time is not common among women here), I encouraged them to come on time by saying that they would have time to color their pictures if they came earlier.

The next day, as I was still preparing for the class, the first colorers arrived. They helped me set up a simple table of sawhorses and planks and settled themselves to the exciting new experience of coloring with crayons, old and broken though they were. Soon more women were standing, waiting for a space to color as a few of us set up more tables. More women came the second day than on the first. On the third day, exactly at two P.M., the first group of women arrived, and after that it was a steady stream. We didn't have enough horses to make more tables, so some women knelt on the floor and colored on the benches. By 2:15, Marcos, our translator, arrived. He asked if we could start because there was no more room for coloring! By the end of the class that third day, I counted forty-five women and young teenaged girls. That is an exhaustingly big group to work with, what with all the crying, fidgeting babies, and little children clamoring for their mothers' attention. I am not sure why the course this time attracted so many women. Was it that word spread that we would be teaching religion (the first time in the course) or that we were giving away free pictures that they could color?

August 10, 1979

These past few days I've had a little time to rest and think about things other than the work I'm doing in town. The Church in

Guatemala has not been hit in its higher leadership (priests, religious) as I had feared would happen after the murder of Father Hermógenes López last year, and the expulsion of a few missioners after that. Maybe the government feels it has accomplished enough by warning us very strongly that it will not tolerate Church activism to get "out of hand." But other organizations and groups have been hit hard. Two civilian leaders of new political parties were gunned down, and with them went the hope of any political change. Labor organizations have been under severe pressure. Hundreds of poor rural and urban leaders who were able to raise and organize people to work for change have died or disappeared. Such leaders are a real threat to those who don't want change, who don't want to lose any of their power or prosperity. It is a tough situation.

In El Salvador, the slaughter is increasing as the army and the National Guard terrorize the population in the name of "National Security." The civil war is very bloody, and disappearances and kidnappings are commonplace. Several Catholic priests have been murdered there recently. Three were killed this year alone, and the last one died just about a week ago. That Church has suffered terribly, with catechists and priests being killed with abandon. Yet the persecution seems to strengthen the resolve of people of faith. It has also united missioners and local clergy and religious, and bonded them to the people even more tightly. They are all subject to the same suffering and suspicion.

What light does my faith shed on this dark time? Jesus has told us that the question on the day of judgment will be: How have you treated your fellow human being? "Whatever you have done to one of these, the least of my brothers and sisters, you have done to me." That is Jesus' only concern. And that is what missioners like us are trying to teach by word as well as by example. And it is what the people with whom we work are taking to heart. And it may be what will get some of us into trouble. We may be called antigovernment, or even more ominously, Communists. So, we plan to prepare the catechists and the parish community—men and women—to carry on without us. It will take time, and I pray we can accomplish our task in our own time frame, and not have to leave before the people feel ready to take over. Whatever happens, I trust in God's guidance.

August 21, 1979

The other day, I went to visit our friend, Vicenta. I called out the standard greeting before entering her house and waited for the "welcome," which came immediately. From the doorway I could see her and her two daughters all sitting on their heels, weaving. I asked them not to stop and took a seat, the only chair in the house, near the door. We chatted about the parish classes and other developments in town.

After about a half hour, I began to make the proper signs of preparing to leave. That was her signal to beg me to stay a little longer and offer me a Pepsi. One daughter ran out and bought a bottle and brought it right back. Soft drinks here are not as expensive as they are in the States, and the bottle is worth more when you return it than the liquid it contained.

I left shortly afterward, thanking her for her hospitality, and she thanked me for the visit. I find these visits very helpful because they get me to know more about the town, its history, its customs, and the people. And I don't disturb people from their work. They can weave and chat at the same time, so I don't feel guilty about taking them from their work.

Magdalena was just here for a visit. She is a remarkable example of a woman who, with all the strikes against her, somehow manages to survive with dignity. I first met Magdalena when the weaving cooperative was forming. She was one of the early members. She also took part in our literacy classes. We learned her story bit by bit, as she stopped by with some rolls or fruit for us on occasion. Magdalena's husband has epilepsy. Although the medicine to control his seizures can be obtained easily from certain government health centers, he doesn't have faith in the daily dose of pills and doesn't take them regularly. Instead, he spends most of Magdalena's hard-earned money (he can't hold a job) looking for cures with spiritists in distant towns. Magdalena can't be more than thirty-two, and yet she looks much older. Their home is a miserable shack of cane and mud. I would venture to guess that it's one of the poorest in town, and this is a *poor* town. Until recently, the couple had three children whom Magdalena worked long hours at weaving to support.

A few months ago, Magdalena gave birth to twins. If she had had a boy and a girl she could have been strongly tempted to allow the girl to die, since breastfeeding both for over a year could ruin Magdalena's health and eventually bring death to herself and both children. But these were both girls, and their mother was fiercely determined to nurse and save them both. She came to tell us of the birth and brought some bread as a gift.

We have been receiving a mixture of powdered milk and corn-meal for our catechist sessions as part of an international Catholic Charities program called Caritas. I offered Magdalena a few pounds to try in the form of a hot drink three times a day, to supplement her own sparce diet. I also gave her a month's supply of multivitamins and iron pills, which she definitely needs. She is such a small, frail and anemic-looking woman, it's hard to believe she'll make it, even with this supplement. But she is a fighter and I think she'll pull it off. I asked her to come back every month for more pills and corn-milk mixture, until she feels strong enough to go without it. She is proud, but realistic. She doesn't come to beg, but rather to share. I'm glad I can share with her, too.

September 19, 1979

There was a funeral a few days ago that was doubly sad. The dead youth was about nineteen years old. He was engaged to be married to a lovely young woman and seemed to be very happy about the prospect of setting up a home and starting a family. Then, one day, he drank insecticide and died an agonizing death! No one knows why. He may have been drunk and drank the insecticide inadvertently. But that is highly unlikely; that stuff smells and tastes so bad that even in a drunken stupor one should recognize what it is. Did he want to get out of the marriage but felt by honor committed to it? I'm afraid that is what the bride-to-be suspects and she is devastated, feeling somehow responsible for his death. Both families are quite broken up about it, especially since no amount of questioning brings answers, and no amount of blaming will bring him back.

In a poverty-bound community like this, drinking insecticide is the handiest and cheapest method of suicide. His is not the first case. Some have succeeded in killing themselves this way. Many more have tried it and failed, succeeding only in making themselves very sick and their families extremely agitated. Recently a wife came for an antidote because her husband had taken insecticide. He was saved by her quick action. I wonder if he is grateful or resentful. Insecticide is something every campesino has on hand for his crops. Maybe these suicides choose it because it is somehow linked in their minds with the hard life of a campesino. Their existence is so precarious that a bad crop can wipe out their food for the coming year. Insecticide is part of the campesino's life, and for some, it is accidentally or deliberately the cause of death.

October 7, 1979

I'm writing from the town of Patzún, where I have just finished the second week of an intensive course in Cakchikel. I covered a lot more material than a beginner would, and with the help of a trained teacher I should be able to master two months of material in less than one month. It's not that I'm a language genius, of course. It's partly because I've been working on this language for a long time. I think my having learned some Polish as a child helped train my ear and tongue to foreign sounds. That is a big advantage.

But one thing that makes it harder is the fact that each town speaks a slightly different dialect of this language. So, while I know how words are pronounced in San Jerónimo, here I have to pronounce them the Patzún way, even though I tell the teacher I'm speaking the dialect of *my* town. He says that Patzún's way is the correct way, and every other way is a degeneration of the pure language. That is an insult to the other towns, but I can't argue; he's the teacher.

Patzún is of interest to me for another reason. It is the home of some remarkable young Indian women. One, in her mid-twenties at the time, decided that she wanted to become a religious Sister. She interested about a dozen other young Indian women in joining her. They looked for a community that would accept them, even though most had not even completed their elementary education. The Carmelite Missionary Sisters, a congregation of Mexicans and Central Americans, decided to experiment with adaptations of religious life to the Indian culture and also provided these women with the opportunity to finish school. The group retains the native dress style of Patzún women. Eventually, they will be given mission work in the Indian area. I hope to meet them some day. It would be wonderful to have them in our area.

November 4, 1979

I returned to San Jerónimo a few days ago. The people here in town are happy because the rainy season is finally over. We had too much rain this year and crops suffered. They say the rain "went" on All Saints' Day. It stops, just like that.

On November 2, All Souls' Day, I looked outside to find the sky filled with beautiful, six-sided kites being flown all around the town. Boys and men had made the kites of split reeds and colored tissue paper. Apparently this is a custom related to the veneration of the dead.

Within a few days, there were many "dead" kites to mourn. They had gotten caught in the electric wires crisscrossing the town, and I guess they'll stay there until they fall apart.

This was the first time I was able to be in our town for All Souls' Day, and I was intrigued to see how the people honor and remember their deceased.

The Acción Católica Committee and Hijas de María worked hard for this day. They removed all the pews from the church, sprinkled the rough brick tile floor with water, and swept it clean. They put fresh flowers in the "vases," formerly powdered milk cans. The air was festive.

Early on All Souls' Day, members of each family brought small boards into church, chose a spot as theirs, and laid the boards down. On each board they stood neat rows of six-inch candles, one for each deceased family member and ancestor as far back as they could remember. Between the candles on the board they scattered bright yellow marigolds, called *Flor de Muerte,* or flower of death. These flowers grow wild and in abundance in this season.

The families lined up their boards near the walls of the church. There must have been at least seventy families represented by the husband, wife, and older children, all of them standing by their lit candles to tend them lest they go out too soon. I would estimate that there were thirty to forty candles on each board. The families lit the candles at the offertory. Within ten minutes, the scent of hot wax filled the church. By the end of Mass, we in church felt like *we* were the ones in purgatory, rather than the deceased represented by all those burning candles! Many of the candles actually melted and fell over. They were too soft to stand upright again. It is bad luck to have the candles blow out, so everything was shut up tight during the Mass and afterward.

After Mass, Fr. Martín stayed in the church to bless each set of candles with holy water and to say a special prayer for the dead. He read every name from each family's carefully preserved list of deceased. A list is usually an old page that was torn years ago from a school notebook, and each person who dies has his or her name added to it. Poor Martín emerged from the sweltering church with the sweat actually pouring from his face. His vestments and alb were soaked. He took off the vestments, put on his jacket, and came over to our house for some hot coffee, because he didn't want anything cold after all that heat. The change in temperature was so great, from the super-heated church to our cool house, that he was afraid he'd get a chill. Meanwhile the families tended their candles, waiting until the last one flickered out by itself. Only then did they leave the church and head for the cemetery, where they continued honoring their dead with special food, drink, candles, and flowers at the graves.

Just so we don't think ourselves superior to these people in their customs for remembering the dead, I'll tell you a story I heard:

A missioner, trying to make a point, said to an Indian man: "Why do you take food and drink to the cemetery? Don't you know your deceased can't eat or drink that food?'' "Well," said the Indian man, "I give *my* dead food and drink just as you give *your* dead flowers. Don't you know your deceased can't smell those flowers?''

November 19, 1979

On my walks through town to visit families, I frequently pass the oven of Ramon, the First Communion catechist and health worker. He is also one of the few bakers in town. I could call him "Round

Ramon" because his shape resembles the buns he bakes. He bakes only twice a week, so I don't get a chance to watch him at work very often. A few days ago, I got to his oven just as he was taking out a batch of wonderfully scented, fresh and hot sweet rolls. He offered me one, and I tossed it from hand to hand until it cooled. There is no need for butter or jam on his bread. It's delicious just as it is, and when it's dry, it is proper and customary to break it and dunk it in your coffee.

The oven is a big white igloo-like dome that Ramon's father built over fifty years ago. It has been patched where the earthquake damaged it, and is still in fine working order. It is made of adobe and the years of fire inside have hardened the adobes to brick. Next to the oven is the room where the dough is prepared by hand. I watched Ramon's muscular son-in-law as he leaned over a four-foot wooden trough, kneading the large mass that would supply the town with bread. When the dough was sufficiently kneaded, Ramon weighed out identical hunks, formed them into hundreds of balls, and put them on trays to rise in that very warm room. When the dough is ready, he takes the trays outside to the oven where a fire has burned down to hot coals. The coals are pushed to the sides and the bread goes in on a large paddle.

Ramon learned to bake bread from his father who may have learned it from his own father. But bread-baking came with the Spanish conquest. The Spaniards would not eat the tortillas, or anything made of corn, as they felt this was beneath them. Indians made the bread for the Spaniards, and learned to eat it themselves. The Indians gained something in learning to make and enjoy the delicious bread. But the Spaniards lost something in not learning to make and enjoy the delicious hot tortilla!

December 27, 1979

December has gone by in a big blur of meetings, preparation for Posadas, classes, then the actual Posadas, and then Christmas itself. I didn't have time to gather my thoughts about the days whizzing by, much less write to you. It's quiet for the moment, and I have time before the next meeting tonight to write you a short note just to let you know I'm fine, in case you were worried.

After Christmas Eve Mass, and the usual visitors, and the traditional tamales, we were able to sleep until about eight A.M., when the visitors started coming again, bringing more of the traditional Christmas tamales. In the afternoon, we went to a neighboring parish for Christmas dinner. They invite us every year, and we are grateful for a touch of our own traditions. We crossed cultures on that day, and it felt right and good. And so we move into a new year. I wonder what it holds for us and our hopes and plans and efforts to form a strong base of informed, living faith among our friends and neighbors in town. Please pray that these seeds we are planting will be blessed with much fruit for the people here, and for all those whom they will touch.

Through the celebration of the birth of Jesus into our suffering and shattered world, may we all work to show that God's justice has truly triumphed. Happy New Year, too.

Chapter Three

The Storm Rages
1980

THE TOWN

It was a gruesome picture on the front page of the tabloid: two bloated bodies stretched out on the street, and two grinning soldiers poking at them with sticks. The caption read: "Guatemalan soldiers exhibit bodies of slain guerrillas."

Pablo studied the picture carefully, then declared, "They're not guerrillas. They're just poor campesinos, like us." Then he looked hard at the soldiers and asked, "Are they Indians?" Without needing an answer he shook his head sadly and muttered, "They're Indians."

He put down the borrowed newspaper and sat in silent thought. Then he looked up at his friend, the Peace Corps Volunteer, and asked, "What can we do? How can we change the situation we live in? How can we stop our people from being used against their own flesh and blood, their own race, by the army?" The only solution he could see lay far down the road, with his own children. "We have to do everything possible to send our children to school. And not just to third grade, like me; I mean all the way, through grade school, through high school, up through college. Maybe my baby daughter will grow up and become a lawyer, a lawyer for her own people. Maybe she will run for Congress, and maybe she will get elected to represent her people. Wouldn't that be great? What if we had five or ten Indians, educated from every town, who could be the doctors, lawyers, and political representatives of their own townspeople!'' Suddenly, Pablo's enthusiasm turned sober. ''But we can't stop there. We need our own military.''

Pablo had been forcibly recruited one Sunday when he was at the market. His next three years were spent in the Guatemalan army. He said the training program had done its best to dehumanize the Indian recruits, but he had managed to retain his humanity. When ordered to train recruits himself, he tried to pass that human decency on to them, treating them kindly.

''We need our own officers if our people are to have a real change for the better. Indian officers could humanize the army by Indianizing it. If we had our own lieutenants, majors, colonels, and generals we could overthrow the government that has been murdering us, and have our own officers take power. They would see to it that we were protected in our fields; not chased and massacred as we are now. They could represent us to other governments because they would be educated and would know the world of politics and economics that we know nothing about.

''We don't want to do anything wrong, and if they'd only leave us alone, able to cultivate our plot of corn and beans in peace, we'd be happy. But they won't even let us do that! God knows, we have so little as it is that we can hardly feed ourselves, but they won't leave us alone! We need our own people to climb the ladder of the officers' corps quietly. That's our only hope. Elections mean nothing. Only a few people in Guatemala City benefit from our ballots. We are obliged to vote, and we do so in fear anyway. We get nothing. If I have a son I'll encourage him to study hard, to work for his people, and one day I'll send him to the military academy. If only I could get other fathers in town to think this way!''

His friend the American asked if he didn't think the guerrillas were doing what he wants already—they have their own army and their own officers. But Pablo shook his head, smiled ruefully, and said, ''The subversives? They're crazy. They've taken on the whole army and the whole power structure from the outside. You can't beat them that way! Look. There are two 'guerrilla' armies: the guerrillas of the rich and the guerrillas of the poor. The guerrillas of the rich have killed off all the leaders of the poor—all our friends, our church leaders. No one is trying to stop them. But the whole army is trying to stop the guerrillas of the poor, killing off whole villages of people in the process.

''Look. The rich can hire a poor Indian soldier for a few dollars a day to guard their house. He'll stand there like a dog outside in the dark and the cold, trembling with fear, while they sleep securely inside. I know, because I have stood trembling, outside one of those houses myself, wondering if the death-squad car would pass and shoot me. I was putting my life between the possible assassins and the victim snoring in his soft bed. The soldier is like a watchdog. That's all he is, really, a dog. They even make us wear these 'dogtags'! And they treat us like dogs, too. Tell me: Who protects the Indian farmer in his field? Who helps him fight off those who steal his land? Nobody! The soldier should be standing with the Indian in his field, not outside the house of the rich man in his bed!''

The volunteer patiently explained to Pablo that international forces, primarily U.S. foreign policy, oppose his solutions and support the armies of the Central American governments. Only Nicaragua has managed to throw off its dictatorship, he told Pablo. And that government is fighting to survive against tremendous pressure from the United States. He explained that while many U.S. citizens would support Pablo's ideas, the U.S. government fears them and supports the governments as they are.

Pablo was pensive for a long time. Then he looked up, with a gleam of hope in his eye. "What if all the countries in Central America were to get together and do the same thing, at the same time; make government changes so that we would all live the same way, in peace with each other and strong; cooperating for the good of all our people? What if we could all, all at once, throw off these governments? Who can I write to, to ask them not to oppose the people in their struggle for change?" He looked pleadingly at his friend. "Please, give me an address. I'll explain how it is here. Maybe that will help.''

LETTERS

San Jerónimo
February 5, 1980

I don't know if you heard anything about the terrible tragedy that occurred in Guatemala City on January 31st. Perhaps it was covered in the U.S. press, but one never knows what they might consider newsworthy, so I'll tell you the little I know.

On January 31st, a group of about thirty campesino leaders, students, and labor union members entered the Spanish embassy in Guatemala City. They wanted to speak with the ambassador, and he met with them in his office. While they were with the ambassador, riot police surrounded the embassy, a large crowd gathered, and TV camera crews arrived. At one point, the Spanish ambassador appeared at the window calling to the police to back off and leave the embassy grounds. He said that he and everyone else were fine and that they were having a peaceful discussion. Shortly afterwards, the police stormed the building. During the ensuing confusion, fire broke out in the ambassador's office. The people in the street called to the police to rescue the people inside, but the police just stood and watched the building burn. By the time firemen came it was much too late. The ambassador and one campesino escaped with injuries. All the others, including the embassy staff and two former Guatemalan government officials who were there on business, died in the inferno.

The Spanish embassy, like all embassies, is international territory. It is supposed to be inviolable by the police or army or government of the country in which it is located. Embassies are universally recognized as places of sanctuary for political refugees fleeing their own governments. But the men and women who occupied the Spanish embassy were not even trying to flee their own country. They were looking for someone to listen to their story. They had tried the Guatemalan government channels, including Congress, and were turned away. The Spanish ambassador gave them an opportunity to speak, but the opportunity proved fatal.

Most of the Guatemalans who died in the Spanish embassy fire were buried on February 2nd, the anniversary of the earthquake that killed almost 30,000 Guatemalans in 1976. The funeral procession started at San Carlos, the national university, because some of the victims were students there. Yet even before the procession had begun to wend its way through the streets, two students were shot dead on campus. Gunmen seemed intent on breaking up the massive funeral procession, but they did not succeed. Fearful of the police who lined the streets, many mourners covered their faces with handkerchiefs to conceal their identities.

Late that same night, the tortured body of Gregorio Yujá, the campesino survivor of the fire, was dumped at the entrance to the university. He had been kidnapped from his hospital bed. Hired armed guards stationed at his door had done nothing to prevent the death squad from carrying him off to a death worse than that suffered by his companions.

If such things can be done with impunity, what else is this government capable of doing?

February 12, 1980

Our catechists and the parish council teams from town and mountaintop villages recently came to a session about the changes in the Church since Vatican II. Since most of them learned their religion by rote-memorization from a Spanish catechism, they found the new emphasis on Bible study and discussion a refreshing change. To vary their presentations and prevent fatigue, the catechists asked a few volunteers to put on a skit portraying a familiar experience: the demeaning treatment Indian people frequently receive from government employees. The story line came from an actual experience of Antonio and his wife Bernarda, who is losing her sight. Antonio was looking for the best place to take his wife for treatment, so he made inquiries at the Society for the Blind and at the national hospital in Guatemala City. He was given an appointment at a government hospital a hundred miles from where they lived. The appointment was for 10 A.M. To be there on time, they had to leave home the previous day, travel by different buses, spend the night in that strange city, and get to the hospital before 10 A.M.

Bernarda speaks practically no Spanish, and Antonio speaks it poorly. They were dressed in their best Indian clothes. They were in the waiting room of the eye clinic at 9 A.M. At 10:30 A.M., Antonio went to the receptionist and reminded her they were there. She told him the doctor wasn't in yet. By 11, the doctor was seeing patients, but Bernarda was not called. At 11:30, Antonio reminded the receptionist again. "I know you're here," she retorted. "Sit down and wait. I'll call you when the doctor is ready to see your wife." Anger and frustration rose within Antonio as he returned to his wife. Other people were going in to see the doctor. What time were the other patients' appointments? By 1 P.M., Antonio left his wife and bought some coffee and bread for lunch. They missed

their tortillas. Every now and then, he'd try to catch the receptionist's eye, but she didn't look up. Finally, when they were the only
ones left in the waiting room, and the last patient had come out of
the doctor's office, Antonio told Bernarda that she *must* be next.
But she wasn't called. He waited. The receptionist was gathering
up the things on the desk. Antonio went to her. "When will the
doctor see my wife? It is four o'clock. We must soon catch a bus
or we will have to stay here overnight." "Oh, I forgot to tell you,"
she answered, putting on her jacket. "The doctor had an errand
and didn't have time to see your wife today. Come back tomorrow,
at 10 A.M. You'll be the first he'll attend."

During the sharing of experiences that followed, it was very clear
that many of the men had similar stories, and they freely expressed
their feelings about it: "They act as if we're *things,* not people."
"They treat us as if we are not important." "They think we have
no feelings. Well, we do. I have very great anger when I am treated
that way. But I can't show it, because it makes things worse."
"They treat us worse than they treat the ladinos, but what can we
do? We have to bear it."

There was a very good discussion after this. We asked what was
it that *God* wanted for them. Some were of the opinion that submission to God's will meant taking humiliation and prejudicial
treatment without complaint. Others didn't agree. The tide turned
when a catechist said that God created all people equal and wanted
them all to live in dignity, treating each other as children of God.
One participant stood up and said, "All this time I have thought it
was God's will that I be poor and have to suffer humiliation. Now
I am happy to learn that God does *not* want that for me, and that
the Church wants to take my side!"

March 17, 1980

Remember Magdalena, the woman with the twin baby girls? She
came by yesterday to visit and, as usual, brought a gift of some
buns. She came to tell us that her mother was bedridden and near
death. That gnarled old woman used to supply us with lemons from
her tree, for a penny apiece. The sick woman and her spunky daughter
are alike in many ways, especially in their ability to face hardship
with courage and a smile. Magdalena's mother sent for her a few

nights ago and said, "Magdalena, I'm dying, and I'll need a coffin. There is no one in the family who can afford to buy me one. Besides, I want to buy it myself and have it here where I can see it. I will certainly die happier if I have my coffin ready. But Julio the carpenter says it will cost $30 to make. I don't have $30.

"Magdalena, you need a better house than that shack you live in. And I need a coffin. I'd like to give you this poor house of mine, which I soon won't need, but I can't afford to give it to you. I have to sell it to buy my coffin. But I don't want to sell it to just anyone, because it belongs in our family and I want you to have it. So, if you can bring me the price of a coffin, I will leave you this house when I die."

Well, the prospect of losing her mother made Magdalena sad. Yet the prospect of having her house as a swap for the coffin brought her hope. Magdalena promised her mother that she would do all she could to get that money. But she was racing against time. Even if she worked extra hours weaving, she would never be able to save that much money before her mother died. So she came to us to ask if we could lend her the money. She assured us she would pay us back within a year.

Burying the dead is an act of charity, we're taught. Lori and I could have given Magdalena the money as part of our Christian duty and told her not to pay it back. But that would certainly wound her pride and make her ashamed. So we gave her the money as a loan, prepared to write it off if necessary as a gift to charity. Magdalena gave us one of her biggest smiles, and assured us at least five times that she would pay it back within the year.

March 31, 1980

It's a week since Oscar Romero the Archbishop of San Salvador was murdered at his altar. The news was a terrible shock. It made me think long and hard about the work of the Church in Central America.

I thought of Romero as a valiant man, a voice, like St. John the Baptist, "crying out in the wilderness." His was a wilderness of terror, disappearances, torture, and sudden deaths. He spoke against these evils openly, at each Mass, which was broadcast every Sunday on the diocesan radio station. When the radio station was bombed into silence, he then recorded his messages on cassettes and sent them to his parish churches in El Salvador. He was the voice of those who had no voice. He felt compelled to speak, in the name of the people and in the name of God, against the escalating violence that led to more and greater violence. Finally, his enemies, unwittingly repeating the steps followed by the enemies of Jesus almost 2000 years ago, decided it was "better that one man should die," and had him murdered. Once, when asked if he was against the government, Romero replied: "I am not *against* the government; I am *for* the people." That was a fine distinction beyond the comprehension of those in power. Both Jesus and Romero were "for the people," and both were killed by parties vying for power in tiny countries of practically no significance on the world scene. Yet Jesus's death had magnificent repercussions throughout the world and human history. I believe that Archbishop Romero's death, too, will have an effect on his country and the world. It will bring our attention back to the importance of love and the evil of hate. I pray that the blood of this martyr will not have been shed in vain. Perhaps, somehow, the people he so loved and for whom he died will find a solution to their problems and a new and better life for all in that tiny, suffering country named for Our Savior. I, who never met the man, still feel the loss personally.

Here in Guatemala, we have reason to watch the events in El Salvador with special interest. The Guatemalan people are currently suffering a severe repression of political, religious, and community leaders—of anyone who looks like a threat in the slightest way. In recent incidents, soldiers opened fire on spectators at a soccer match and in a market place, and they continue terrorizing the countryside.

Some bishops have spoken out against the disappearances and murders in their own dioceses. These bishops run the great risk of being silenced, once and for all, like Archbishop Romero; yet their faith and their role as shepherds of God's people requires that they speak out, denouncing the injustices and inhumanities inflicted on their people.

The true struggle in these Central American countries is not between the people who love democracy and freedom and those who want to bring Communism. It is between the "haves" and the "have-nots." The "have-nots" see clearly that they have not enough to feed their families; that they have not enough land to grow enough crops to earn a living; that they have not a chance for education and betterment; and even that they have not a chance to participate in the political life of their country. They don't need outside agitators to show them what they have not. And they are intelligent enough to see that the "haves" don't want to give up anything that they have, be it power, wealth, or privilege. Common sense shows that when only five percent of the population are the "haves" and the very great majority cannot find enough work or pay even to feed their families, there is an extremely grave injustice being done—one that cries to heaven. And the loving God of heaven and earth expects us to work to correct those injustices in creative, loving ways.

The season of Easter is upon us, a time of rebirth, a time of renewed hope, a time when we ought to feel that life is worth living. It is the time when we celebrate the Resurrection of the Lord Jesus and hope to participate in that resurrection in our own lives. And yet, we may feel a bit of foreboding in this desire, because we know all too well that resurrection is preceded by suffering and death.

April 27, 1980

About a week ago, Magdalena came to tell us that her mother had died. We tried to console her for her loss, but how does one do that? The best we could do was to listen to her story and offer her a hug. She said that with the money she had borrowed, she went to the carpenter and asked him to make her mother a nice coffin, painted black, with a cross carved on either side. It took him a while to do, and it arrived in the house none too soon. Her mother was failing very quickly, but seemed to hang on till the coffin was in her house, and she had some time to contemplate it and give her approval.

Shortly before she died, she called in some people as witnesses, had a bill of sale drawn up, and transferred the house to Magdalena for the sum of $30. Both she and Magdalena signed it. The old lady signed with her thumbprint, and Magdalena painstakingly signed her own name, a skill she recently learned in our classes.

Magdalena plans to move into her mother's house when the nine-day mourning period is over. She invited us to visit and promised to start repayment soon.

May 5, 1980

I must tell you that there has been a good deal of harassment of Catholic church workers this year in the country. I haven't told you before now because I didn't want to frighten you. But now I think you should know the latest development. On May 1st, Labor Day, there was a huge demonstration by workers. They were elated by the recent successful strike of sugarcane and cotton workers on the coastal plantations. Thousands had struck for higher wages and the government finally raised the minimum wage for farmhands from 1.25 Quetzales to 3.20. They had asked for 5 Quetzales, but were happy to get any raise at all. That wage is per *day,* you realize, not per hour!

A lot of people, including priests and church workers, supported the strike as a just demand for a living wage and better working conditions. Among them was Conrado de Le Cruz, a Mission-hurst missionary priest from the Philippines. He went to the Labor Day demonstration with some of his parishioners and his sacristan. They were kidnapped in broad daylight in Guatemala City around lunchtime, and haven't been heard from since. The priest was thirty-two years old; his sacristan, Herlindo Cifuentes, about twenty. Conrado was pastor of a parish in the province of Escuintla, where the strike affected the sugar plantations. It makes me wonder if some plantation owners wanted to get rid of him and make an example to others who might want to support the rights of the poor farmworkers. I pray they will turn up alive, but I fear that this will not happen. On Friday I'll attend a Mass in Guatemala City for them celebrated by their bishop. Hundreds of ''little'' Church people, catechists and parish workers, have suffered disappearances, torture, and death. They are known to their communities and families and friends. But when a priest disappears or is killed, that event makes bigger ripples. And it gives the rest of us professional Church workers much food for thought. It tests our faith.

May 13, 1980

When I went to pick up my mail at the post office today, I was greeted with: "Isn't it awful about the pastor of Santa Lucía?" "What about him?" I asked. "He was shot crossing the plaza." I stared in disbelief. "When?" I asked. "Today. I just heard it on the radio."

Walter! I last spoke with him on Friday after the Mass for Conrado de la Cruz and Herlindo. I had wanted to leave a letter with him for someone so I looked for him after Mass. The sacristy was jammed with priests getting out of their albs, but Walter wasn't hard to find. He was a tall and lanky Belgian who stood out above the rest. I called to him, got his attention and a big grin of recognition, and handed him the letter. And now he's dead! Eyewitnesses say he was machine-gunned and fell, convulsing, in the street. Walter Voordeckers, another Missionhurst, had not only taught in the Atitlán Radio School leadership program, but also worked in his parish to set up agricultural cooperatives. He had supported the cane-workers' strike and preached strong sermons on social justice. I wish I could attend his funeral, but I have no way of learning when or where it will be.

So, two Missionhurst priests from two different countries have given their lives for their flock. I can only wonder who will be next. Their bishop, Mario Rios Mont, is also a target. A small man with a powerful voice, he didn't need a microphone to give the homily at the memorial Mass for Conrado and his catechist, Herlindo. And he challenged any spies in the audience to take his message to their bosses. He said the Church would not be silenced and that the work for the rights of the poor would go on. Bishop Rios Mont is one of the bishops in Guatemala who stand beside their clergy, religious, and lay workers. They are all in this evangelization effort together, and they will suffer together.

May 19, 1980

I have written to you about the murders of several Church-connected people over the last few months. It is clear to me that these are not random killings, but rather a part of a planned persecution of the Church here in Guatemala. Now the Guatemalan bishops have written a response to this persecution. I will give you highlights of their statement, which is a courageous denunciation of the violence done against church people and Guatemalans in general:

The Actual Situation

We believe that rarely in the history of our nation have there been days as bitter as these: all hearts are gripped by fear, anger, and desperation. Each day violence takes an alarming toll of victims: disappearances, tortures, murders. Bands of hired killers move and work throughout the country. No group or class escapes this uncontrolled wave of violence. . . .

The Catholic Church, to which belong the majority of Guatemalans, has suffered with the people in its long and painful passion. Innumerable catechists and Delegates of the Word have been murdered; others have had to flee, abandoning their communities. Various priests, Brothers, and Sisters have been threatened with death. Now, in these recent days, we have painfully experienced the loss of . . . Father Walter Voordeckers, who was assassinated in broad daylight. . . . A few days before, another priest, Father Conrado de la Cruz, was violently kidnapped along with a young catechist, and we have no news as to their fate. In a short time we will be celebrating the second anniversary of . . . Father Hermógenes López. It is especially painful and discouraging to see the impunity with which these bloody acts are carried out. . . .

Our Voice as Pastors

We bishops, who have the mission of caring for the flock Our Lord has confided to us, cannot remain indifferent and insensitive to the pain and desolation of our people. . . . We strongly remind all Guatemalans, especially those who foment and maintain violence and have their hands stained with blood, that no one has the right to take the life of a neighbor, since human life is a sacred gift that no one should violate with impunity. The voice of God resounds in our nation and cries out: ''Cain, what have you done to your brother, Abel!''

It is, therefore, most urgent that we call a halt on this road to self-destruction. . . . Neither the fear of communism nor the exasperated desire to change the actual unjust structures of our society can be the pretext or justification to murder. . . . It would be indeed sad and shameful if the Christian faithful remain insensitive to the persecution and vilification of the priests, Brothers, Sisters, and catechists who struggle for them and who dedicate their lives to serving them. . . .

Conclusion

We beg God to help us pause and reflect on Jesus' message: . . . that the only valid road for the resolution of the social, political, and economic problems is found in respect for the human person, human values, and human dignity.

Please pray for the bishops, the church workers, and all the suffering people of Guatemala. The majority of them are poor, simple campesinos, dedicated to cultivating their land, caring for their families and living their Faith. Many of us missioners and native church workers have chosen to accompany them in this time of trial. Their Faith is being tested to the extreme, and Christ's words have a very real meaning for them: "Brother will betray brother to death, and father, his child; children will turn against their parents and send them to their death. All will hate you for your allegiance to me; but the one who holds out to the end will be saved . . . A pupil does not rank above the teacher, nor a servant above the master. The pupil should be content to share the teacher's lot, and the servant to share the master's" (Mt. 10:21–24). And we are all too aware of the lot of our teacher and master, Jesus, these days in Guatemala.

May 26, 1980

I don't think I told you about our latest catechist sessions. In March, we introduced the men to the book of Genesis. To wean them away from the strict literal interpretation of the Bible, we talked about the story of the Flood. Five town catechists divided the thirty-five participants into groups of six, and gave each group a slip of paper with a text from the Flood story to read, discuss, and report on to the whole assembly. The men who could read (the minority in each small group) found the text in the Bible and read it slowly to their companions. They painstakingly took notes on the information the text gave them and discussed it. When we called them back to give their reports, the fun began, as I asked:

"Group one, how many pairs of animals did Noah take into the Ark?"

"The Bible says Noah took in one pair of each animal into the Ark."

"Are you sure, group one?" All six members of the group nodded in unison. They were sure.

"Group two, how many pairs of animals did Noah take into the Ark?"

"The Bible says Noah took in seven pairs of clean animals and one pair of unclean animals."

"Are you sure, group two?" All six members of group two nodded but looked a bit perplexed, as the men in group one began to demand a rereading.

I asked the reader of each of the groups to read aloud the text his group had studied. When the conflicting stories were read, I asked, "Which story is correct?" and no one could answer. Before getting bogged down with the first two groups, we called upon the rest of the readers to give their responses to other texts, and similar conflicts surfaced. By the time we finished, confusion reigned and tempers began to show as personal honor and the Bible's dependability were hotly defended.

I called for order, and when the class quieted down, I asked once again, "Which story is true?" and repeated all their answers. A couple of men smiled then, and one began to chuckle. Then a ripple of laughter became contagious until the hall was filled with laughter. One man shouted, "All the stories are true, or none of them is true!" And from there, the discussion developed until the point was clear to everyone: Not every detail in the Bible is factual. We must look for the overall message of each story, asking, "What is God saying to us in this story? What message can I take away with me? How can this story help me know God better, and live more like God's child?"

June 7, 1980

I don't know whether to continue writing to you about what is happening here in the Guatemalan countryside, because I don't want to frighten you. But if I don't tell you, you'll find out somehow, so I'd rather be the one to say it.

I was in Huehuetenango for a meeting when I heard the news about another priest being killed. This time it was in the province of El Quiché, in the northern part of the country. He was a Spanish Sacred Heart Father named José María Gran, and he was just thirty-five years old. The other priests there pieced together the story of his death.

He had been out on what is called an *aldea trip*. That is a tour of several settlements that are far from the town. An aldea trip can take a priest away for a week or two. On the way back to town after a ten-day trip, José María and his sacristan, Domingo Batz, were shot off their horses. It was a while before they were missed, but their bodies were finally found, lying off the road.

Why was he killed? I don't know what he may have been doing personally to call the murderers' attention to himself. But his group, the Sacred Heart Fathers, have had missions in the province of El Quiché since the mid-50's. Their work of organizing the people through Acción Católica is famous. Many of the priests have come to see the great suffering of the poor Indians who are landless and dependent on others for work. The priests have developed cooperatives and have fostered settlement of government-sponsored colonization zones, giving the people a piece of land they call their own. This is where "new owners" appear at times, driving the Indians off the land, claiming it as theirs by a deed issued in some government office. A few of the priests were working on land titles for the colonizing campesinos. Maybe José María was involved with that kind of work for the people. Maybe he was killed simply because he was a member of that group of priests. His parish is in a zone where there has been confrontation between army and rebels, or army and unarmed people. There is terrific suffering there now, and many of the people dying are catechists and leaders who were trained by the Sacred Heart Fathers.

As I had wanted to go to Walter's funeral in May, so I wanted to go to José María's now, but again I couldn't. I had no car, and the trip by bus is hazardous and very long. So I joined with some friends in a simple prayer service remembering this new martyr of the Church in Guatemala, praying that his blood water the seeds of the peace and justice his community and the people of El Quiché so desperately long for.

The situation for the Church is very tense. We are all looking over our shoulders wondering what will happen next, and hoping this is the end.

And into this situation are coming two U.S. Dominicans, women I don't even know. They wrote asking if they could help us with a literacy program for a few months this summer. We are glad to have the help and the chance to share the mission work here with these women who have been working in the South Bronx for years. That's about as different from here as you can get, yet there are similarities, with the people being poor and exploited in both places. These new teammates will come to join us in early July. We'll set them up in our office with some cots, and that will be their home while they stay with us. I just hope they don't get too frightened with what is happening around us!

June 23, 1980

Yesterday, when Fr. Martín came for Mass, he brought us another statement by the Guatemalan Bishops' Conference about the situation of the Church in the country. The statement was prompted by the latest murder of a priest. This is a huge step for the bishops to take because, although they don't name names, they strongly hint at an official policy behind the campaign to slander or discredit the Church. They denounce the capture, torture, and murder of the numerous catechists, prayer leaders, and other Christians. They say that the pastoral agents (priests, religious, and lay people working directly in Church work) are continually watched; their sermons are taped by spies, their actions are checked. Many have been threatened or expelled from the country.

The letter says that the Church is frequently accused of being a vehicle of atheistic Communism. The bishops reject this accusation as absurd and false. They say that the Catholic Church, with its teachings founded in the truth of the Gospel, has a message above and beyond any human ideology. The Church has condemned all atheistic materialism, be it Marxist or Capitalist or the ideology of the National Security State.

They give special thanks and praise to missioners, many of whom have left homeland, comfort, and family to serve the people of Guatemala, even in the remotest parts of the country, and who now face persecution. They call on all people to accept the value of their own dignity and that of others as well, and to look for peaceful solutions. They exhort us to intensify our prayer, asking God for fortitude and for the capacity to love and forgive those who persecute us. They tell us to pray for the courage to continue to live out our faith.

So, you see, we are all involved in the suffering of the People of God. Only now we are becoming more aware of what that really means here in Guatemala. And to help us feel more united with the people and the other pastoral agents, there is to be a national congress of priests and religious at the end of June in Guatemala City. Lori and I are planning to go. I wonder how many will be able to attend. Right now we really need to share our experiences, our fears, and our faith.

July 15, 1980

We are now four women living in our tight quarters, since our Dominican volunteers arrived over a week ago. Fortunately, we enjoy each other and get along very well. The day I went to pick them up at the bishop's house, I walked right past the place where they were seated on the stairs. How was I to know that the slender, curly-headed blond and her auburn-haired friend were Gerry and Pat, the Dominicans I was looking for? They wore old jeans and beat-up shoes, carried back packs, and looked like they had just come in from a twenty-mile hike! Even the bishop's cook, who told me my guests were waiting inside, wasn't too sure they were "nuns." When I welcomed them to Guatemala, they lit up in smiles. Mine was the first English they had heard in a long time. They had just taken the bus from Mexico City, a trip of over thirty hours. They were ready for a good meal and a long sleep.

Gerry is about forty-three, and has been a Dominican Sister for twenty-five years. Pat, her former student, is a Dominican lay associate. Both teach in a parish school in the South Bronx where most of the students are Hispanic. I am learning a lot about that poor urban ghetto area, and of the church workers dedicated to the people there. I have dubbed Gerry and Pat "inner-city missioners."

Just before Gerry and Pat arrived, Lori and I attended the national congress of religious. It was held at a Catholic boys' school in Guatemala City. Over 600 priests, Sisters, and Brothers—Guatemalans and foreigners—attended. It was very important for us to meet at this time of open attack on the Catholic Church leadership. After each speaker's talk, we broke into small groups, where we could share our experiences and thoughts and support each other. We had no illusions about the danger we faced as Church workers. Hanging over the podium in the auditorium were huge portraits of the five priests murdered since 1976. Maryknoll Father Bill Woods was included because most Church people here believe his plane was shot down, and didn't crash accidentally as the authorities claim. Many of us bought posters with the pictures of the five priests and the words of Archbishop Romero: "You can kill me, but not the voice of Justice." The congress ran through Army Day, an official holiday. That morning we could see soldiers goose-stepping in formation as they paraded down the avenue near the school. Planes flew overhead that day, and helicopters frequently hovered over the school during our meetings.

Many of us left feeling united with each other in our determination to live our faith witnessing to the message of Jesus, in the face of threats and harassment. But we didn't know how soon we'd be tested. Just five days ago and less than two weeks since the congress, another Sacred Heart priest, Faustino Villanueva, was murdered. He was forty-nine years old. And people who knew him said he was a rather conservative fellow, not at all radical. He was shot in his parish office in the province of El Quiché. He is the second priest to be killed there in less than two months. I didn't know about it in time even to think of getting to the funeral.

It's strange. Each time I hear of a killing of a priest I have a strong urge to attend the funeral—not out of any morbid curiosity, but because they are my brothers in mission. We all came here for similar reasons, and we stay for similar reasons. Now we have to be even clearer about why we are here and what we are doing. The message of Jesus has to be paramount in our lives and in our witness. Seeing the rapid succession of murders of priests, I can't help wondering: "Where next? Who next?" And I think of the men who come to our classes and who are preparing to be catechists and teachers of religion. Will they also be marked men? Where is all this leading us? It is becoming clear that every time the bishops make a public denunciation of the situation, another priest is assassinated. Will the bishops be silenced this way?

July 30, 1980

We are using our volunteer literacy teachers, Gerry and Pat, to the hilt. Last week I took them with me to a settlement an hour away up on the mountaintop. There the clouds roll in at 3:30 P.M. and envelop the village in a cold, damp fog. We stayed until the prayer service and community Bible study session ended at 9:30 that night, then came home. I was impressed with their efforts to understand the learning mode of the young Indian men they were teaching to read. A couple of sharp young mothers joined the reading group after the first day. I am sure Gerry and Pat's classes far surpass mine, since they are schoolteachers. They enjoy their students, and the students are very faithful in attending the classes.

For the night sessions, when all the people in the settlement came to the chapel, we showed filmstrips on the life of Jesus. One night we had a Celebration of the Word, to which I brought Communion from the parish church. The people really liked it and want to send their catechists to learn how to conduct their own Celebration of the Word. That's what we want, too. Soon we hope to have people trained for the Celebration of the Word in all the communities we serve. Then, in case something happens to us, they are prepared to continue.

For the final night of this course we told the people we would have something very special for them, and the chapel was packed. The history of this "special" teaching method goes back a few months to our catechist sessions. We were teaching the lives of famous Old Testament figures and had the bright idea that acting them out would be better than reading about them. Even though none of the men had ever done any acting before, they took to dramatization like ducks to water! We encouraged them to put on these dramas (done with a bare minimum of props and lots of creativity) in their own mountaintop communities.

On this night, in their small, cement-block chapel lit only by one kerosene lamp hung from a rafter, the catechists acted out the story of Moses in the Bullrushes. The actors, all men, borrowed most of the props from their wives: lots of shawls to wear as skirts and head covering for Pharaoh's daughter and her attendants; a towel, folded and tied in the form of a baby; and a tortilla basket to lay the "baby" in. The flowers from the altar became the bullrushes. The community, gathered around the actors in the middle of the chapel on that cold and windy night, was quickly transported to sunny Egypt. There, on the Nile River, a basket carrying a baby floated slowly past the flowers on the river bank right into the hands of Pharaoh's lovely daughter. (Special effect: the basket "floated" because a string attached to its base was pulled by a man in the audience.) While the people watched the play, I watched the people. They were totally caught up in the drama, their faces registering concern, surprise, and delight as the story unwound. I doubt these folks will ever forget this Bible story.

Tonight is the third and last night of our mini-Bible course here in town. The town catechists (those who had the most study and training) presented this material in the monthly catechist sessions. Now they are giving a condensed version to the parishioners. On the first night, they introduced the Bible and gave explanations. On the next two nights there were enactments of the stories of the sacrifice of Abraham's son, Isaac; Joseph being sold into slavery; the rescue of the baby Moses from the bullrushes; and the escape of the Israelites from Egypt. The parishioners, who have never seen a skit or play, find this top-notch entertainment.

August 17, 1980

Mom, in your last letter you said that the day you wrote was the first day you've had to yourself in three weeks. What a busy life a grandmother lives! But, knowing how you love your grandchildren, I'm sure you really enjoyed the time you spent with them. I can also appreciate your busy-ness. I've been going nonstop for almost a month. First, I went to that meeting of Religious in Guatemala City. Then Gerry and Pat came. Lori and I had to prepare for their arrival and then help them break in. We planned a lot of courses for the time they are here, and have been with them most of the time, giving literacy classes. Some of the classes were on top of the mountain, and it was very COLD. We wore long-sleeved shirts, sweaters, jackets on top of the sweaters—and still we were freezing. The people were so faithful to the classes that they didn't want to take even a ten-minute break in the classes that lasted two and a half hours! Both of our volunteers were very impressed with the hunger for learning and the stark living conditions of that mountaintop community. We were there for a few days and suffered from the cold and damp, because a fog rolls in at about 3 P.M. and stays around until it burns off at about 11 A.M. each day. These folks live here all year round, and suffer the cold all the time. And they don't have the warm clothes we have. Most women have just one shawl, frequently occupied by a baby slung on the back.

While we are at a course like this, the community provides our food. Feeding three or four strangers is a big expense over a three-day period, so we chose to go home every night; it was about an hour's drive. That way they only had to give us lunch and supper. The meals are much more than they themselves eat at one sitting. We got fresh hot tortillas, black beans, an egg, some rice, some chopped tomato and onion, and coffee. I was amused to see how Gerry held the hot tortillas in her cold hands, hunching over them like a Girl Scout over a dying campfire, trying to warm up. She and Pat have a great respect for the people, and they have adapted quite quickly to our life here.

August 26, 1980

I am on vacation at Likin, an ocean resort where a group can rent a small cottage for $30 per day. We are six Sisters in our cottage; and Gerry, one of the Dominicans, is with us for a few days before she goes back to the States. Her partner, Pat, left already. They are wonderful people, and I am grateful that I got to know them. Their work in the South Bronx, where they teach in what looks like a bombed-out war zone, must be difficult. Theirs is a special calling to serve the poor in that setting.

Because all four of us lived so closely and did everything together in San Jerónimo, I didn't get to know Gerry well until now. We've taken long strolls along the beach talking about our youth, our families, and the reasons we chose to join our religious communities. We discuss our thoughts, feelings and hopes about our work and the people with whom we share life. Although she is sorry to be leaving Guatemala, she is eager to get back to her students in the South Bronx. She is so convinced of their dignity and worth as children of God that they catch the conviction from her and begin acting and studying and working, knowing that they really are important to their community and to God. Outside of school, she is on two Justice and Peace committees, one in her Dominican community and the other in the South Bronx. So, while I'll miss her, I gladly send Gerry back to the people she loves and serves so well.

I'm writing you about the violence here because I don't want you to be alarmed if you hear about it in the news. I am sorry to have to say that the American prized "Freedom of the Press" actually allows for slanted and one-sided reporting. The reader is manipulated to form an "acceptable" opinion. Just a few decades ago, every small town in the U.S. had its independent newspaper. Perspectives varied. Now a few massive corporations own almost all of the communications media. They decide what belongs on the front page, and Guatemala is just not front-page news. The Spanish embassy massacre got a few lines on the back pages of some major newspapers; that was all. How would they have treated that story had it occurred in Cuba?

A recent *Time* article gave a lot of space to reporting the assassination of a respected Guatemalan journalist from a conservative newspaper who was killed by leftists. The story was true. However, they didn't balance that story with the fact that several journalists of other, more moderate papers, have also been murdered recently by right-wing death squads.

Over the last few months, the forces of the Right seem to have been trying to provoke the Left into a civil war. In the process, simple, innocent people have been killed or have disappeared. The U.S. and Guatemalan press appear to classify anyone who is poor and a leader as a "Leftist." But they don't refer to those who are rich and leaders as "Rightists." They are warping public opinion while forming it.

Last year, during the first ten months, the *police* records showed that over 1250 people were killed by the Right and that only 87 were killed by the Left. So, if you hear about "leftist violence" in Guatemala, multiply that by 15 and you'll know the amount of violence the Right is inflicting on the people of this country.

Most of us who work with grassroots organizations and Church groups know that many of the people killed by the Right are doing nothing more subversive than developing their God-given talents and using them. They don't work for personal gain, but rather to serve their neighbors and communities as catechists, health-promoters, cooperative leaders, agricultural advisors, and other agents of human development. Many of them received their initial training in parish programs and view their service as an expression of their Christian faith. It is their way of following Jesus, who said: ''I have come that they may have life, and have it in abundance.'' They don't receive pay; they work in their free time and make big sacrifices to study at courses to improve their knowledge and skills, to serve their communities. That seems to be enough of a threat to some people in power who label them ''Communists'' and order them killed. Government troops frequently arrive in a tiny town or village and treat the people as if *they* were the enemy, so the common people fear their own army. And the tragedy is made worse by the fact that almost all the foot soldiers are Indian boys, who are forced into the army for two or three years. They are brutalized and stripped of their Indian culture and values and are built into an efficient, brutal fighting machine, capable of perpetrating horrors against their own people, in the name of saving the Fatherland from Communism.

I am reading *Dragonseed* by Pearl Buck. Maybe you have read it, Mom, since you like her books. In the story, a villager, who is expecting the foreign conquering army to march into his village soon, thinks, ''When a man becomes a soldier he ceases to be a man and goes back to the beast he once was in some other life.'' Humanity is trampled by this army, its own and that of the populace. We don't know when it will stop, but we are praying and ask your prayers, too, for this suffering people.

August 31, 1980 (10:30 P.M.)

Dear Gerry,

As you can see it's my bedtime, but I felt like writing anyway, because it takes two weeks for a letter to reach you, and in two weeks you'll be so involved in your life in ''Da Bronx,'' that our little town will be part of a dim, dark past. We've got to keep the spark of recognition alive!

The catechist session went well today. I'm just sorry you weren't able to stay a few more days to be here for it. You really enjoyed helping prepare the Bible skits in the last one, even though you didn't understand much of the Spanish. I hope your Spanish was helped by your stay with us, because our work was certainly helped by your stay. We ended the session at about four P.M., but by the time we cleaned up, had the evaluation with the teachers, and attended to all those who had questions or business, it was 5:30. I sat down to supper and had time to read a few chapters of the book you left me, *The Scarlatti Inheritance*. Then the knocking on the door began for the night. Young Angel came to tell me that he would be preaching over the parish loudspeaker to the town only on Saturdays and Sundays now, rather than every night (thank God!). I told him he was wise, because he might otherwise run out of material quickly, and he replied with that big smile: "Exactly!" In his case it's true that a little knowledge can be a dangerous thing. After just a few courses in that parish in the City (and not understanding very much, from what I could gather), he read from his notes every evening over the loudspeaker. Remember how we'd cringe when he'd start? But Angel is so good-hearted, how could anyone cramp his style? I'm glad he made this decision by himself.

Then Santos, that little boy with the impish smile, came with his friend to play with the kittens. They stayed an hour. Others came and went, until it was quite late. But I couldn't sleep without cleaning the floor a bit first, because the kittens had had a field day while we were gone! There was strong evidence that the little darlings frequently romped through their milk.

I want to tell you what happened when I left the airport after putting you on the plane. I had a feeling that something was missing all the way back to the car. I checked my purse, but everything was there, especially the car keys, which I am prone to leave in the ignition! I checked my luggage in the trunk, but that was all there. Finally I looked at the seat next to me and I knew what was missing: YOU, that's what. I realized suddenly that I had grown accustomed to your presence. Then I saw the note you left on the seat. When I read it, I realized you were still present. Thank you for all the kind thoughts, the prayers, and the sharing of so much of yourself with us. Thanks most especially for befriending me while my trusty partner, Lori, was gone. Ordinarily I enjoy being alone in the house, staying up till all hours, doing repairs or typing without worrying about disturbing anyone. But this year is different. I think

I'd have been depressed all alone here all that time. There is so much evil all around, so much suffering. Sharing the knowledge of it and venting our feelings was very healthy. Do you recall the Cakchikel greeting: "La utz awech"? ("Is your presence good?") Your presence here was *good,* believe me, Gerry. You and Pat became part of our lives so quickly and so unobtrusively; and you know how hard it is to be unobtrusive in our tiny house! You appreciated so much the little things that make up our lives, and so, when I got home, I found myself thinking of you frequently: when Carlos came to the door, as he always does at 4 P.M., for his piece of candy; and when Angel came to check in, and when I did the dishes; and when I stood outside tonight with some neighbors looking at the Milky Way. Little things have great meaning and value for me, whether they be little bits of obsidian dug up in my garden and shared with a friend, little and unknown people like these townsfolk, or the billions of "little" stars making up the Milky Way. I feel that little things also hold great meaning for you, Gerry. So I'd like to tell you that the Milky Way has shifted. Remember how it appeared to our left when we stood looking at the sky right outside the door? Well, now it's to the right. From July to September it moved all that much. It's a shift that starts one thinking about the marvels of the universe. I'm sure an astronomer would have a simple explanation, but I don't really need it. I accept it as it is, as one of God's wonderful mysteries. Another little thing: when I led the singing in the catechist session today, I thought of you and smiled. You're the first person ever to tell me I have a good singing voice!

Well, this *is* a wordy letter. I will bring it to an end. By the time you get this you will have seen Lori in New York. Have an ice cream sundae for me. Good-bye for now, have a wonderful year, keep us in your prayers (as you said you would) and write if you get a chance.

September 6, 1980

Dear Gerry,

In one of the Ludlum books you left me, *The Osterman Weekend,* one character tells the other that he will find himself operating on two levels simultaneously, and will adjust to that strange situation. Well, ever since you left here, I've realized *I'm* doing just that: operating on two levels. The difference is that Ludlum's hero was living the truth and a lie. I am living two truths—the common everyday truth of our little town and the terribly uncommon, manic depressive truth of the Guatemalan national situation that is affecting all of us. I find myself wanting to share both truths with you, perhaps too much. I write my thoughts and feelings much more eloquently than I speak them, and much more verbosely as well! No one who has visited here has responded as you did, and that response to the suffering of the people and the nation has unlocked the floodgates of my pent-up thoughts. I've been in a stream-of-consciousness writing mood ever since. Because you asked me to write, I gladly will. But I certainly don't expect you to respond in kind. Maybe the frantic pace of my letters will soon die down. But now I want to share with you my thoughts on some recent developments. This letter will be in diary form; with jottings daily until I can get to mail it.

I'm sure you heard of the bomb that went off in front of the National Palace in Guatemala City. The force of the blast was felt on the outskirts of the city, yet it damaged only the exterior of the building. Several innocent bystanders were killed and many other people were injured. I believe it was a warning from some rebel group, to dissuade people from participating in the "Rally for Peace," called by the president to be held in front of the National Palace tomorrow. That rally is a government-imposed show of solidarity with itself, if you can believe it.

I first learned about this rally a few weeks ago when a full-page ad appeared in the newspapers, inviting all "freedom-loving, democracy-cherishing" Guatemalans to attend. It didn't say it was to support the government, but that it was a rally for peace. Since then, the radio has broadcast frequent ads about it. Today a plane buzzed us again, dropping more flyers, by the thousands, calling on people to be patriotic and oppose the *subversives*. These folks don't even have the word "subversive" in their vocabulary, so it's one they will have to learn. It is being used more and more by the government.

An order has gone out from the government to all the provincial governors, requiring that each town be well-represented at the rally. Since all the governors are also military men, they will certainly do

their best to "show that we support the government." Our mayor
(and every other mayor in the country, you can be sure) used the
full weight of his authority to fill his quota of men for the rally. No
excuse was accepted, no right to refuse acknowledged. Of course,
some may decide not to go, but what will happen to them if they
are not present at roll call?

Luciano, the husband of María of the quiet smile in your writing
class, visited me last night. He was very troubled. He said: "I was
called to the mayor's office this afternoon. He ordered me to go to
the rally. He said it was my duty. Our town has to send a busload
of men to prove our loyalty. Madre, I have never refused an order
from the mayor. But I don't want to go. What do you think?" I
supported his right to refuse, since there is no law saying he must
attend a "voluntary" rally. But we discussed the possible consequences: a fine and a few days in jail in town if the mayor feels let
down. The consequences could be much worse if the government
or army want revenge. He left shaking his head, saying: "I don't
know what I will do. I just don't know." The mayor met with the
chief military commissioner and his aides today. You may remember that they are civilians from town appointed by the colonel at
the army base to carry out *his* orders in the town. Everyone here
knew of the meeting and I sensed that we were all walking on eggs.

At about 6:15 this evening a delegation from the military commissioner came, requesting to use the church's public address system. Fortunately, that is not in my realm of authority. Eduardo, the
new president of Acción (and my former Cakchikel teacher), cautiously but graciously let them use it. They went on and on about
"your patriotic duty, democracy, love of country, defense of freedom, support of the government, and free bus fare." After they
finished, Eduardo took the microphone and tactfully announced that
the message came from the governor and the mayor, not from the
Church. He also decided that, because so many men would be at a
meeting with the mayor tonight, it would not be wise to have night
prayers in church. He didn't want to give the authorities any reason
to think we were in competition, or worse, opposition. I've never
seen Eduardo so subdued.

Carlos, our retarded friend, came with his rattle to play with the
guitarists in the evening prayer. He was also affected. When the
parish council left at 7:15 after the announcement, Carlos looked in

and asked to see the kittens. But he hardly looked at them. He sat quietly on the stool by the door, smiling nervously when I smiled at him, picking apart his beat-up sweater, thread by thread. When a polite space of time had passed I bade him good night. "I'm afraid," he said, something I had never heard from him before. He felt the tension in the air and would not go out into it. He felt safer in our house. There was an awful, eerie silence outside. Finally, a youth came on an errand and Carlos, hat on head and rattle in hand, was up and at the door, smiling and saying good-bye, as he left with his newfound protector.

Mateo, a vendor from a nearby village, joined me for coffee yesterday. He is selling *rosquitos,* small, hard cookie rings, in front of school these days. Mateo is a catechist in his village, and is a village elder. He told me three of his neighbors were kidnapped from their homes and that no one knew why. He said the governor told the people of his village that a busload of them would have to go to the rally because, as he said, "maybe that will guarantee your village's loyalty and there will be no more disappearances." I wonder if that was a threat or a promise. Mateo said that the mayor received orders to commandeer the cars and trucks in his village to carry the people, but he just commandeered one small bus. When that's full, that's it. Mateo's own son is on the list to go. He hopes that his fellow villagers come back alive. He, and many other pawns in this evil chess game, fear the worst: a confrontation tomorrow between the government and opposition forces, and themselves caught helplessly in the middle. Mateo dunked his roll in his coffee, looked at me with eyes that have lived much more than his fifty-nine years, and said: "We have to support this government, but we also have to ask God to bring better people into power. Those who are against the government, those who want to take the power from this government—how do we know they will be any different? I don't think I will ever stop being an Indian for them, and working like an Indian for them, do you?"

Remember your handsome literacy student, Miguel? This afternoon he came by. His wife is that bright young mother of two from your class on the mountaintop. Remember she came by to see our reading class and finished a whole book in one day? Well, Miguel was in town when the plane dropped the leaflets about "subversives." He wanted to know what it was all about. He also asked me a flood of questions: "Why are there no more priests, Sisters, or a bishop in the Quiché diocese? Why are Catholics persecuted? Why is even the American Evangelical missioner in a nearby town preparing his congregation for his eventual absence?" We talked for a long time. He told me the whole story of his small community's conversion and how they are now united, and none will ever give up the Faith.

A group of catechists in his area met to discuss what to do if any of them or other leaders were sought in the community by strangers who might kill them or carry them off. Well, Miguel was so impressed that he met that night with his community and discussed what they would do. They all decided that they would not give out any information. The very next day, three strangers arrived, and stopped at the house of old Esteban. They wanted him to identify the catechists, the president of the parish council, and other leaders. They said they wanted to offer these people a course in being health promoters. The old man played his role marvelously.

"Señores," he said, "we are all simple Indian people in this village. No one wants to study here. No one cares to learn anything here. We just work our fields as our fathers taught us. What more do we need?" The visitors told him they would return for a list of names of the leaders who might be interested in becoming health promoters. They would send the names to Guatemala City. That night, when Esteban told the assembled community about the visitors and his answer, they commended him for his brave response. Luckily, the strangers never returned, but the community was on the alert for other such visits.

"Madre," Miguel said, "I have heard a rumor that all priests and Sisters will be put out of the country within a year. What will happen then? Will we catechists be able to marry people and baptize the children?" I assured him we would prepare them for that, and I whispered a prayer that we might be here long enough to fulfill that promise. We also spoke of the possibility of suffering for the Faith and he said, "I think about it, and I know I have to die one day. I could die in a bus accident or something. It would be better to die for my Faith." Miguel is no more than twenty-four years old, has a lovely wife and two beautiful little daughters.

Antonio and Alejandro came by tonight to prepare for the catechist session. Antonio told me of a recent dream: He saw a soldier in full battle gear single him out and then thrust a dagger into his heart. But our gentle friend Antonio whipped out a knife in this dream and thrust it repeatedly into his assailant's throat, saying over and over again, "I won't die; you will!" At that point he woke up. Sitting on his reed mat, he prayed to God that he would not be afraid to die if the situation came to that. And he smiled that big smile at me and said, "Now I'm not afraid. There are times in your life when everything seems black and you can't see where you are going. Then, there is a sudden flash of light, and all is darkness again. But now you know where you are going, and you are content in the dark."

Right now I know where I'm going: to bed! It's 11:30. I hope and pray the rally tomorrow is peaceful, even though it is a fraud. I hope you interpret it properly if it makes the evening news in the Bronx.

* * *

Sunday noon

Well, it's over. I just heard the tail end of the rally speeches on the radio. All the stations in Guatemala "spontaneously and freely" broadcast the speeches throughout the country. Among other things, the president lamented the fact that many more people wanted to come to the rally but couldn't. At least fifty times, he said that his was a democratic government, that Guatemala had all sorts of freedoms, including freedom of speech, and that it is the bad Guatemalans and the Communists who are slandering the nation beyond its borders. One of those "bad" Guatemalans is the vice-president, Francisco Villagran Kramer, who just resigned in disgust and shame. He is a respected civilian, the former head of the national university, a leading intellectual and moral force who gave the government a semblance of respectability. He waited until he was outside the country to resign, which was probably a wise move. Once he resigned, he described the terrible abuses and corruption of the government that prompted him to disassociate himself totally from the Romeo Lucas García regime. In his speech, President Lucas called all his accusations lies.

The president thanked all those who freely came to support his government in this rally. I wonder how many there were who really came "freely." All public school teachers, postal workers, and other public employees were obliged to go. At one point in his speech, the president spoke a few words to religious and priests. He said that those who didn't dedicate themselves to serving souls would be expelled.

This morning we had a Celebration of the Word in Church because Father Martín couldn't come for Mass. The Sunday readings were about seeking wisdom and the teaching of Jesus that, to be a disciple, a person has to take up the cross and follow him. In the homily, I tried to make the point of considering seriously what our faith is all about. It requires a definite commitment to follow Jesus. We have to make that commitment seriously and wisely. I invited Mateo, the vendor of *rosquitos,* to talk about his village's recent experience. Mateo looked pensive as he left his seat and came up to the lectern. "Blessed are the persecuted," he began. "In my village, we all feel persecuted these days. Never in the memory of even the oldest person in our village have things been so bad, or has life been so cheap. In our village, three young men, good boys, were kidnapped from their homes at night. No one knows why. No one knows where they are. Our only consolation is that they are known by God, somewhere, alive or dead. Our faith is our strength, and if those young men are alive, their faith is also their strength. Let us pray, brothers and sisters, not only for them, but for all innocent victims of this persecution."

What a contrast: the vivid reality this simple man portrayed of a betrayed, confused, and suffering community, and the president's portrayal of a united, protected, and democratic national community. The president makes a hideous mockery of the national reality. God must have some very interesting comments on all this, and I hope this president hears them when he goes to his final reward.

* * *

Monday

Today I had to take some of our catechists to catch a bus in the next town. They are going to a second course in Huehuetenango. On the way, where there are some pretty tight curves in the bumpy dirt road, one of the men said, "Be careful, Madre. There are rocks around the bend." Sure enough, there were several big boulders, but I could still squeeze by with my little car. I commented, "How could there have been a landslide? We haven't had rain for weeks." He replied: "It's no landslide. Those rocks were put there. A slide would have dirt and smaller rocks. These rocks appeared here early Sunday morning, and there are more further on. They were there to prevent people from going to the rally in the capital. They had to be moved so the bus could take the people, and the bus just barely avoided going over the edge of the road. In other places, trees have been felled across the road and there are rocks on the highway. It must be the work of the rebels." I mused that the rebels might not have been able to keep the people from going, but they had a night of mischief trying!

On my way back to town, I gave a ride to a teacher. I asked if she had gone to the rally. She replied that she had a little baby and didn't want to jeopardize her life. She said that she knew about the order to go. Teachers were threatened with loss of pay for the month of September if they didn't go. But since her supervisor did not personally give the command to the teachers in town, none of them went. They can plead ignorance.

I talked to a man at the road-workers camp. He said he used the excuse that he couldn't leave his post as watchman. He told me none of the other road workers in his gang went either. They were hiding out! Then I went home, turned on the radio and learned this astonishing news: 1) Never in the history of the nation had there been such a large gathering in support of the government; 2) no one was obliged to go, all were merely invited; 3) all enthusiastically supported the government and its policies to wipe out subversion and Communism in the nation.

Last Tuesday we had a diocesan meeting. To it were invited two of the priests who had to leave El Quiché; they came to explain why all the pastoral agents had left the diocese. They were a fine example of missionary dedication. One of them hoped to be back in his parish in six weeks. They told us some horror stories about what they, their people, and their bishop, Juan Gerardi, had experienced.

After two Spanish priests were killed this summer within about six weeks of each other, the pastoral agents got together with the bishop and divided the diocese into zones to cover the pastoral work. The bishop was to go to a designated town every Sunday. One Sunday, he was delayed in Guatemala City and couldn't make it back to the diocese in time, so another priest went in his stead. About a mile from the town, a man warned this other priest not to go any further because an ambush was prepared to kill the bishop, but they would kill this priest instead. Of course he didn't go. When the bishop learned about it he called a meeting of all diocesan personnel to decide together what to do. They shared experiences: In a very short span of time, a convent had been machine-gunned by the army for fifteen minutes; at least three priests had been threatened with death if they stayed; one of the Sisters was expelled, and an attempt on the life of a priest and two Sisters had failed narrowly. As a result, they all decided to pull out temporarily in protest. The bishop viewed their action in a very practical light. He said it was useless being martyrs out of stupidity. Rumor was that, if they had stayed, a plan to kill all priests would have been activated.

Of the two priests killed in that diocese a few months ago, neither could be buried in his parish. In the case of Father José María Gran, the people had expected the funeral to take place in their town, Chajul. But word came that this would be prohibited by the army. His funeral Mass, concelebrated by over thirty priests and two bishops, was in Chichicastenango, where he was buried. When his parishioners learned this, they decided on a brave course of action. They said that, if they couldn't have his body, they could at least have his blood. So they went in procession way out to where he had been killed, dug up the blood-soaked earth and put it in a small wooden box. They proceeded to the church, had their own funeral service, and buried the box beneath the altar.

In the second case, the body of Fr. Faustino Villanueva had been expected by the parishioners of Joyabaj. When church officials learned of possible trouble with the army, they changed plans. The parishioners then decided to have their funeral service without the body. They had a prayer service in church, followed by the recitation of the rosary. Then they recited another rosary in procession around the town square. That may not sound too heroic, but the central square was fortified with four mounted machine guns, one at each corner, and they were fully manned. That procession took courage and great faith. ''The blood of martyrs is the seed of Christianity,'' and the response of those heroic Christians to the death of their martyrs is a lesson to all of us who think we know what it's all about!

Dear Gerry,

The youth of the parish are getting ready to celebrate a fiesta soon. I'm sorry you can't be here to help us celebrate in typical Indian style. This youth group has begun to meet and study the Bible together twice a month. There is a wonderful spirit among them and they are full of ideas about entertainment for the fiesta. I dropped in to see how they were doing and saw several mothers in the group—well, actually grandmothers! The youth are well chaperoned!

The kittens are now leaping onto the chairs in one spring, walking on the window sill, climbing up to momma who takes refuge on chairs, and are always doing something under the beds. At this age, they play most of the time that they aren't eating or sleeping. They will be six weeks old tomorrow, but I don't plan to have a birthday party for them. They are going to have to get used to the customs around here; people don't usually celebrate birthdays, except the first birthday of a child. However, I did go to Julian's birthday party.

Julian is fifteen but looks about eleven years old. His parents, Victor and Juana, worry that he isn't growing, although he eats well enough. For the party his parents requested a Celebration of the Word at their home, and Victor asked me to select a Bible text. I chose the first six verses of the Book of Sirach which speak of heeding and revering mother and father. A fifteen-year-old boy could do with hearing such words, don't you think?

After the prayer service, the musicians, catechists, and guests were served tamalitos (small, dry tamales) and turkey. Someone said they cooked at least two turkeys and used about seventy-five pounds of corn! This corn is not only for the tamalitos, but also for the sauce served on the turkey. Don't think of a typical U.S. butterball turkey dinner, with mashed potatoes and green beans accompanying sliced breast of turkey. For a fiesta in this town the turkey has been strutting around for a long time before being killed. You need a tough turkey to make a good soup. Even though it is cooked all day, it's still tough. The turkey is served with a thick gravy and some tamalitos. That's it! But they served me such a big piece of turkey that I had to take most of it home; it made my dinner for three nights! I noticed how one of the men, whose wife is due to have a baby in about a month, unobtrusively wrapped his piece of turkey in a leaf from the tamalito and put it in his pocket. I know who is getting that piece! Meat is a real luxury for these people. In fact, most of them may eat meat only once or twice a month, and some not even that frequently. The usual main meal consists of six to ten tortillas each, with some greens or black beans, and coffee. Turkey brought home from a party is a real bonus for the family of the invited guest.

Gerry, my letters to you tend to be filled with reports about things and people you knew while here and the little things that make up our lives. I hope they will help you remember us here in Guatemala. It's easy to share these thoughts with you because you were a part of us for a while. But I certainly don't want to be one-sided! I'm interested in what you are doing, and in the people who are part of your life. I think of you so often, knowing how you are trying to help those kids in school, climbing those five flights of stairs to do it. It's like my climbing the hill! I think of your students' language handicap when I try to communicate with a Cakchikel-speaking woman (which I did fairly well yesterday for about ten minutes). I envy your artist friends when I see a beautiful sunset or a scene of people in daily life worth capturing, and I have to resort to my camera. And whenever I drive out of town I smile to myself as I bounce down that steep rocky hill, recalling how I tried to alleviate your fear by distracting you: "Could you find some nice music on the radio?" By the way, can you keep your car from sliding backwards down the hills in the Bronx yet? There is so much of Guatemala that you didn't get to see and so much of the town I didn't think to share with you, because (of course) you came to work! Maybe there will be a next time.

This morning I saw my first scorpion in this house. It came from under the wardrobe and headed for my bedroom, where I was standing in my slippers. I thought, "Well, it's either you or me, and I don't want it to be me.'' I reached for my shoe and gave the poor little animal a good whack. May it rest in peace.

I'll close this letter for now, hoping that the school year begins well for you and your students.

September 22, 1980

Dear Mom and Dad,

Lori and I just finished a five-day retreat on Friday afternoon, and on Sunday we had a meeting. After that we began another round of courses for women in communities in the mountaintop settlements. I have a chance to write you this morning since our classes are only in the afternoon. Lori said that she did get to talk to both of you by phone while she was home on vacation. Then I got your note saying that you talked to her and enjoyed hearing all about me. It's wonderful to be appreciated, and I want to thank you for being all you are to me.

I'm glad you also had a chance to talk with my friend Gerry from the Bronx. She told me she would call you when she got back. We appreciated having her and Pat with us. They both live such different lives from ours here in this Indian village, but they are serving God's poor there, just as we are, here. Gerry and I were alone here for about two weeks, since both Pat and Lori had gone to the States. We got to know and truly appreciate each other in a very short time. Only time will tell if our friendship will last, since being in two different countries and living two very different lives is not very conducive to lasting communication, much less to lasting friendship.

September 22, 1980

Dear Gerry,

I'm sitting in your old room, which is also our office, wondering if I should write you all that's in my head again. I told Lori that you asked me to write, but that I didn't think it fair to burden you with all that is happening. She strongly encouraged me to write and share what I can, so I will for now. But if it gets to be too much, just let me know.

First, I want to thank you for your note and the book, *The Hiding Place*. I read it during my retreat and found it very appropriate for this time and place. The persecution of Jews in Holland during the Nazi occupation, portrayed in the book, is similar to the persecution of the Church and population in Guatemala right now. The witness of those courageous Christian Dutch women, Corrie and Betsy Ten Boom, in hiding and transporting Jewish fugitives also finds its echo here, now.

I keep wanting to tell you things and find it frustrating that I can't pick up a phone and call you once a week. But that's part of the life we two have chosen. We both belong where we are, where we're needed right now. And I, from where I am right now, have so much to tell you. Yet, at each paragraph I stop and stare at the page. It keeps getting shorter and I know I have not yet begun— where to start? How much to share? How not to impose on you or burden you? And yet an inner voice urges: "Bear one another's burdens." That means I should bear yours, as well as share mine with you. So, I guess I'll begin with our retreat. You unwittingly had a lot of input into it through the book and excellent article on Guatemala you sent me.

About twenty of us Maryknoll Sisters spent five days of a retreat reflecting on and praying about our situation as part of a Church that serves the poor in Guatemala today. The retreat was bracketed, so to speak, by death: the recent drowning death of our Sister Carla Piette, and the impending death of our Sister Alice Morrison by cancer. Both had planned to be with us for this retreat. You and I heard about Carla's death while we were on vacation at Likin last month. When we learned that she died when her jeep was caught in a flash flood while crossing a river at night, you said: "What a terrible way to die." Our Sister Ita Ford, Carla's friend and companion in the jeep that night, was saved when Carla pushed her out the jeep window. Ita, a small, intense woman, still frail from her battle with the raging river, was with us for the retreat. Alice was in New York bedridden, with a very short time left. I ached because I knew I'd never see her again. Carla and Alice were dedicated to serving the people of Latin America; both were about my age; both were well-loved; both deserved a long and fruitful life.

But death comes like a thief in the night, and resurrection can come only after the suffering and death that precedes it. With that sobering thought, I began the retreat, whose theme was "Justice and Faith."

The daily themes of the retreat were these: Experience of God in our lives; God's life in the People today; the Cross of Christ; Resurrection; Religious Life as a Response in Justice to the Process of Liberation of God's people, the Poor. We began the retreat with morning prayer and the singing of Pescador de Gente (Fisher of People), the song you tried to learn as we drove to the airport the day you left. So I had you in mind as we sang, and wondered if the melody stayed with you long enough for you to teach it to your students. You were very much a part of this retreat for me, and I'm glad you were along in spirit.

Although no one intended the retreat to dwell so much on death, it was unavoidable. First, as Ita grappled with "Why Carla? Why not me?" we all grappled with that sudden death. Ita taught us "Lord of the Road," a song she and Carla wrote for their jeep trips over El Salvador's bumpy roads. Singing that song frequently during the week reinforced our awareness of death. We also listened to a song taped by our Sister Alice. It brought tears to our eyes. Such a beautiful, talented person, with such a lovely voice; her absence is such a great loss to us and the people she loved in Guatemala. Added to that was the bad news we heard from other parts of the world about how good struggles against seemingly insurmountable odds to overcome evil. It is an eloquent reminder of our human helplessness in the face of suffering and death. At about that point, I began reading *The Hiding Place*. I was impressed not only with the matter-of-fact courage of that family and so many others, but also with the possibility of any or all of us who were making the retreat being called to similar action very soon.

On Wednesday morning, at coffee break, we learned of the violent death of the deposed Nicaraguan dictator, Anastasio Somoza, and I just couldn't work up a feeling of sorrow. I could not help feeling he got what he deserved. I know that is a very un-Christian feeling, not at all like the forgiving stance of Betsy Ten Boom in the book. It's true that "Vengeance is mine, says the Lord, I will repay." But God acts in history, through people. Could Somoza's assassins be God's instruments? Terrible thoughts! I am angry and bitter towards him, but God is God, not me. Somoza will be judged by God, not me.

The following day, just before Mass, we got word that the lawyer of a bishop we knew was shot dead in front of his office, as he stood next to his little daughter! This was not only an attack on the lawyer; it was also a warning to the bishop and the diocese. That afternoon I looked out my window and saw a man digging something that looked suspiciously like a grave. It gaped at me for a whole day. I was relieved and pleased to see that he finally filled it with good, rich earth and planted flowers! (Am I paranoid?) At about that same time I finished the book, and we retreatants were being prodded into thoughts of life, resurrection, joy in the Lord.

The day we reflected on life and resurrection, we had a Mass that lasted all day long. At noon we had the offertory, in which each of us placed a symbol of his or her life on the altar, giving a short explanation about why we chose that symbol. I used the autumn scene from my October calendar as my symbol. The fall has always been my favorite season, and I spent many happy years with my family in our home in the woods. Giving up family and the change of seasons was a big sacrifice for me, but one I gladly made in exchange for the opportunity to live and work among the people of Guatemala. At the end of that offertory, many had tears in their eyes and I had a lump in my throat. We all knew the truth of the symbols, the fragility of life, the dangers of the Christian witness we are called to give.

One night, we sat in small discussion groups, sharing our thoughts on the retreat, and immediately the topic of death surfaced. A Sister doctor had "lost" a patient just before coming on retreat. She was very upset because she had worked so hard that she expected God to save him when she couldn't. She realized at this retreat that she wanted a God of Power who would right all wrongs and step in and save those she could not. Now she was trying to penetrate the mystery of the God of Love who doesn't intervene, yet loves totally. She can't find meaning in death unless God's love somehow gives it meaning. Another Sister is battling with the whole faith aspect of life after death. No one can prove it even exists. She is still upset by the shooting in her town of a woman lawyer, killed right down the street. The lawyer was a woman dedicated to serving the Church.

As you can see, everyone was struggling with the problem of death in a very real, very personal way. More than the problem of death, though, was the problem of finding meaning in one's death. A death without meaning is a bad joke. One of the retreat directors told us of a poor Indian man in the Quiché area, who spoke to him about life and death. He said: "We are not free to avoid death; we are free to give meaning to our death. I know I may die trying to help my people. If I do, my death will have meaning and may give life to others." Two weeks later that man died in the burning of the Spanish embassy.

I think the Indian man had the key. He said in a few words what it took the philosopher Heidegger chapters to explain. Heidegger says you cannot fully live your life until you first embrace your death. Not just accept the fact that you must, like all living things, eventually die. No, he says we must go forward to meet our death and embrace it. Once you do that, you can really *live* your life. Jesus did that, it seems, when he "resolutely set his face for Jerusalem." That acceptance, that embracing of his death, enabled him to do what he had to do, and finally to embrace the whole world on the cross. Although he suffered the terror and blackness that preceded his death—"My God, my God, why have you abandoned me?"—he soon found God's hand in that darkness: "Father, into your hands I commend my spirit." One doesn't embrace death at the last minute; one must do it while still fully alive.

A question I had at the beginning of the retreat is still with me, and it is not a morbid question: Am *I* capable of embracing my own death—now? It is that embrace that will make me more alive, more human, more compassionate, and more willing to hand over my life when God's hand is there ready to receive it.

Why do I say so much to you, Gerry? I can't recall ever having written like this before. Why do I find it so easy; why am I compelled to put these thoughts on paper and send them to you? Why am I so confident they will be received reverently? Something happened while you were here, Gerry. It triggered this flow of energy in my spirit. When I try to stop, a new thought comes, a new urge to share it with you. Please put up with my madness a little while. And thank you for allowing me to—no, for *asking* me to share my burden with you.

Thanks also for the article by Alan Riding in the *New York Times*

Magazine. It is one of the best pieces I've seen on today's Guatemala. One sentence jumped out and slapped me in the face: "No one has ever succeeded in organizing the Indians, but if anyone does, God help us." My reaction was, "That's *it,* of course!" The businessman quoted was speaking of Indians organized to fight against the power structure, but I also saw in that statement the great fear at the bottom of the campaign to kill *anyone,* especially any Indian, with leadership potential, or anyone belonging to a group whose aim is betterment of life for the community. Acción Católica, agricultural cooperatives, labor unions, radio schools, and much more are lumped together as subversive in the minds of those who jealously guard their privilege and power. What do they care that such organizations are expressions of the democratic freedoms to speak and organize guaranteed in the Constitution? I was struck by the realization that people with many privileges tend to view those privileges as rights, while they treat the basic rights of the poor and powerless as mere privileges. They would readily deprive the poor of livelihood, land, home, family, and life itself.

October 3, 1980, 9 P.M.

Dear Gerry,

I just tried to shut my door and learned that the cat's tail was there. She screamed in her own, inimitable way and shot out the living room window. A bit earlier, Lori had waltzed into my room to leave some more reading material in my overflowing box. After commenting on the lovely music coming from my tape recorder, she hulla-ed out of the room. It was her waltzing, actually, that let the cat in, which led to the tail incident.

You may wonder why such strange behavior is coming from your usually sedate friends. Well, the sad truth is that your friends have been imbibing spirits a bit these days. As you have already noted, neither of us is much of a drinker. But we do have some partially filled bottles of spirits, namely bourbon, Canadian Club, and wine. These were brought by friends as gifts from the good ol' U.S.A. The bourbon arrived during Holy Week. The Canadian Club came in January. In addition, when I was home a few years ago I splurged on some instant drink mixes and we still have most of them. Well, not really. We had most of them up until a few nights ago. That was when we realized that, since the guerrillas have been visiting the nearby towns during recent weeks (oh, yes!) they may well visit us soon. Not that they will try to rob us. They are reputed to be well-mannered fellows. But the pattern is that after the guerrillas leave an area, the army comes to pay a visit. And the army soldiers are not just rumored to be, but they are *known* to be *very* bad-mannered fellows. In fact, they are taught to be very bad-mannered and do their mean act on command, just as they can pass out candy to children as part of their act. They are very obedient soldiers.

Well, we thought to ourselves (out loud, of course) that it would be a real shame to lose that good alcohol to soldiers who prefer the local moonshine anyway. So we decided to get rid of as much of it as we could before either group arrives to visit our town. Rather than pouring it down the sink, we decided to imbibe in moderation, a bit each night. That in itself was a momentous decision, since we drink very rarely. Every night after supper, around 8 or 9 P.M., if we have no meetings or visitors, we go through a new ritual. I take out the bourbon, the instant drink mix, and the cherries, and mix a *very* light drink for each of us. We then sit and enjoy each other's company for a few minutes. We are down to just one daiquiri mix for the two of us for tomorrow evening. Then we'll have just bourbon—and what? Well, that will be Lori's problem, because I'll be gone all of next week. I know she doesn't drink alone. Maybe she'll share some with the cat.

So you see, Gerry, there are some funny things still happening around here, really (though I miss your wonderful sense of humor and hilarious stories). My recent letters have been very heavy, a cheerless batch, it seems to me. But there is a lighter side to life here and I try to see it whenever possible. Laughing is a rarity these days, such that we really notice when one of us does actually laugh out loud. Sometimes we need a good, long and contagious laugh to brighten the day and our spirits.

Pablo, a thirty-year-old ex-soldier, now a catechist, was here before supper. He brought two nice bunches of onions. I mentioned that we would like to have a meeting of town catechists on Thursday to prepare for the coming sessions and retreat. He hesitated, then said: "I have a meeting that night. I volunteered to be an advisor to the new youth group. They plan to meet every Thursday.

I want to keep my word to them.'' Pablo is also a member of the beekeepers' group, and they meet every Sunday night. But he told us that he had set his priorities, and that the catechist work is *first*. God bless him! At a time when catechists are being killed, he says he puts that work at the top of his list!

Lori and I crossed Lake Atitlán a few days ago to visit the newly arrived Carmelite Sisters in the parish of Santiago Atitlán. That town is a must for all tourists to the lake region because of the beauty of the trip and the picturesque costumes of the people. The pastor, Fr. Stanley Rother, was raised on a farm in Oklahoma and speaks with a hint of a drawl. I envy his reputation as an excellent missioner who has been totally accepted by the people, even by the traditionalists. Stan speaks the Tzutuhil language very well and is working on translating the Bible into that language. He already says Mass and celebrates all the sacraments in Tzutuhil.

Stan has been the only priest in the parish for several years. Of course he has a well-organized team of catechists and other workers from town, but he hasn't had permanent full-time pastoral agents with him until recently. It was a happy coincidence that he was looking for some Sisters to work in his parish, and this group of Carmelites was looking for a parish to work in. They are native Indian women from the town of Patzún. I first learned of them when I studied the language there. They have just made vows and wanted to go, all together, to one parish to work and to continue their formation as Sisters. There are about eight of these young women, trying to live religious life and still retain their Indian culture. They wear their native Indian costume, in shades of brown and tan for the Carmelite connection. The Sisters will work in the catechetical program, visit families, and otherwise lend their services. They will have to learn the Tzutuhil of their new town.

Thank you for your letter, which arrived yesterday. I enjoyed hearing about what's going on in ''Da Bronx.'' I saw your favorite chubby kitten yesterday at Vicenta's house. She is still fat and sassy, but doesn't like to eat tortillas. If she doesn't learn to eat them she'll get skinny, because that's all Vicenta can give her, except for some greens once in a while. I am giving your greetings to everyone you mentioned in the letter as I see them, and they are thrilled that you remembered them by name. You are really a ''people person.''

Your schedule sounds overwhelming. I'm glad I'm in such a peaceful little town. I couldn't handle all that activity myself. I guess I'm getting acculturated to life here. But I'm glad that you are doing what you so want to do—to serve the poor. And please, don't feel you have to answer every letter I send you, Gerry. I'll be glad to hear from you whenever you can write, even if it's a shortie. I'm in a rare frame of mind these days, partly due to the terribly unjust situation here, partly because I've had time to write, and partly because I have such an understanding friend to write to. I have written some things to my parents, but as things get even worse I hesitate to tell them all the bad news because they would worry. And since you were here with us and know the people and situation, and feel as I do about it, I can pour it out freely to you. I just hope I don't depress you with my last few letters. The next will be cheerier, I promise!

October 5, 1980

Dear Mom and Dad,

I have two of your letters here to answer, but first, before anything else, I want to put your minds at ease. The articles you read about Guatemala in the paper and sent me are scary, but please don't worry about my safety. I want you to keep up on what is happening here and I tell you a lot myself because if I were to tell only the good news or funny stories I would be presenting a very one-sided picture. Then if anything really bad happened, like civil war breaking out, you'd be totally unprepared. This way you'll be aware. I truly appreciate your concern and prayers, but I really don't think I have anything to worry about for myself. I'm not a priest, nor an activist. I try to be a follower of Jesus Christ and to help the people here prepare, psychologically at least, for what may come. Things have quieted down in some ways for the church. That mainly means that no more priests have been killed. I've heard that over fifty have left the country because of threats, since they know those threats are backed up with machine guns. One of the priests who gave our retreat left a few days afterwards, because his life had been threatened more than once.

Guatemala has spent millions of dollars internationally to lure tourists, and many arrive daily. These guests view the people and the countryside from sanitized tourist buses and air-conditioned hotels, untouched by the tragedy all around. Yet, in some places and to some people here terrible things happen. We are a bit out of the way in our town, and neither side seems to think us important enough to bother with. But I can't remain comfortable in my security when others are suffering so, and I guess I can't let you be comfortable in your security, either! You know, the people who are suffering and dying for their faith here in Guatemala and other Latin American countries are a lot like our Polish ancestors. They suffered long centuries of persecution for political reasons, and the Guatemalan people are suffering for political reasons, too. But I don't think Jesus sees ''political'' reasons the way those in power do. I believe he sees reasons like greed and lust for power on one side and suffering and martyrdom on the other. I feel very united with the Guatemalan peasant, the *campesino,* especially the Indian Catholic campesino, at this time. Some people who have studied the rise and decline of religion in various societies see that the U.S.A. and Europe are in a period of religious decline. The Catholic Church in rich countries may be secure financially, but it is in danger of dying out among the middle and upper classes of people. As people move into that economically higher class, they tend to become more selfish, think less of helping others, and may think they don't need anyone else, not even God. But Catholicism is flourishing in Latin America, especially among the poor. Some predict that Latin America will bring about a new flowering of Catholicism in the Western hemisphere. In twenty years, they will be sending missionaries to the United States and Europe to re-Christianize *them!* It is an interesting theory and I can see some truth in it. When people have to live their faith in an oppressive situation, and may even have to die for it, the faith either becomes stronger and more meaningful, or it is relinquished. In the United States, we are so free to practice our religion without persecution that we don't even realize what a precious thing that faith is. St. Paul says of our Faith: ''We carry this treasure in clay pots.'' In a time of religious persecution, Christians have to look into their clay pots to see just what it is they have in there. Do they see it as a treasure, or as a liability? If the fragile clay pot is going to be smashed, the treasure had better be worth it!

October 11, 1980

Dear Mom and Dad,

Happy Columbus Day!

This is a short note to welcome you back from your trip. I know I'm sending it before you even leave, but by the time it arrives you will most likely be back! See, I am planning ahead. I'm in Guatemala City for about a month, helping to give some Bible classes. I'll return to San Jerónimo at the end of October, so you can phone me here until then.

We Maryknoll Sisters, scattered all over the highlands, will celebrate Thanksgiving together, provided nothing happens to change our plans. Travel is not too safe these days, with rebels stopping cars and taking money, or even taking the cars, and the army patrolling and stopping and searching everything. I look forward to Thanksgiving. We will not only eat together. We'll also pray together, play together, and relax together, as well as catch up on the latest news from different parts of the country—most of it bad news, unfortunately.

Soon it will be Christmas! But before that comes Election Day in the U.S.A. Many analysts are predicting that Ronald Reagan will win easily. I'm sure he has many good qualities, but one great problem I foresee is his strong support for governments in Central America that justify their tyranny in the name of "anti-Communism." There is more in the newspapers here these days about the U.S. electoral campaign than about local politics. The rich and powerful are counting on lots of military aid from the Reagan administration to continue pressing down true democratic, grassroots reform. The U.S. government seems to believe that a strong military in these countries will guarantee democracy. In truth, it murders democracy. Those of us who work at the grassroots level, working in education, health, or empowerment motivated by the message and life of Jesus, shake our heads in dismay. How can we all be Christians, on all sides of this terrible struggle? What does Jesus have to say to us? "Those who live by the sword will die by the sword." What does the Magnificat of Mary say? "God has pulled down the mighty from their thrones and has exalted the lowly. God has filled the hungry with good things and sent the rich away empty-handed." Are we even reading the same message?

This is much longer than I had expected. Bye for now.

October 11, 1980

Dear Gerry,

Here's more of the same, to think about and share with anyone interested in events here in Guatemala.

Last night I learned that the Christian Brothers' school in Guatemala City was forcibly entered and ransacked by the secret police. They were looking for God knows what and finally made off with some stencils that were probably supposed to contain subversive ideas. Any truth printed nowadays is printed on mimeograph machines and hand delivered. The Right is putting out terrible slander, lies, instigations to kill "subversives," personal attacks on the reputation of certain individuals, and threats on the lives of still others. You can be sure the secret police won't be investigating these tactics of the Right!

Also, at least one Guatemalan Sister has had to leave the country because of threats to her life. She had been on the board of directors of the Conference of Religious of Guatemala. I know I don't have to ask you to keep these people and all of Guatemala in your prayers. Thank you for caring.

You know, Gerry, I have just come to realize that what I write to you is like a journal. I had never been any good at keeping a diary. I couldn't just "talk to myself" like that. But now that I have begun writing to you, I see it is a journal of significant events and reflections on them. And since almost everything that happens these days is significant and needs to be reflected upon in the light of our Faith, I'm writing to you very frequently. I also know that you are very committed to issues of justice up there, and I want to share justice issues with you from down here. But these "journal entries" can be depressing if you keep getting them and can't do anything about them except share them with others. Well, don't feel too bad. We can't do anything about them either, except speak this truth to anyone who will listen. And you are a very good listener. You didn't really know what you were in for when you asked me to write to you, did you? Neither did I!

Things are relatively quiet in the country these days. Headlines about murders are few, and rumors or tales about disappearances are not so frequent. Some think both sides are taking stock of themselves and each other, and maybe something big will blow up soon. If it comes from the Left, you'll be sure to hear about it in the news. If it's from the Right you probably won't, so I'll tell you.

October 26, 1980

Dear Gerry,

How shall I begin this letter? There are so many interesting jumping-off points. For example, just this minute the cassette I'm playing is "Night on a Windy Mountain," by Moussorgsky. I didn't even realize that the piece was on this tape, so it's pure coincidence. It reminds me of the very rewarding two weeks we spent teaching and coming to know the people in the village on top of that very cold, windy mountain. Another jumping-off point is the mule that just hee-hawed outside my window. If I could record it and send it to you, you would be amazed at the sound of a donkey. They don't hee-haw at all! But I guess I'll actually start with this: It was wonderful to hear you and Pat on the phone last night.

The phone connection was excellent. I wish the one I had a few days ago from home had been equally clear. For a few minutes I was afraid the worst had happened to my father. The call came in the morning, just as I was leaving the house. I recognized my mother's voice and her tone was not happy. When I asked her what was wrong she started with "Well, . . ." and from there on I heard only fragments of what she was saying. The connection kept getting interrupted with spots of silence, dropping out parts of words or several words at a time. It was terribly frustrating. I got words like: "Dad . . . hospital . . . attack . . . don't worry . . . operation . . ." Then my sister got on the phone and it was as if we were on a different phone line. I got every word she said. Maybe it was because Mom's voice was subdued and my sister's voice was strong. It was really strange. Anyway, she relieved my anxiety with the news that my father did not have a heart attack after all. I thanked God for that. And I wonder how your mother is doing. I know you told me she had had a cancer operation a while back and things seem to be going well now.

October 30, 1980

Dear Gerry,

Your letter mailed on the 21st arrived yesterday. It took just eight days, a record! Sometimes mail takes up to fifteen days. Today I received a letter from my sister mailed on the 23rd. That even beats yours. I wonder why the mails have speeded up.

It was delightful getting that call from you. It pays to be in the big city sometimes! I do prefer rural life and work, and had gotten used to not having a phone in our town. But I do relish using the luxury of a phone when it's available. I feel the same frustration you mentioned about not being able to say everything we want on the phone because the phones may be, and probably are, tapped. Just the possibility of the phone's being tapped, and the awareness that what we say, however true or innocent it may seem to us, could cause trouble, is enough to control our conversation. The paranoia built into this system is a great control in itself. They wouldn't have to spend the money to bug the phones. They would just have to spread the word that the phones are bugged to have the desired effect.

Here is the latest bad news. The director of the Radio School "La Voz de Atitlán" was assassinated over the weekend. I wrote you recently about the Sisters who just moved into that parish, and about Fr. Rother, the pastor. The murdered man was Gaspar Culán, well-known throughout the lake area for his fine work with the programs for education and information as well as for entertainment on that radio. What a tragedy for his family and his community, and what a loss for the people who benefited from the radio he directed so well. It broadcast in Spanish, Tzutuhil and Cakchikel, and had a wide listening audience. It seems that radio schools are fair game for the antisubversive, anti-Communist forces in the country. It is subversive to teach the Constitution of the nation over the radio, it seems. It is subversive to help people understand the labor laws and their rights. It is apparently subversive to have programs with reflections on the Bible, especially if the topics have anything to do with daily reality here. It's not at all illegal, mind you. But those with power to order and accomplish assassination, preceded most often by torture, are hardly deterred by legal technicalities.

Gaspar was an Indian who was fortunate enough to have a high school education, and he was very concerned about the need for Indians to receive basic education. Most people in the area are lucky to make it to the third grade. Gaspar had been threatened and was spending his nights in hiding, while going to work at the radio station during the day. One night, the fatal night of October 24th, he went to his own home. Masked armed men kicked in the door and shot him in his bed, wounding him, and dragged him off to a waiting vehicle. He has not been seen or heard from since. Fr. Rother strongly condemned the kidnapping of Gaspar at Mass on Sunday. It takes great courage to speak out like that because there are spies for the police or army who report whatever a priest says in church.

The young Guatemalan Indian priest of the town of Cerro de Oro, near Santiago Atitlán was threatened. And an American priest who works in the province of Chimaltenango barely escaped an assassination attempt. He has left his area, and may already have left the country. He had worked for ten years in *comunidades de base* (basic Christian communities) in his parish. He also formed a Guatemalan missionary team for the whole province to do education and consciousness-raising among the people, Indian and non-Indian alike.

I went to a meeting recently of people working in women's promotion, especially for Indian women. We were twenty-two women: ten religious and twelve vibrant, highly intelligent and articulate young Indian women from all over the country. The meeting's purpose was for us to get to know each other a bit and share our experiences. I was truly impressed with the suffering and the commitment of the Indian women. One who spoke a lot about her experiences introduced herself as "Juana from the province of Chimaltenango." She said she didn't want to say exactly what town she was from, and I am not too sure her name is Juana, either! Among other things, she said that it used to be fashionable and exciting to say "I work in the promotion of women." Now it is neither. It is a difficult and dangerous thing to do, but that is all the more reason to do it. The need is that much greater. She said that she and her companions, other Indian women, have to face the fact that the more they work, the more they will be known and the more danger they will face. If they continue to wear their hand-woven, highly visible and distinguishable native dress, identifying them as from specific places in the country, they put themselves in greater danger. She said: "We have had to make the choice, the very hard choice, of giving up our native dress. We wear the dress of other towns, changing our style frequently. We go to our meetings with other women in disguise, dressed as market women, weavers, or whatever else can give us and the women in the group protection. To help our people, we will do this." They are risking their lives to serve their people. And they are Catholics, acting out of a faith commitment. Yet, even in this group, I wonder how many were there out of sincerity, and if at least one was not really a spy. One cannot trust too readily or speak too freely to strangers these days. We all end up doing an intricate dance, mentally and verbally, trying to communicate well without saying too much.

There is the need to find ways to help people care for injured or wounded family members or neighbors when help from the usual sources will be impossible. A flurry of first-aid courses is being given at present, a sort of civil-defense preparedness course. While people back in the States might find a first-aid course an interesting diversion a few nights a week, these first-aid courses are being taken in deadly earnest, because the unspoken question is not, "What if something were to happen?" but rather, "When such and such happens, what can we do?" People are receiving crash courses to teach other people and spread the knowledge fast. It is all being done as quietly as possible, of course, not to attract attention from the wrong places. It is strange to face the realization that we are in a near-war situation without knowing who the enemy is. In a clear-cut nation-versus-nation war, the government mobilizes all the groups it can to prepare the civilian population to protect itself. Here, the government would suspect any civilian group that undertakes such preparation, labeling it subversive. It's a crazy turnaround! The government suspects the great majority of the population to be enemies of the State. These "enemies of the State" are mostly people like those you met up on the mountaintop: simple, poor, illiterate Indians who are trying to better their lives. That seems to be an unwritten crime these days in Guatemala. Only the powerful, it appears, are allowed to better their lives and organize to assure success. Others who try that are called Communists or subversives.

I read in the paper that the army has formally requested the Guatemalan Congress to pass a law allowing it to bomb the *altiplano,* the highlands that are mostly Indian territory. They say they want to flush out the guerrillas hiding in the mountains. That means, of course, indiscriminate bombing of civilian populations, destruction of their homes and crops, and, as a consequence, famine. And all in the name of *defensa de la patria*—defense of the fatherland. What is the *patria* if not the majority of the people, the land they farm, the homes built from the earth with their own hands, and the food they produce for their families and the rest of the nation?

November 21, 1980

Dear Gerry,

How was the Solidarity Weekend you attended? I'm eager to hear all about it. I'm impressed with the fact that you joined the Guatemala committee. See? You really are a missioner. Keep it up, if you can find the time and energy to spare, but don't wear yourself out, please.

We had a catechist session a few weeks ago. A couple of young men attended from the next town. One was a man who worked for the radio school La Voz de Atitlán. The other was the president of Acción Católica in his town. Both men asked if they could talk to us when we were free. They had some news about the death of Gaspar Culán and later developments.

They told us that about a week after Gaspar was kidnapped, his mutilated body was found on a roadside. His murderers had cut out his tongue and gouged out his eyes, an obvious punishment for his effective work as the eyes and voice of the Indian people in the area. Soon after that, the radio school was ransacked by three carloads of "unknowns" who took whatever they could carry off and destroyed whatever they couldn't take. Francisco, one of the men telling us this, was on the board of directors of the radio school. He said he was leaving town, and that another fine young man connected with the radio (a father of three) had already gone, taking his family with him. They feared that, now that the records were in the hands of their enemies (whoever they were), it would not be safe to stay home. He didn't ask us for anything, but simply came to say good-bye. What a great person he is. I was touched that he thought to come and tell us personally of his decision. We offered him a little money, which he accepted gratefully. Jorge, the president of Acción Católica there, said he was worried about himself and another man, Raúl. A few days before, three cars came roaring into town and the men in them started asking for people by name. He and Raúl were on their list, as well as those men connected with the radio school who lived there! Jorge's wife had just given birth a few days earlier and they have customs that must be strictly kept that require twenty days of bedrest for a new mother. The men in the cars said they would return on November 22nd. The army also gave out the word that it would be in town around the same time. After talking to us and to each other, they decided not to try to leave the country, but rather to hide out for a while. Poor men, caught in an evil power struggle, in a real religious persecution.

December 3, 1980

Dear Gerry,

I'm back in town after a month, and it's good to be back.

I never know what will happen when I leave for that long. When I left, our little town was a backwater with a bus only to the next town, and when I got back I found we have daily bus service to the capital! That is real progress!

Lori and I enjoyed your Thanksgiving card and were touched by your message. She said, "Isn't it strange that we, as well as Gerry and Pat, sense the same deepness of enrichment by having known and shared life with each other?" It is one of those unexpected blessings in life.

On November 30th, we had the retreat for the catechists, which you helped me prepare while we were on vacation. About twenty men came. We broke them up into smaller groups, each with a catechist from town as a guide in the discussions. It was well received and, as one participant said, "It makes your commitment to

Christ even stronger.'' They had to think a good bit about the call to be a prophet and the suffering that prophets must endure to speak God's message. It is very appropriate for this time and place.

Thanks for telling me about the people you work with, Gerry. You've got an awful lot of love to give, and it's reaching a lot of people. Just don't wear yourself out too fast, and don't get a heart attack from overwork, please!

December 10, 1980

Dear Family and Friends,

I have been thinking of you constantly throughout these last days of horror, numbing sorrow, and growing rage. The murder of the American missioners Maura Clarke, Ita Ford, Dorothy Kazel and Jean Donovan in El Salvador on December 2nd came as a terrific shock. The pain was deeply personal for me, because two of them were Maryknoll Sisters. Just a few months ago, Maura Clarke and Ita Ford participated in a retreat with us Maryknollers who worked in Guatemala. My last visual image of each of them is still fresh; Maura, flashing me a big smile that made me feel I was someone special; Ita, hands in her jacket pockets, hunched over in the cold morning air, walking pensively on the gravel path.

Lori and I heard about the disappearances of the four women from an American priest early on December 3rd. Later that day we caught a news bulletin that the bodies had been found in a shallow grave. We quickly decided to try to get to the funeral and were very lucky to get our visas the very next day. By ten A.M. we were in a car with two more of our Sisters, heading for El Salvador. We arrived at the church in San Salvador shortly after the funeral Mass was scheduled to begin. As we walked toward the church I noticed two black Cadillacs near the entrance and wondered who was important enough to come in those. Then I realized that they were two of the four hearses. I was struck by the irony. These women had lived and worked with poor refugees. They drove around in jeeps and vans transporting food and medical supplies over rocky roads. They never would have chosen to make their final trip in a Cadillac!

The newspapers, radio, and T.V. are probably still talking about these murders. You can learn whatever is officially being said in statements issued by the governments of El Salvador and the United States. You can get something more truthful from statements put out by the Catholic Church. But, now that I'm back from El Salvador and have thought about my experience there, I want to reflect on what has happened.

What do these latest murders mean to us women missioners? I guess it means that the powers of evil have crossed another boundary line. Once upon a time, in what seems the dim, distant past, the death squads felt they could kill civilians and laity with impunity, but not clergy. Then they got a taste for killing clergy in El Salvador and Guatemala in large numbers. Afterwards, they aimed at and felled an Archbishop, Oscar Romero. Each step was another boundary crossed. They began killing foreign priests in addition to native priests. And now, they have singled out American women missioners, both religious and lay, and killed four at once. It looks as if there are no more boundaries. As the Bishop of San Salvador said when he celebrated the funeral Mass of the four women: "Now our Church's offering is complete."

You may have heard about liberation theology. It is a way of coming to theological insights out of life situations, reflected on in the light of the Bible. I recently read an article in which an important American business executive said something about liberation theology that sent a chill through me. He said that it was really a Communist tool to lead the people of the Catholic Church in Latin America away from our "traditional values based on the free enterprise system," and that the Church needs to be guided back onto the right road. The fact that religious groups who own stock in a corporation have dared to unite and speak at stockholders' meetings about issues that affect other human beings (wages, safety standards, dangerous pollution) annoys this type of businessperson. It seems that the money of religious groups is welcome but their opinions as stockholders are not.

Theology here in Latin America continues to evolve and develop along uniquely Latin American lines, in response to the reality. At the same time, we have learned to read the Bible in a new way. For example, in the story of Abraham's attempt to please God by sacrificing his son, the writer really wanted to teach the Israelite people about sacrifice. He wanted to say that their God, unlike the gods of their neighbors in Palestine, did not want human sacrifice. The God of the Israelites is a God of life, not of death. The idea of the God of life is so obvious and clear to us here, but to many others it says nothing. They are people who worship the god of power without pity; the god of wealth without wisdom; the god of pleasure at all cost. All these gods demand human sacrifice in some form. While the people who serve the God of life struggle to bring about some semblance of the Reign of God here on earth, those who serve the gods of power, wealth, and pleasure have united forces to supply their gods with rivers of human blood. We may be tempted to think "they hold nothing sacred," but that's not true. They hold their gods sacred: Wealth, Power, Pleasure. They also hold sacred their servants: National Security, Strong National Defense, Free Enterprise. They also believe in their own sacred texts: "If you possess more you will *be* more"; "Some people (like themselves) are born to rule, and the rest are born to submit"; "The survival of the fittest." The value of human life doesn't enter into the list of what they hold sacred. For them, human life is a commodity, bought and sold on the open market; it is something to be used to serve their purposes, then discarded. Torture and murder are tools to control human beings. The atrocities committed in the names of the gods they serve, the gods that bring death, are merely means to an end. And the end? Appeasement of their gods. They would never admit it, but their actions prove they believe it. By sacrificing thousands of human lives on the altars of wealth, power, and pleasure, they believe they will be guaranteed *more* wealth, power, and pleasure. They believe it with the strength of religious fanaticism. Yet these blind servants of murderous gods scoff at those who live and act out of religious principle and conviction. They believe they are above being duped by religion. They don't even *know* they are simply serving different gods!

Meanwhile, we who serve the God of Life, who truly believe that Christ came among human beings "that they might have Life, and have it in abundance," continue trying to help people find that life. We believe in the gospel statement: "Whatsoever you do to one of these, the least of my brothers and sisters, you have done unto Me." We are armed with love, a desire to share, a willingness to receive as well as to give. We long for the day when true justice will reign, and God's Will will truly be done *on earth* as it is in heaven. That reign of God begins right here on earth, and it begins with *us*. We desperately want to make Jesus' last prayer our own: ''Father, forgive them, for they do not know what they are doing.'' It is not an easy prayer.

The gods of death are many, the God of Life is one. We must continue to trust that God's reign will come some day, and we must continue to work and pray for its coming, in the face of threats, and in the face of death, as did these four women, and as did the thousands of Salvadorans and Guatemalans who preceded them and will follow them as martyrs for the Reign of God.

December 15, 1980

Dear Gerry,

At our December catechist session we studied the prophets. Each group of about eight men took one of the four prophets: Amos, Isaiah, Jeremiah, and Ezekiel. They had four questions to answer as they studied and discussed the prophets. For the question: ''What were the evils of the time of the prophet?'' each group carefully wrote down what its prophet condemned. Afterwards, all the groups came together to listen. These were their findings: Jeremiah urged his hearers to do what was right and just, and to stop oppressing widows and orphans and shedding innocent blood. Isaiah condemned those who wrote oppressive decrees, who deprived the needy of justice, and who robbed the poor of their rights. Ezekiel denounced those who took bribes to shed innocent blood, who exacted high interest on loans, and who robbed their neighbors. Amos railed against those who cheated in commerce, who rigged the scales in their favor, and who sold inferior or tainted food as first grade. The group then compared the evils condemned by the prophets with what the country is going through now. They concluded: ''The evils of the prophets' time were the same as those of our own. We must be like prophets, speaking out against these evils in our own situation.'' I was surprised at the forthrightness of their answers!

At lunchtime, they came to the kitchen to eat. There, as you may recall, we had hung a big blackboard with pictures of martyrs. Since you were last with us, we have added the pictures of Maura, Ita, Dorothy, and Jean to those of Bill, Hermógenes, Conrado, Walter,

José María, Faustino, and Archbishop Romero. We even had a small picture of Gaspar Culán, whom most knew. I had hung a crucifix above the board. On the board, above the pictures, I had written the words of Jesus at the Last Supper: "This is my body, given up for you." Below the pictures I wrote, "Prophets of Today." The men gathered around the board to look silently. They stood quietly in line for their dish of beans and rice, then worked their way over to the benches at the tables to eat. After eating, rather than following their usual routine of getting up, thanking everyone, and leaving, they just sat, looking at the pictures. I saw their interest and explained who each person was, when and where they were killed, and what their prophetic stance had been. We talked a bit about Archbishop Romero, and most of the catechists knew who he was already. Finally, I explained about the newest additions, the four women. They listened quietly, then asked some questions and made some comments. They were a very sober group that afternoon. After they got up from the tables, they gathered once more around the pictures, examined them more closely, and read the newspaper clippings. Some who could read, read painstakingly the clippings aloud to the others. I felt as if I were in a chapel then, seeing the respect and reverence with which those men listened and questioned. They got the message better that afternoon than they would have through any number of talks we could have offered.

Back in the classroom, we read them the message of solidarity sent by the Pope to the Guatemalan bishops and people. Then we read some excerpts from the letters written by the bishops after priests had been killed. Both the Pope's and the bishops' letters called for an end to the violence and the persecution of the Church, as well as for positive reforms. Those letters fit in perfectly with the texts we chose from the prophets. Each man received a copy of the letters from the bishops and the Pope. They were duly impressed. I am touched with their deep faith that keeps them coming to these sessions in the face of such danger. Such a faith commitment can cost one's life these days. They are great people!

As for me, my martyred Sisters are constantly on my mind. I go to bed thinking about them and I wake up thinking about them. I don't think of them lying dead in the field, or in their graves; nor about the anguish of their last hour. They are just very present to me, always. Maybe it's a vague realization of eternity and the trust and hope I have in the Resurrection. Maybe they are making themselves present to me. It's probably a bit of each of the above. I am proud and happy to have known some of them. I know they are as much saints today as St. Agnes, St. Lucy, or St. Cecilia were when they were martyred in the early Church.

It's strange, now that I think of martyrs. When I was young I used to pray to St. Tarcicius and St. Sebastian each night. I gave that up along the way. Maybe I'll pick it up again. They have taken on a very real presence with our preparation of the catechists and people for a possible absence of priests and religious, and with the possibility of martyrdom never being far away.

In one of my letters, I promised I'd comment on the book you sent me to read, *The Gemini Contenders*. That was just before the women missioners were murdered in El Salvador. After all the real violence and killing going on all around us here, I don't need Robert Ludlum's fertile imagination. Many of his characters have the same attitude about human life as is held by the people who form death squads. I copied out a few lines from this book because they said so clearly what many power-hungry people believe.

"The most difficult part of this work (killing) isn't the *doing,* it's the getting used to the doing. Just accept the fact that it's real. We've all been through it—go through it constantly, as a matter of fact. It's all so bloody outrageous, in a way. But someone's got to do it, that's what they tell us."

"Never admit. Never explain. Take the objective. The rest is no strain."

"One disposed of hostages when they no longer served a purpose."

"Only fools kill indiscriminately. Death is an instrument, a means to be used in reaching an objective or completing an assignment, and that's all."

—And who decides when the instrument is to be used? *YOU*?"

"*Yes!* and men *like* me!"

So, men like him continue to kill to take the objective of more power, more wealth, more pleasure. I want so much to believe that it is all fiction, but I know better. Murdered women and men—

catechists, campesinos, union leaders, priests, religious, and lay people—are a testimony to the effectiveness of that philosophy. But Ludlum's imagination isn't fertile enough to match reality down here. I think I'll switch to Agatha Christie. She presents you with a nice, neat, clean murder, and one that is solved in the end, with the guilty party brought to justice. Her fiction doesn't try to imitate reality.

I'm getting carried away again, and I'm thinking of the murdered women again, and I'm getting angry, and the tears are smarting again, and I guess I'd better stop. Thanks for your support, your caring, your prayers, and your love.

December 26, 1980

Dear Mom and Dad,

I wish you a Merry Christmas, and a very Happy New Year!

Christmas for us was a bit different this year. We could only get a priest to come at 4 P.M. on Christmas Eve, so we had no Midnight Mass. But the people asked if we couldn't still have something at Midnight, a Christmas Celebration of the Word. Since we were already planning with the catechists to do just that, they were delighted and asked if we could have a solemn Celebration of the Word, with lots of prayers, incense, singing, a talk, etc. They wanted it to be long and meaningful. So, at about 11:45 P.M., Lori and I went over to church and found it pretty full already. The manger scene was all set up, complete with big pine branches and twinkling lights, and everyone in church eagerly awaited the arrival of Mary and Joseph from the last house of the posadas. You may recall the Spanish custom of taking the statues of Mary and Joseph in procession to a different house each night for nine nights. This night, at midnight, they would come to the manger where the Infant would appear. This baby Jesus (El Niño Jesús) was dressed just as a baby of the village would be, in traditional costume, complete with a baby's stockingcap! The Niño Jesús was the size of a medium-sized baby doll, but it was not treated like a doll. It was treated very reverently, carried to the altar, and placed on a pillow, awaiting its parents' arrival.

When the procession entered the church, it was led in by guitarists and singing people. The bearers of the statues of Mary and Joseph placed them in the manger scene. We then began the Celebration of the Word. Right after the reading of the Gospel, which told of the birth of Jesus, one of the catechists very reverently took the figure of Jesus in his arms, like a real baby, and gently carried it over to the manger and placed it in the spot prepared between Mary and Joseph. As he did this, another catechist explained about Christ's birth. It was done with such care and respect. All the people were caught up in the awe of the birth of God among us as a helpless child. He looked like their own children except for the statue's blue eyes and fair skin.

We continued with the Celebration of the Word, and we gave Communion to many people that night. Lori and I finally got to bed at about 2 A.M. Fortunately, there was no Christmas morning Mass, so we could catch up on our sleep. There was no waking us up for tamales, this time, either.

Dad, I'm thrilled to know that you have a good report from the doctor, and that your heart shows no sign of trouble. I guess the old ticker is still ticking along just fine.

Mom, I'm happy your church Christmas bazaar went so well. I think you should work on making things for it all year long, so that you won't have to rush so much as the time comes close.

I am glad you are praying for all of us missioners these days. We need every prayer we can get! I can't say, "Don't worry." If you will, you will. But don't worry *too* much, O.K.? I'm fine, and I have a lot of support from Lori, my community, and the people who surround me here in town. We all pray that the Prince of Peace bring true Peace to this battered but faithful people, who seek nothing more than the life of human dignity God wants for all people, and for which Jesus came into the world. He can show us how to live as children of God. But showing isn't enough. We must *do* that living each day.

Chapter Four

In the Eye of the Storm
January 1981–March 1982

THE TOWN

The army arrived in town yesterday. They came in battle gear, on foot, strung out along the road—over seventy soldiers, hot, tired, thirsty. As soon as the first ones arrived, they headed for the nearest stores and asked for beers and Cokes. They get a salary, but they asked for free drinks and they got them. What storekeeper wants to get on the bad side of the army these days?

They were spotted by two women while still a long way off. The women had had previous experience with soldiers in another part of the country. It showed. They huddled together, hunched over ever so slightly, with their voices lowered to a whisper. They repeated over and over again, "The soldiers, the soldiers." They asked if they could hide in a back room. When asked if they thought the soldiers were coming after them, they laughed a bit nervously, said "no," and headed for the back room.

What does a small town do with seventy soldiers? It feeds them as long as they are there. It provides them with a place to sleep, a place to bathe and to wash their clothes. It provides them with amusement of sorts, as they watch the girls go by on their errands. It tolerates their boisterous shouting, it fears their gun-toting drinking. It wonders why they've come, where they have been, where they are going. It tries not to think about all it has heard through the grapevine about what happened to other towns the soldiers vis-

151

ited. It treats them nicely and hopes they will soon go away, leaving the town and its people intact.

A group of young soldiers stood talking with the storekeeper. They were drinking his beer. One said it was a nice town. Another mentioned he thought the church was pretty. A third said he had just seven months left to finish his hitch in the army and hoped he'd make it. Someone else mentioned that he used to be a Catholic before he entered the army and still liked to hear the church hymns. The storekeeper's son took out his guitar and strummed. As he began to sing a familiar hymn, most of the soldiers joined in. One protested, saying he preferred Mexican cowboy songs. All the others turned on him, saying if he didn't like it he could leave. He stayed. After that hymn, there was another, and another, and a mood of nostalgia overtook the group. Almost all of them were Catholics, or at least, had been. When the storekeeper's son asked why they were no longer Catholics, a soldier said that, when they entered the army, they were told amid kicks, punches, and curses, that in the army there is no God, just the devil, and they had better get used to it. One brave young recruit said that whenever they are in a town where there is a Mass, some of them try to sneak into the church, hoping not to get caught by an officer.

In church on Sunday morning, a handful of worshippers clustered near the altar. All faced the altar but the catechist, who faced the congregation and, beyond them, the open church door. As the service began, he could see the officer in camouflage uniform framed by the church entrance. He could see very clearly everything that the officer did. It was a distraction during the service, but a fascinating distraction.

The congregation rose, sang a hymn, and began the service.

The officer stood watching a minute, then turned, sat down on the threshold of the church, and took off his back pack.

The congregation prayed in silence, asking forgiveness for any offense they had committed against God or neighbor.

The officer opened his back pack, rummaged through it, and noisily emptied its contents around him. He pulled out several items wrapped in plastic bags. As he opened each bag, to check its contents, the sound rustled up to the sanctuary. Some things he rewrapped, and others he placed on the steps for further reference. He looked over his shoulder at the congregation.

The congregation stood, listening attentively to a scriptural reading. It spoke of the death of Jesus at the hands of soldiers. It told of how, after he was already dead, a soldier stabbed him in the chest.

The officer pulled out his blanket, spread it, shook it, checked it for fleas, folded it up and shoved it back into its plastic bag.

The congregation sat in silence, reflecting on the reading, its meaning, and its implications for their own lives.

The officer untied his combat boots and took them off, plunking each down soundly on the church step. He removed his plastic shower slippers from a plastic bag and put them on.

The congregation shared their thoughts on the Gospel reading. One man told of how his brother-in-law had died two nights earlier. The brother-in-law was asleep in his house, he said, when big men with big guns broke in and demanded money. They shot him and he died on the floor of his home. He was shot in the side, about where Jesus was stabbed.

The officer stood, scratched his chest and sides and took off his belt. He unbuttoned and removed his shirt. He threw his arms over his back and began to pull off his khaki t-shirt, then stopped and turned to look again at the congregation. His glance met the eyes of the catechist. He paused, then bent down and picked up his clean shirt and pants. He called another, younger officer and left him standing in the church entrance as he walked away.

The congregation spoke of the loving forgiveness of God, of the love of God's son, shown by his giving up his life for us, and of the need we have to forgive and be forgiven.

The officer returned and dismissed his subordinate. He stood, hands on hips, bare-chested and in clean camouflage pants, staring into the church. He stretched, yawned, scratched himself, bent over his back pack and rummaged again. He turned his back to the altar and, once more, sat on the threshold of the church.

The congregation stood, thanked God for the gift of Jesus and the gift of life. They begged the Creator's blessing on all peoples, the sick and dying, all who work to make this a better world. Then they shook hands all around.

The officer picked up his automatic rifle, examined it closely, checked to see that it was fully loaded, and then laid it across his knees.

The congregation prayed a closing prayer and sang a final hymn.
The officer shouted and a soldier came running. He gave an order, then picked up his towel, threw it over his shoulder and clip-clopped down the stone steps.

The congregation filed out of church, stepping around the officer's back pack, and past the soldier who stood guarding the pack and the gun at the church entrance.

A priest came for Mass that Sunday afternoon. The church was filled with townspeople; the back pews were full of soldiers. Soldiers also lined the back walls. They all carried their guns. Some didn't seem to know what a Mass was, and were the last ones to stand, sit, or kneel, following the congregation's example. They laughed a lot and chewed gum during the Mass. Several more soldiers ran into church during the Mass to escape a downpour. They hovered near the entrance, just waiting for the rain to let up. Of the over twenty soldiers in church, two took a risk in the face of possible disciplining by their officer and certain mockery by their companions. At Communion time, they rose, laid down their rifles, filed up the aisle and reverently received the Eucharist, the Body and Blood of their Lord, Jesus Christ, who gave His life that humankind might learn to live as Children of God.

LETTERS

San Jerónimo
January 2, 1981

Dear Gerry,

Thank you for your letter. I am grateful for your immediate response to the murder of Maura, Ita, Dorothy, and Jean in El Salvador. I *do* know that you were thinking of Lori and me and the many other women missioners you met while you were here. We're all equally vulnerable now, it's true. The response of American women religious was immediate and powerful. Thank you and your own Sisters for being so united with us now. It can't be very pleasant going to stand every Wednesday night in front of the Salvadoran Embassy, calling for a halt to military aid to that country. It's *cold* in New York in January!

You know, you scare me. You have done *almost* what I thought you might do, but *hoped* you wouldn't. I feared you would write to Maryknoll to find out if you could volunteer to replace one of those martyred women in El Salvador next summer! You have gone even further by asking to be accepted as an Associate Maryknoll Sister! If you decide to enter that program, who will I have, besides my family, to write these letters to? And no one can take your place in the demonstrations, protests, candlelight vigils, fasts, and prayer services for Central America. There will be no one like you to get on the phone to start things moving, to send telegrams, to write letters and organize and mobilize people to respond to the injustices done in the name of the people of the United States. Oh, I know there will be other people doing all those things, Gerry, but you are unique and irreplaceable! And you might end up in Tanzania or Taiwan, far from Central America, or from the Bronx, for that matter. Well, I am praying for you each day, that you resolve your dilemma and that the decision really be the best for you. I recall that you wrote in late October that you were beginning to "discern God's will for me in my ministry." That sounded serious to me. I think of you as perfect for the South Bronx, doing what I could never do. Yet you said then that, "although I love my work here in the South Bronx, in Guatemala a peace and closeness to God occurred in my life that I cannot explain. Maybe all the work I did there with adults, and literacy, and catechists, and the Celebration of the Word, was a preparation for a new ministry for me. I am confused and yet I still feel that very deep peace within me." You asked my prayers then to help you work through this serious step. I have had you in mind and heart since, but I guess I thought that it was a held-over glow, like the Northern Lights, that would eventually fade with the coming of a new school year and all its involvements. It hasn't faded, obviously. And even though you speak enthusiastically about your eighth graders, it is clear that your heart is not settled yet. So I'll keep it under my hat and in my prayers for now.

January 15, 1981

Dear Gerry,

Here I am at the same table in Likin where you helped me work on the catechists' retreat. It wasn't even four months ago, but so much has happened since then. The militarization of the country is being given a bizarre twist here at the beach. I was walking along the water's edge today and almost got hit by a jet fighter that swooped down so low along the shore that I felt I had to duck! I suppose I could have looked the pilot in the eye had I wanted to.

Here in Guatemala it seems that the death squads took their Christmas vacation, because things were quiet for the most of December. Now they are back on the job. I heard from a neighbor just before leaving town that ten bodies were found at a major crossroad nearby. I know an Indian woman whose father and two brothers were just assassinated, too. It's "business as usual."

On our way here several days ago, I had an experience I have been dreading for a long time: I saw my first bodies. They were three young Indian men. I was driving and since a small crowd was gathering, I passed very slowly but didn't stop. I took one long look, though, which was enough for a lifetime. Three young men, the one nearest to me with a gash from jaw to collarbone, bigger than my open hand could cover, were lying faceup. Nameless bodies, food for vultures, who not long before were living, hoping, laughing young men. Each was someone's son, someone's brother, perhaps some girl's boyfriend, or some child's father, leaving behind a wife who didn't yet know she's a widow.

I have seen, almost touched, the violence up close. Not only that. I may have seen the killers. Those bodies had just been dumped there, because people were just beginning to gather around them. We may have passed their murderers in a police jeep, on the highway. If those plainclothesmen chauffered by a uniformed cop were the killers, just doing their job, then they and the men lying on the road are bound together forever, as executioners and victims always are. A strange new interpretation of a quote from the gospels comes to me now: "What you bind on earth shall be bound in heaven."

I'm reading the Book of Wisdom these days, preparing for a catechist session. It has become one of my favorite books of the Bible. Only in this situation do I comprehend its message. Chapters One through five are particularly clear regarding death from God's point of view and from the perspective of evil men:

Death was not God's doing, he takes no pleasure in the extinction of the living. *To be*—for this he created all

But the godless call with deed and word for Death. Counting him a friend, they wear themselves out for him. With him they make a pact, and are fit to be his partners, for they say to themselves, with misguided reasoning: "Our life is short and dreary, nor is there any relief when man's end comes, nor anyone known who can give release from the land of the dead. In time, our name will be forgotten. Nobody will remember what we have done; our life will pass away like wisps of cloud. . . . Come then, let us enjoy what good things there are. . . . As for the virtuous man, who is poor, let us oppress him; let us not spare the widow, nor respect old age, white-haired with many years. Let our strength be the measure of virtue, since weakness argues its own futility. Let us lie in wait for the virtuous man . . . let us test him with cruelty and with torture . . . let us condemn him to a shameful death."

This is the way they reason, but they are misled; their malice makes them blind. They do not know the hidden things of God; they have no hope that holiness will be rewarded, they can see no reward for blameless souls. Yet God made man imperishable; he made him in the image of his own nature; it was the devil's envy that brought death into the world, as those who are his partners will discover. . . . They will come trembling to the reckoning of their sins, and their crimes, confronting them, will accuse them. Then the virtuous man stands up boldly to face those who have oppressed him, those who thought so little of his sufferings. And they, at the sight of him, will shake with coward's fear . . ."

I can see why people hoped for justice after death, when there was none for them in life. I believe in a God of compassionate love. But God is also just.

We are packing to go and will leave here tomorrow morning, back to the real world. I'm looking forward to hearing from you. Oh, by the way, please don't worry, if you can avoid it. You say that, with all the scary news, you "still haven't mastered the faith aspect." Neither have most of the rest of us, here in the midst of it. It's an ongoing process, but we get a lot of help from seeing the faith of the people with whom we live and work. You and we and they are in this together.

January 21, 1981

Dear Gerry,

I keep receiving gifts from you, sent with anyone you hear of who might be passing through Guatemala! Thank you for the hand-carved jewelry box, and the poster of a snow-covered tree with the words, "Faith is the substance of things hoped for, the evidence of things not seen." Since I won't see snow ever in Guatemala, I have hung it in my room by my desk just to remind me.

How good it was that you and Pat were able to attend Dorothy Day's wake at the Catholic Worker. I never met her, but I knew a lot about her. Through her living the Gospel daily she was certainly a great symbol, a beacon of Christian witness in a world darkened by selfishness. I wonder if anyone will arise in the United States to continue bearing such lifelong witness. I know there are many "little people" doing it, but we lack a charismatic figure who sums it all up in one person. We'll have to wait until God raises up another Witness of her stature.

Thank your friends for us, please, for that very generous check they sent for our work. I can't believe you got that much from a potluck supper and slide show on Guatemala!

I am anxious to hear the results of your inquiries into our Sister Associate Program. You said that you feel very strongly drawn to the people of Latin America. I guess that the program would be a good way for you to see if you can realize that attraction. Your faith is strong, and you know that God is at work in this decision. If you are to go, you will. And that first-aid course you signed up for may just come in handy!

January 31, 1981

Dear Mom and Dad,

I am writing you this, hoping you will share it with the rest of the family. It comes from the pain in my soul over our government's double standard in dealing with different countries, and it comes from my Christian perspective of what being a child of God really means.

Today is January 31st. All over the U.S.A., people are preparing to remember the people of Poland tomorrow. I know that our government has prepared a spectacular TV Special, as well as a broadcast on the Voice of America called "Let Poland be Poland." The programs support the human rights of the Polish people and protest martial law there. Rallies will be held by U.S. labor unions supporting the Polish workers' right to form a union called "Solidarity." President Reagan will appear on the TV program and will also attend some solidarity rallies. Under other circumstances, I would say, "Wonderful!"

But living in Guatemala gives me a point of view that is distinctly different. Because of what I see, I have a hard time fighting back the tears of anger and frustration when I hear all the broadcasts and U.S. government statements on defending the rights of the Polish people, while U.S. policy doesn't consider the rights of the Guatemalan people.

By coincidence, today, January 31, is a special day here in Guatemala. Today is the first anniversary of the massacre at the Spanish embassy, when over thirty peasants, labor leaders, and students died in a fire after Guatemalan riot police stormed the building. What was their crime that they merited such a horrible death? They were trying to get help in finding their husbands and sons and brothers who had been kidnapped by death squads. They were asking for an investigation into the murders of those who were found, tortured and disfigured. They wanted justice in their legitimate claims for the land on which many of them were born. To keep them silent, the army made the people of that area virtual prisoners in their own towns. They were brazenly and systematically being killed off, not by the army of a foreign enemy, but by the army of Guatemala, which was made up in the main of young Indian men, of their same race and culture.

In Guatemala, as in some other Latin American countries, recruitment resembles a roundup of wild horses. Young men, off to market or coming from church on a Sunday morning, are chased by recruiters or soldiers. They are grabbed, beaten, kicked, tied up, and carried off to the army base where they are reduced to obedient automatons. They are taught to despise their Indian languages and culture and to hate Communists. Without a clue as to what *Communist* really means, the usual soldier believes that "Communist" equals "enemy," and that "Indian" is close to "Communist." They think this especially of those "subversive" Indians who are educated and organized.

Daily, the newspaper details horrors that should be unspeakable, pictures that ought to be unprintable. And the worst cases never even get to the papers. Those stories are passed in whispers from horrified witnesses to equally horrified listeners. The stories are spread by terrified people who are torn between not speaking and getting the story out lest it fester within them. They speak to share the horror so it will not be their burden alone.

I want to cry over the hypocrisy of our American leaders. Why do they shut their official eyes and ears in the face of truth from some countries, like those in Central America, and open them wide for others, as is the case with Poland? They defend Poland before the world with one hand, while devastating Central America behind their back with the other. In the name of fighting terrorism we teach the armies and police of Central America to terrorize their own people.

I've experienced that terrorism myself, in ways that just brushed me, but that I will never forget. Recently, I was coming home on a bus. It was an old, rickety bus, with a hole in the floor through which I could watch the road slip past as we rode along. It was a bus for poor people. As I got on and made my way to the back, I spotted an empty seat. A young Indian man rose, smiling, and gave me his seat near the window; he took the aisle seat. He began to chat with the man across the aisle as the bus cranked up and rumbled on once again. But it barely got going when it was stopped by an army patrol less than 200 yards ahead. Soldiers got on, yelling, "All men, off!" Old men and little boys, along with the able-bodied young men, stood up and filed off. From my window seat I watched the men line up along the length of the bus, fishing in their shirt pockets as they went, pulling out identification papers that were carefully wrapped in plastic bags. I knew the men had been subjected to such searches innumerable times before and were well practiced. As some soldiers went down the line checking papers, frisking the men who stood with arms raised, another soldier got on the bus and poked at the bundles on the overhead racks. When he got to me and my beat-up old denim tote bag and camera bag, he was curious. "Whose are these?" he shouted. "Mine," I said. He told me to get them down so he could search them. When he finished rummaging, he got off the bus while I repacked and closed my bags. The men filed on again, tucking their papers into their pockets. Relief was apparent on many faces. But as the bus started, I missed the man next to me. I had the whole seat to myself! I looked across the aisle and asked the men in that seat what had happened to him. They looked at the empty seat, then at each other. One said simply, "They took him from the group." "Why?" I asked. "He didn't have his identification papers." They seemed startled themselves. Then I noticed that the whole seat in front of those two men was also empty. "What about those three men?" I asked. "Who knows?" was the helpless reply.

The bus had been full when we were stopped. Now four seats were empty. Four men were in the hands of the army. Looking at those four empty seats was like looking at four coffins. Being taken off the bus in Guatemala at this time is not a mere inconvenience. It can frequently be fatal. If there had been rebel activity in the area, you might think those men were guerrillas. But that army checkpoint is a permanent one. It's been there a long time, just down the road from the usual bus stop. People who travel that road know that. My seat companion and those other three men could have easily gotten off the bus when others got on, before the checkpoint. None of them did. Why not? They had nothing to fear, apparently. They were unsuspecting victims.

The man across the aisle from me looked about sixty. He said he hadn't known the young fellow who gave me his seat. "I'm from Santa Ana," he said. My heart went out to him. Santa Ana and other nearby towns and villages had been "swept" by the army when they were looking for guerrillas. In the process of the sweep, many innocent people had been killed. Other towns were completely abandoned when word got to them of the fate of their neighbors.

As we rode along in silence, I felt the oppression of the empty spaces around me. It felt worse than sitting with three passengers squeezed into a space made for two. I kept wondering about that young man. What was he thinking, praying, worrying, saying right now? How much would he suffer? Would they kill him? What of his family who waited for him?

Once in a while I'd glance at the empty seat with a pang of regret. Not only did I not know his name, but I never really had looked at his face. I can't remember what he looked like. The least I could do in his memory is recall how he looked! But I can't. I pray for him and refer to him as "the man who gave me his seat."

These days I've been reading the Book of Wisdom as I prepare for our catechist sessions. Until I lived through a period of wickedness myself, I could not really comprehend the message of that book. But now I see it as the book of hope for the helpless, innocent children of God. In the end, the virtuous one triumphs, at least in the Book of Wisdom. It gives hope of some justice being done after death if none is done before. And when daily injustice is what a person faces, the hope of some justice *some day* gives one courage to go on living:

> . . . Grace and mercy await the chosen of the Lord, and protection, His Holy ones. The virtuous man who dies condemns the godless who survive, and youth's untimely end condemns the protracted age of the wicked. These people see the wise man's end without understanding what the Lord has in store for him. They look on and sneer, but the Lord will laugh at them. Soon they will be corpses without honor, objects of scorn among the dead forever.

I'll end with a plea for your prayers for us and the suffering people of Guatemala and El Salvador, and the request that you listen critically to what our government says, and make your outrage known.

February 5, 1981

Dear Gerry,

Lori and I returned from Guatemala City last night and I trudged on down to the postoffice at 6:30 P.M. to check for mail. To my surprise and delight, there were your two letters waiting for me! I've been a bit depressed this last week, and getting your letters perked my spirits. Today is a free day (we'll see how long it lasts) and I'm dedicating a good bit of it to writing to you. I don't know where it will go, as I have so many thoughts; they just come tumbling out when I start writing.

So, my friend, you are beginning to come out and speak openly of your desire to work as a missioner in Latin America. I'm glad your friends are so understanding and supportive. I know they hate the thought of losing you to another part of the world. Your conviction since December 2nd, of setting yourself on this new path, is scary to them, I'm sure. You say you feel a special bond with Maura, Ita, Dorothy, and Jean and that you pray to those four martyred women to help you in your decision. I'll pray too.

We are preoccupied these days with the idea of self-defense. So much has happened to innocent people who have no way of defending themselves. Lori and I both keep a small bag packed in case we have to leave suddenly. After a lull around Christmas, the terrifying "midnight visitors" have begun to pay calls on innocent, unsuspecting families once again. Three men have disappeared from the town up the road. In the town across the ravine, cars have been going in and out for months almost each night between 12 and 3 A.M. Just a few days ago, the men from one of those phantom cars entered a house in town demanding to know where certain people lived. The poor woman, alone in the house, didn't tell them anything, so they gave her a punch that sent her reeling. They ransacked her poor little house, took $2.50 (her budget for the week), and said they would be back. Their tactics are to sneak up on a house, drag the victims out and either kill them outright, or, more usually, shove them into their vehicles and torture them to death elsewhere. They dump the bodies far from where they lived, so the families can't even bury them.

Some of the death squads are composed of soldiers or police, both on duty and off. I was told by an ex-soldier that the men in his outfit were frequently asked to volunteer for special, unofficial assignments, which were to be done in civilian dress. He never volunteered, but said that the bullies of his outfit frequently did, and returned laughing and bragging. They are like the Gestapo in Nazi Germany, but they lack the honesty to wear their uniforms openly. This official terrorism is no secret here. Why is it unknown to the White House? I am so ashamed of my government's policy of support for this military government. Poor Indian peasants ask me why such terrible things are happening. How can I explain the United States' role in their government's terrorism? How can one even begin to make sense of it in terms of Cold War, East–West struggles, when they simply want to know why their own government singles them out for extermination?

Some of these people have come recently with their simple stories, and I have to fight back the tears as they speak. In their poor, broken Spanish they eloquently convey their experiences and their dismay bordering on despair.

—The other day, Lorenzo (you met him a few times in that community on the mountaintop) came to visit us. He wanted us to accept a simple gift. Digging down into his woven rope shoulder bag, he pulled out a huge bundle, wrapped in his wife's hand-woven red napkin. I opened it and found two huge cooked yams and several oranges. We thanked him profusely. Lori put a kettle of water on the stove to heat and invited him to share coffee and bread with us. Then we listened to his story, trying hard to follow as he spoke his Mayan Indian thoughts in halting Spanish.

"I came down to town today to pay my annual one Quetzal tax for 'beautification of the town.' At the same time I'm getting my older children's birth certificates. I heard that children from ten on up who are caught walking along the road without identification papers are picked up, and that the government has no obligation to give them back to their families. Is this possible, Madres?" he asked. It was the first time I had heard of such a thing, but anything is possible, and I told him so. "Da lástima," he said, shaking his head; "how sad."

"A parent can't even send a child on an errand any more," he mused. "I'd be afraid he wouldn't come back. Can they walk to school down the road safely? Can they visit their grandmother across the road?" He is faced with new kinds of problems, questions, worries. He went on to talk about the war in El Salvador, to which he added another "da lástima." He had heard of the death of the four women missioners there, and knew we had gone to the funeral. He had really been quite worried about us, and hadn't slept that night because he had been so worried. He thought the women were killed because "the Sisters and priests were giving the people opportunities to learn things—new ideas—to improve their lives,'' and that "there are people who don't want the poor to get any new ideas.'' He finally thanked us for our efforts to help them understand their faith better and to live it more fully. As an afterthought, he thanked us also for the literacy classes and the women's classes.

When he left, it was my turn to say "da lástima!'' To think that such people must live in fear of kidnapping and torture and death, just because they want to improve their lives and live their faith more fully! Folks on the mountaintop have been warned by the army not to be wandering in their fields or on the roads between 6 P.M. and 8 A.M. because they could be mistaken for guerrillas. That's hard for a man who has to walk an hour or more to reach his farm plot, because he will lose several hours of valuable work time a day. But they take the advice of the soldiers seriously, because they fear becoming victims of such a terrible "mistake.''

—A man I didn't know came to visit us yesterday. His clothes were patched patches. He was barefoot, and in his hands he held the remains of a weatherbeaten black felt sombrero that was stained by the rains. His wife had sewn its crown and brim together with green embroidery thread. He also had come to town to pay his one Quetzal tax. Like our earlier visitor, he lives on the mountaintop, and was getting his children's birth certificates. He said his name was Manuel. He told us that a few weeks ago the army picked up his twenty-two-year-old brother and their cousin right down the road from their homes. The young men were going rabbit hunting for the family meal. Manuel's brother, Beto, carried a .22 rifle in a sack, a most unwise thing to do. A witness in a cornfield saw them being questioned by an army patrol. Then they were grabbed; their hands were tied behind their backs, and they were shoved into the jeep.

The family has searched unsuccessfully for them at several army bases and outposts, and they were treated rudely. "I love my brother,'' Manuel said. "He used to come to visit me. We'd talk about the crops, and how to treat our wives and children, and what the Word of God tells us. He used to play the guitar and sing in the chapel when our community gathered for evening prayer. We miss him so. *Da lástima,*'' he said, in typical Indian understatement.

"How is the family?" I asked. "My mother can hardly eat two tortillas," he replied. "I sold my shoes to pay for the bus fare to go way up north to look for Beto. I looked for him on the Atlantic coast, and on the Pacific coast; wherever there are army bases I've looked, but I haven't found him. And Beto's pregnant wife and two little children are always so sad. And look at me: I'm all patches! I try to treat my children well, and if we have meat, I try to see that everyone gets a little bit. I try to see that they are clothed. But my brother's children? Who cares for them? We all try to help, but we are all poor. His wife tries, but it's so hard! When he disappeared he left his fields and they need tending. We cultivated and harvested his corn. And now my parents are giving us their inheritance. My father has three acres and it must be divided among six of us children. But my poor brother will miss his share, because we don't know if he's dead or alive. If he ever comes back, I'll give him some of mine, because he's my brother, and I love him. What can we do? We'll keep looking as long as we can. Because he's my brother, and because '*da lástima.*' "

(Gerry, can you take any more, because I have more to tell you. I have to tell someone.)

—With all the news and rumors of phantom cars, disappearing men, appearing bodies, and the realization that the Catholic Church is being persecuted directly (aimed especially at the simple, poor Indian peasants who happen to be community and church leaders), many people wonder if they are marked for death. Each puzzles the question, "What can I do to prepare for the night they come for *me*?" I gleaned the following from a meeting of such men at 9 P.M., in a windowless room behind the parish hall, where they played a radio so loudly that no outside eavesdroppers could hear. Paranoid? No, prudent. This was the conversation:

"Well, my brothers. We are all here now because we all have the same fear: 'They may come for me some night.' Cars without lights come into town late at night, and strange men walk around town at that hour. We have good reason to fear. Those strangers may be just trying to scare us, but they may also be looking for our houses. What should we do to protect ourselves and each other? Please speak from your hearts, brothers."

"I think, if they come to get one of us, a neighbor should run and warn the others."

"It would be better if we could somehow unite to keep watch at night, so that we can give warning in time, so they don't find us in our homes."

"But how can we give a warning in time? If we ring the bells, or do something else like whistle, we will arouse suspicion among the neighbors. If we stand watch, we may be suspected of helping the guerrillas at night. Paid spies can be anywhere."

"What about our families? It is impossible, even with a few minutes warning, to get your wife and small children out of the house and safely someplace else. Do they kill families, too? Or will they just kill me? If they just kill me, 'da lástima' to think that the family and especially the children have to see. If I run away, maybe they won't touch my wife and children, but they would be defenseless. If the strangers are angry that I am not there, they may kill my wife and all my children to get even with me and make me suffer."

"I don't want to die. I have three small children. I want to give them better than I had. My eldest little girl is in first grade. I'm already planning for her education when she finishes sixth grade here. If I am killed, how will my wife support herself and the children? I have no land, but I have a good job. It is because of my job that I can plan for the future; and it is also because of my job that they will want to kill me! If I quit my job I may save my life but have no future. And if I don't quit it, I may lose my life, and have no future!"

"I have sent my younger children to live with their grandmother, and the older ones stay with us in our house. I'm worried about what they might do to my sixteen-year-old daughter. I'm considering sending her to work as a maid in Guatemala City.

"How can we resist if they come for us? Let the air out of their tires? But that could be dangerous. They would surely have a guard at the car. They have big machine guns; we have only our machetes."

"My brothers, can we make a plan together *tonight*? What about using flashlights to signal each other? We will all have to be committed to take a turn as lookout, because we will be responsible for each other's *lives*. Last night, around 2 A.M., I heard a car enter town. I got up and looked out the window. There was no moon and the car had no lights. It went to the end of the road, turned, and left. They *are* coming, brothers. What can we *do*?''

—We are preparing to finish our course on the Old Testament, with a touch and a taste of Wisdom literature. Antonio has a very hard time with Spanish and can't get the material he is to teach without great effort. But he struggles and puts in hours going over it with me. I gave him what I thought would be the least difficult part, from the book of Ecclesiastes, where it says ''Vanity of vanities, and all is vanity.'' The author of Ecclesiastes sees no fulfillment in what the world values. Having tried it all, he finds it all wanting. He lives in a time when life after death is a madman's dream, not a belief of intelligent people. He sees life's rewards in living according to God's will and enjoying the simple things.

Well, I sat down with Antonio and began trying to give him a feel for the mindset and problem of the author. I thought it would take an hour of plodding to do it. In fact, it took three minutes! First, he read the text Ecclesiastes 1:12–18. This passage begins: ''With the help of Wisdom I have been at pains to study all that is done under heaven; oh, what a weary task God has given man to labor at!'' The passage ends: ''Wisdom has been my careful study; stupidity, too, and folly. And now I have come to recognize that even this is chasing of the wind. Much sorrow, much grief, the more knowledge, the more sorrow.''

After he labored over this reading, Antonio looked at me and said simply, ''Madre, I don't understand this reading.'' I paraphrased it in simpler terms. Then he read it again and began a commentary the likes of which I've never heard before.

''I can understand the author's feelings,'' he told me. ''I too, have racked my brain on the meaning of life. I feel sorry for the author since he didn't even know that life after death was possible. It is certain that what we have on this side of death can't ever satisfy us.'' Antonio can understand the futility the author expresses. He himself, who believes in a life and a reward after death, doesn't really *know* for sure if it exists or not. He said, ''Life is like a chance you take on some prizes at a fair. At the fair, however, you can see the prizes up there on the table: First Prize, Second Prize, Third Prize. Seeing the prizes makes you all the more eager to buy as many chances as you can to win. But in the gamble we call life, we can't *see* the prizes. We don't even have an assurance that there *are* any prizes at the end! Especially with the new element of danger and threat added to our lives, those of us who have chosen to be teachers of the Word of God want even more assurance that the gamble is worth it. We need to know that the chances we take are not foolish, and that the prize awaits us. But we don't *know*—we just don't know.''

We went on to the next text, Ecclesiastes 2:1–11. Here the author says he decided to try everything that promised to give pleasure, and at the end, he found it all meaningless. At this, Antonio said, ''But it is a common experience, and I have felt the same way many times. And this man, this writer who suffered such mental anguish over the meaning of life—he didn't suffer in vain after all. He wrote it down, and today I am reading it, and I can agree with what he says. I can see that other people have the same questions and problems; they felt this way so many hundreds of years ago. It gives me courage and strength to go on, and I say 'thank you' to the man who wrote this book.''

He agreed with Ecl. 3:1–8, that there is a time for everything under the sun, and then we went on to 4:1–3, about the suffering of the oppressed:

> Then I looked again at all the injustice that goes on in the world. The oppressed were crying, and no one would help them. No one would help them because their oppressors had power on their side. I envy those who are dead and gone. They are better off than those who are still alive. But better off than either are those who have never been born, who have never seen the injustice that goes on in the world.

Antonio looked at me then, his sad eyes glistening. ''I guess I agree with that, too,'' he said, ''nowadays.''

Gerry, I've been a bit depressed these last days, and getting your two letters was a great boost. I count on your prayers very much.

February 17, 1981

Dear Mom and Dad,

The government has begun a nationwide literacy campaign that is affecting the life of almost everybody in the rural areas. I think it is an attempt to go through the motions of attacking the problem because Nicaragua has done a great job in its literacy campaign.

A census was taken in each Guatemalan town to find out how many people between the ages of fifteen and forty-five couldn't read or write. In this town *alone* there are 435 women who fall into that category, and that doesn't include the men! Next, the mayor told all those women that they would be obliged to attend the classes, to learn to read and write. The Ministry of Education is supposed to provide copy books, pencils, blackboards, etc. But so far, no materials have arrived, and I doubt they ever will. The women are buying their own materials in the local stores, which are having a hard time keeping copy books in stock.

Lori and I have already offered the women a two-week literacy course each year. Those who studied with us will be ahead of the rest. It will be hard, because most women have a baby at the breast and another by the hand. They have to be away from their homes from two to four P.M. three days a week. They are obliged to go, and if they don't go they have to pay a fine. I doubt the fine can be enforced once the initial fervor has worn off. Illiterate men will study from 5 to 7 P.M. each night. Besides the school, any other place large enough to handle big groups, like the co-op and our parish hall, must be made available. "Volunteers" have been pressed into service, especially men who taught literacy through the Atitlán radio school program. Most Indian women speak only their native language. Yet they will be learning to read and write in Spanish. I expect they will at least learn to write their names, which will make them proud. But because of the literacy campaign, we must cancel our year's courses for the women. They can't afford more time out of their busy lives as homemakers.

Remember Gerry, the Sister who stayed with us last summer? Well, we've developed a close friendship almost entirely by letter. She dropped a bombshell in a recent letter saying she feels called to be a missioner in Latin America! If she gets into the Maryknoll

Sisters' program she mentioned, she'll be ready to go to a mission at just about the time I'm scheduled to return to the States for a few years. We'll miss each other! And when I finish what I'm doing in the States, she'll be finishing her three years in the mission and we may just miss each other again. It will be an unusual friendship if we never see each other.

P.S. I hadn't sealed this yet because I wasn't going to mail it until tomorrow. I just got news that another priest has been killed. That makes five since last May. You may hear about it in the news, then again you might not. His name was Fr. Juan Alonso, and he is the third of his congregation, the Spanish Sacred Heart Fathers, to die in less than a year. Remember my telling you that the bishop of the diocese of El Quiché withdrew all his priests and Sisters in protest over the violence and murder of church people, including laity? Well, after many months Fr. Juan Alonso got permission to go into the Quiché diocese from another part of the country. His superiors and bishop thought he would be safe. They were wrong, and he is dead.

The American pastor of Santiago Atitlán, Fr. Stanley Rother, had a narrow escape. He was lucky to shake a jeepful of armed men who followed him on a wild chase through the Capital. He was there arranging for his exit visa and plane ticket to leave the country after taking the latest death threats seriously. He's been in Santiago for thirteen years, and has learned the Tzutuhil language. He respects their ways and is rare in being accepted by the leaders of the traditional religion. They'll miss him.

Sorry to close on such a sad and scary note. Maybe next time I'll have good news to tell you.

March 11, 1981

Dear Mom and Dad,

We had an interruption in the town's water supply for three days. Some animal had gotten into the reservoir tank, up on the mountaintop. The mayor sent his teenaged helpers, the *alguaciles,* to clean the tank. They had a great time, splashing around, removing a snake from the pipe as well as the animal from the outflow spout. They scrubbed the tank while swimming in it. I wonder how long it will take for the water to be safe to drink after all that?

Our cat is gone. She disappeared a few weeks ago while we were away giving courses in two villages. She was not only fun, she was functional. She kept the birds out of my garden and the mouse population down. When she didn't have kittens to feed she would occasionally bring a mouse and leave it at Lori's bedroom door. I didn't get any mice from her, just fleas. I'll miss Balam.

Tonight and every Wednesday night in Lent we have a special Celebration of the Word to help the people think about what Lent really means. It allows us to give some extra attention to the Lenten readings. Luckily we have some men who are willing to take on the work of translating the readings and to give a homily in their own language. We have been working up to this for years, and now our plans and efforts are bearing fruit. We just sit there, presiding, and we also give out communion. The catechists do everything else, and none too soon!

Several catechists are beekeepers. Their group recently brought in its first batch of honey. I asked Antonio how the honey harvest went. The men did it as a group, ten men with eighteen hives. They borrowed the parish kitchen, brought the heavy hives in from a mile away on their backs, and spent a week extracting the honey with homemade equipment. The first few days went smoothly, but when the bees got wind of it they dive-bombed the workers and crash-landed in the honey trough. After the harvest, the men took the hives back up to the mountainside, but some bees hung around the kitchen for weeks.

The group sold the honey to the townspeople for Q.1.50 a bottle. Everybody is stocking up for the Holy Thursday custom of sharing bread and honey. They were paid according to the number of hours they worked making the hives, inspecting them in the field, and harvesting. Antonio got 48 Quetzales, which went back into the project to pay the cost of the hives, equipment, transportation, and family support for their teacher. Antonio considers it a good investment. He is teaching his sons the art of bee-keeping.

April 7, 1981

Dear Gerry,

I can't recall the last time I wrote. It's been *that* long. Sometimes there is so much to say, as you know, and sometimes there isn't very much. I began a letter to you a while back, never sent it, and can't recall what I last said as a result. But it will all work out.

First, I share from afar your anger and anguish over the apartment-fire death of your students' mother. Since so much of the arson in the South Bronx is designed to "clear the block" so that the buildings can be leveled and insurance can be collected, her death can be called murder. The poor kids lost both father and mother within a year, you said. But their father's death to cancer is at least within the realm of illness. Their mother's death is a violence done to them by other people. I'm sure you will always remember standing with your arms around that sister and brother on the street watching the building burn, knowing their mother was trapped inside. You experience that violence in the Bronx, and I experience it here, but in the end it's the same: power-seeking people causing the death of powerless people.

Thank you for the pictures, especially of the two of us at the beach. You can tell which of us stayed under the umbrella researching the retreat for catechists, and which stood in the water calling, "When are you coming in?" Gerry, you look like a slightly tanned lobster, and I look very pale in comparison! I'm glad we had those days to share.

Well, you have finally made the break from the Bronx to the Latin American missions, at least on paper. I'm glad your mother took it so well. You will be missed at school! I'm sure you have a lot of questions and a lot feelings to sort out. But the worst is over, the bridges are smoldering, and you can look forward now.

Thank you for the book *Way of the Cross, Way of Justice,* by Leonardo Boff. It's a wonderful birthday present, and I'll use it in our town's Stations of the Cross every Wednesday and Friday.

Although the violence has calmed down in our area since my last letter, it is still going on elsewhere. I just read the headlines in the paper: twenty campesinos were dragged from their houses in a town in the province of Chimaltenango. They were shot dead and left there. Their neighbors buried them in a common grave. A picture of the scene filled the whole front page of the paper. There have been about 200 people killed in that town, called San Martín, in a very short time.

Well, I must run. Mass is about to start. Thanks for being so concerned.

April 7, 1981

Dear Mom and Dad,

I'm a bit late in answering your letter and birthday card, and I want to thank you. I had a nice, quiet birthday. Lori planned a little party and baked a small cake in our toaster oven. We shared it with several of the men who work closely with us in town. They enjoyed the crazy American custom of putting little candles on the cake, lighting them, and blowing them out!

This morning I was called to pray over a baby that had just died. The poor little girl was only four months old and had looked and seemed perfectly healthy. Yesterday she developed a slight cough, but that's common among these little children. In the morning she was dead, and no one had even thought her sick enough to worry about. Her great-great-grandfather just had his 100th birthday two weeks ago. Strange, that a 100-year-old man will bury his four-month-old great-great grandchild. The young mother, Francisca, sat very still at the side of the small table on which the baby lay. The tiny body, a red cap on its head, its face uncovered, was wrapped in a blanket. Candles burned at the head of the table, the customary way of waking babies. They will put the little one into a small white coffin and she will be buried at 4 P.M.

Dad, thank you for the virus-resistant tomato seeds. I will plant them tomorrow. They ought to fare better than the other tomatoes I've been frustrated with. And Mom, that blue wool cap and sweater set you knitted and sent is just the right size for the new baby of a young widow I know. Her husband and his cousin were walking along the road near their house, were picked up by an army patrol, and were never seen again. She is struggling to earn enough to support her children by selling fruits in the market and by weaving at home, but it is very hard. She was surprised and touched by your generosity. I'll send you a picture of her and the baby wearing the outfit. Thank God they live in a Christian community who are really committed to living their faith. That includes caring for orphans and widows. But if they are all poor, as these folks are, it will be hard for all of them.

May 10, 1981

Dear Gerry,

I guess it's my turn now to say, "It's a long time since I've heard from you!" I'll be away all next week giving courses, and a letter might come from you during that time. I sure hope so.

I can see you are anxiously hoping for an assignment to Guatemala through the Associate program, but you are a long way from an assignment yet. You have just begun the first steps! And the situation for Church workers here in Guatemala and in most of Central America is so precarious that no one knows how long any of us will be able to stay, for all sorts of reasons. That is a hard fact that must be taken into consideration. I'll give you as much input as I can to help you make your decision.

Our little flower garden looked nice for Holy Week, and the lilies bloomed as if programmed for Easter Sunday. I still find it surprising, after all these years, to see Easter lilies, carnations, geraniums, and chrysanthemums all blooming at the same time in our garden. My vegetable garden is doing as poorly as ever, yet I still enjoy fighting each problem, trying to get better results.

Not long ago, a man named José came to visit in the morning, along with his ten-year-old son. They live on top of the mountain. He is dirt poor, suffers from crippling attacks of arthritis, looks about fifty, but is actually in his early thirties. I have never seen him be anything but sober, yet this day he was a bit under the influence, with good reason. His four-year-old son, Gregorio, was dead. José came to share his grief and perplexity. He told us that Gregorio got sick during Holy Week. He bought some medicine at the drug store but it didn't help. Then he took the boy to a doctor at a parish clinic, where they treated him but said they couldn't keep him because they were closing for the final days of Holy Week. So, José took his son home, and did all he could, within his limited means, to save him. But the child died.

José sat there, shaking his head: "It must be my luck. I don't know what it is. I work and I work and I work, and I keep getting poorer. I work hard, and I try to give my children what they need, and they die. He is the fourth, my little Gregorio. There was one who died at five, and the next at ten, and one died at six, and now my little Gregorio. How he loved to dance when the radio played. He would just stand in the middle of the floor and dance and make us all happy. Now he's in the cemetery. I don't understand!''

Then José shared another grief, which came as a shock to us: ''I heard on the radio at 5 A.M. today that the Franciscans and all priests and all Sisters are going to be put out of the country. Is it true?'' I assured him I didn't know. No one had told us to go, but it did make both Lori and me start thinking about our future plans! He said: ''I saw a neighbor on my way here today, and he said he heard it, too. I said to him, 'Who can give that kind of order?' He said, 'I don't know.' '' José said, heatedly, ''Only God should be in charge. He's the one who should say who goes! The government is supposed to do good for the people, but they don't do good. They should keep the commandments, but they just break them! They want to take away from us the people who have helped us, who give us good ideas, who teach us how to better our lives. It's wrong for them to do that. Why do they want to do that?'' The pained questioning look in his eyes will stay with me a long time. How can anyone answer him?

May 17, 1981

Dear Family and Friends,

I am writing you as a group because I know this will be a long letter, and I know how much you care.

As you know, the Pope was shot on Wednesday, May 13th. This was front-page news all over the world; prayers and Masses were offered for his recovery and messages of support began arriving at the Vatican almost immediately. Those were shots heard around the world.

The next day there were some more shots. They left a Guatemalan priest lying in the street a block from church, where he was going to baptize a child. Carlos Gálvez never had a chance. He was shot in the head by his assailants. No security guards or police chased the killers; there were only helpless stricken neighbors. His life spilled out onto the cobblestones. When his body was removed, some people made a circle of rocks around the blood of their pastor. Soon there was no blood. It had been reverently gathered up with the dust of the road and carried off by hundreds of people, as a remembrance of the martyrdom of yet another priest in Guatemala.

These shots, fired on Thursday, May 14th, were not meant to be heard around the world. They weren't even meant to be heard much in Guatemala. They were meant as simply another step in the program of eliminating Catholic priests from the country (eight priests have been killed in the past four years, six of them since May 1, 1980). The Catholic Church and its pastoral agents are supposed to be terrorized into cowering submission and silence.

The news of Father Carlos' death spread like wildfire. Lori and I were giving a course when we heard it from one of the catechists. We talked it over with the people and decided to cancel the classes and go to the funeral.

The next day we joined a long line of mourners in church, filing past the casket before Mass. We met Sisters and priests who had traveled as long as seven hours to be there. I talked to a Guatemalan Christian Brother whose own blood brother was recently taken by a "disappearance" squad. The eight young Indian Carmelite Sisters had caught a 3 A.M. bus out of Santiago Atitlán and had to catch a second bus to Tecpán, making it just in time. These women are natives of Father Carlos' hometown, Patzún. I'm sure if Stan Rother, their pastor, had been in the country he would have piled them all in his jeep and driven to the funeral. But he had to leave in January because of death threats. One Carmelite told me he came back for Holy Week to "test the waters," and then left again. He may return in time for the parish fiesta in July.

Just before Mass began, the priests in long white albs and cinctures slowly worked their way through the crowd to the altar. They passed the coffin and each paused to look through the glass window at the face of Carlos, the latest addition to the roll of "priest and martyr." As I watched them I couldn't help wondering if one of them would be the next victim. The congregation was as mixed as any I'd ever seen. There were wealthy, middle class, and poor ladinos of both sexes, mixing with Indian men and women in complete native dress; there were people of all ages. This priest had been in

Tecpán just a year, but had already endeared himself to so many people.

In the homily, delivered by his friend, a Franciscan priest, I was struck by a simple line: "Father Carlos was murdered because he was a priest."

At the end of Mass, we all sang what has become the theme song for martyrs. *Pescador de Gente* (Fisher of People). It is the song of one called to follow Jesus. One verse says:

> You need my hands,
> My weariness, that others might rest,
> My love, that wants to go on loving.

I realized, as we laid Carlos to rest, that those words applied directly to all of us present.

After the funeral Mass, the coffin was placed in a hearse for the trip to Patzún. Lori and I drove behind the hearse as we left town on a dusty country road.

It was a pretty ride, through rolling hills and pine forests, with mountains in the background. People lined the road for quite a distance, reverently waiting for the hearse to pass. One woman signaled the hearse to stop. As it did, she solemnly emptied a basket of flower petals on the roof of the hearse and scattered more inside on the coffin. Then she stepped back, covered her face with her hands, and began to sob. Several other people reached in to touch the coffin.

When we reached the town, a great multitude wanted to carry Carlos' coffin, even if for a few moments, in procession to the cemetery. He was, after all, a local boy. The crowd of mourners walked in a hushed reverence. Suddenly the silence was pierced by the wailing of an old Indian woman. She was the only one I saw who mourned in the old, time-honored Indian fashion: she had taken enough *aguardiente* (strong alcohol) to free her of restraints, and then poured out her grief to all who passed by, walking back and forth, wailing, raising her hands repeatedly to heaven and then pointing them at the casket. It brought to my mind the line from the prophet Jeremiah: "Look, all you who pass by; is there any grief like my grief?" Most of the mourners expressed their grief quietly, in tears and whispered words. Behind me a pair of old

Indian men exchanged a very simple tribute to Father Carlos Galvéz in their own language. "He was a good man." "Oh yes, a very, very good man."

Carlos' burial in the family tomb was simple. We all left the cemetery, each with his or her own thoughts. Mine were simple: "Why, O Lord, and for how long?" These are answerless questions, questions that faith must somehow overwhelm with the absolute surety that God writes straight with crooked lines, and that the blood of martyrs is the seed of the Church.

May 25, 1981

Dear Gerry,

I feel like a voice crying in the wilderness: "Is there anybody out there?" I'm sure you're still alive. If you weren't, Pat would certainly advise me. And I suppose she'd tell me if you were sick. So I guess you are very busy with end-of-year work and preparations for leaving school. But the empty-handed walk back from the post office gets longer every day! In your last letter you were worried about not getting a letter from me for a few weeks. And that was almost two months ago! Just want you to know I do miss hearing from you.

The news is depressing, as usual, so maybe you shouldn't want letters from me more frequently. All sorts of atrocities are committed against families and whole villages in the name of anti-Communism. I know one priest who, in a three-day span, saw 147 bodies, of all ages and both sexes, in the hospital morgue. He had gone to bless and help identify them, because many were his parishioners. All the bodies showed signs of torture, and most had been hacked to death with machetes. A few days later he went to get a haircut and passed out in the barber's chair. How much can one human being take of this horror?

Here we are still able to work without any major problems. We don't do any more work at night outside of town, though, and we have to be very careful traveling on the roads, even in the daytime.

NEWS FLASH!!!—YOUR LETTER JUST ARRIVED

I just received your letter dated April 28th and mailed two weeks later! So it's with a lighter heart that I continue this heavy letter.

First, I am happy for you that you signed on the dotted line in the Maryknoll Sisters' Associate Program. That makes it official. It was a tough decision, I know, but your note gives me the impression that you are at peace with it. I'm sorry your Mom isn't feeling well. As you said, it may be a nervous reaction to the news of your going. I certainly will keep her in my prayers.

I heard recently about a young doctor who worked in a parish clinic. He treated the poor with respect, as real people, and they flocked to him. Well, he was kidnapped on his way home from work one evening, and hasn't been heard from since. It appears to be another one of those disappearances perpetrated by "unknowns." The pattern of such disappearances is pretty similar all over the country. The kidnappings are done with impunity. There is never an investigation. If the victim turns up, he or she has usually been tortured, murdered, and dumped in a ravine or along a road far from home. Most bodies are never identified, because families have no idea where they might be. The body is always stripped of identification papers, is frequently disfigured, and is buried within twenty-four hours, in nameless graves marked "XX." I'm afraid the cemeteries will eventually contain more people called "XX" than have names.

It's terrible how one can go from being "somebody" to "some body" within forty-eight hours. These "somebodies" had mothers who brought them into the world, who nursed and loved them, who remember their first steps and their childish pranks. They are somebodies who had thoughts they shared or kept to themselves, but whose minds were whole worlds. They cracked jokes, laughed and cried, and prayed. They had jobs and they were important in the lives of a few or perhaps many people. And within forty-eight hours they disappear from here and turn up there: unrecognizable, horrible, attractive only to stray dogs and the ever-present vultures. They were once "somebodies," and now they are just "some (more) bodies": "XX."

You've got a very morbid friend tonight, Gerry. I guess the thought of death is so pervasive that I get used to it and don't even know I'm morbid! Down here we have a war mentality, even though there is no official war going on. We all know people who have disappeared or who have been found dead. We all have experienced clashes between the regular army and guerrillas. Helicopters fly over town frequently. The rectory and convent in a town about 100 miles from here were caught in the crossfire between rebels and army; their roofs have huge holes in them. When the fighting was over, eighteen soldiers were dead and several guerrillas, including two women, had also been killed.

And persecution of the Church continues unabated, with catechists, parish lay leaders, community organizers, and teachers, as well as church professionals being murdered on all sides. I would like to suggest that you think about choosing another Latin American country than Guatemala, Gerry. That's my opinion, but you make up your own mind. I pray your choice be the best for you and the people to whom you will be sent.

I just had an odd thought: we've had this "friendship by correspondence" for so long, I may not know what to say the next time we meet. I may resort to writing you notes across the table!

June 2, 1981

Dear Mom and Dad,

This is a short letter. I want you to get a letter from me so you won't be concerned. I also want to say that I hope all the May birthday people in the family enjoyed their special day in a special, family way.

Lori and I will soon be flying up to the northern part of Guatemala, called El Petén. We will visit the famous ruins of the Mayan civilization that was at its peak around 900 AD, then fell into decline. Archeologists still don't know why that civilization died. But the ruins of that city, called Tikal, are awe-inspiring. I was there once, years ago, when I was still in language school. Lori has never been there and is anxious to go. It is a short break, a chance to get away for a bit, from all the pressures.

My friend Gerry's mother is very ill. I just learned today that she has cancer and probably will succumb soon. Gerry's main difficulty in choosing to go to another country as a missioner was leaving her widowed mother alone. She made the decision after her Mom had apparently recovered fully from an earlier cancer operation, and had given her blessing to Gerry's desire to go to another country for three years. Once that decision was made, though, her

Mom developed another tumor. Strange, isn't it? Please pray for that family.

June 11, 1981

Dear Gerry,

I, who sometimes pride myself on my ability to express myself well in writing, find now that I have nothing to say. What is there to say in the face of the greatest mystery of our lives—Death? I have written you many thoughts on death in general, in the abstract, and my reaction to the deaths of several people. But this time it is a death *you* are suffering through, a tremendous loss, the loss of your mother. What can I, who have not yet lost a parent, say to you, who have lost both?

When I called you the other night, I dreaded the news, because I somehow felt she had already died. Maybe you were broadcasting your grief through every pore, and the message reached me. But when I heard you say what I already suspected, I couldn't say one word of comfort. I wanted to pass through the phone and stand by you in silent support—words were a barrier at that moment, poor stumbling things, unequal to the task. Yet on the phone all there are are words and tones of voice. Maybe the tone conveyed what the words could not: my love, my concern, my shared grief, my sadness at your bewilderment, my prayer.

Whenever I write a note to a friend or relative on the death of a person dear to them, I like to enclose a few lines from the Book of Wisdom. Although familiar, they are not trite. They give us hope, and they challenge our faith in Christ's promise of life after death:

> The souls of the just are in the hands of God,
> The torments of death shall not touch them.
> In the eyes of the unwise they seemed to die,
> But they are in peace.

I truly believe that, and I know that we are the unwise. How could we be otherwise? We know from experience only the shutting of the door of life as we know it, and can't comprehend that while it shuts to us who are left behind, it opens, to the one leaving, a whole new world worth entering. We know that only through faith, and faith at times of deep loss is extremely difficult. The thousands of questions that batter our faith may give us some relief in the asking, but there is no answering, and the faith may be weakened by the battering—or it may be strengthened.

Yet we all know, though we may not want to admit we know, that from the moment of our conception we were destined to die, and life is a journey toward fulfilling that destiny. We meet many people, some related to us by blood and others by friendship, who help us make sense of our lives and our destinies. How beautiful it is when the people related to us by blood are also our friends, as you and your mother and your sister obviously are. Letting go of those people is a wrenching, agonizing pain, and yet, the very letting go is part of our growth in understanding and appreciating life and its culmination in death leading to New Life, forever, in joy and love, without barriers, no words needed.

If only there were a way to be parted from each other that was painless! In one sense, although your mother suffered greatly, and you suffered because she did, you were fortunate in the way she died. It was not so sudden that she was gone before you even knew it. You both had time to say what you wanted to say. Yet her illness was not prolonged. Her suffering was relatively short. And she had the comfort of knowing you and your sister were with her, talking to her, holding her hand, just being there. She didn't die alone, or unloved. She died deeply loved and knew it. What a way to go! Loved so much on this side of that door called Death, and deeply loved on the other side. She went from life to Life, from love to Love. She was a woman of love and faith, and she gave those gifts to others, especially to her children. Now she can help your love and faith grow in new ways.

I will say no more in this letter that I started, thinking I had nothing to say. Another letter will follow soon. You know my prayers and thoughts are with you constantly. Take care, get some rest, and try to enjoy the summer.

June 14, 1981

Dear Mom and Dad,

Lori and I took a trip to the northern part of the country, called Petén. It's a trip you have to plan well in advance because the area is mostly uninhabited jungle. There is a very poor road from the capital to the city of Flores, an island on the lake Petén Itzá, and the "county seat" of that province. A bus trip costing $15 could take from thirteen hours to three days, depending on the weather and road conditions and other factors. A plane trip costs somewhat more, but not excessively more—about $20. So we planned to go by plane.

Our flight took off right on time, 12:30 in the afternoon, Wednesday. It was a smooth flight and in about an hour we got off into the steamy heat of jungle weather. We got our bags and hiked over to a cab. The cabbie drove us to the bishop's residence, where we had reserved rooms. It's a big old musty place, used now by the priests, Sisters, and lay missioners in their comings and goings from there to the Capital. We slept as well as we could in that heavy heat, and caught the bus for Tikal at 6 A.M. in the market of the town of San Benito, right across the causeway.

The ride to Tikal took about an hour on a dusty road of white limestone. We arrived at the Jungle Lodge, a small hotel resembling something out of the movie *African Queen,* at about 8 A.M. We rested for a few minutes, sipping Orange Crush, and then headed into the jungle.

The path was clear as we walked beneath the thick jungle greenery. I saw some brightly colored birds and wished I had bought that little book *The Birds of Tikal* I once saw in a bookstore. In a few minutes, we reached a clearing and stopped to absorb the scene ahead. From the east and west ends of an enormous central plaza rose a pair of steep four-sided Mayan pyramids, built of white limestone, over 200 feet high. At least 100 narrow, high steps were cut into the center front of each pyramid, and at the top of each was a small temple, shaped like the typical Mayan hut, topped with a carved stone crest. To encourage the faint-hearted to climb to the summit, Tikal park authorities had fastened a heavy chain to the top of the taller pyramid, "The Temple of the Jaguar," and ran it down to the bottom. It doesn't take much nerve to climb up holding the chain in one hand and a camera in the other. But coming down, I wanted to drop my camera and hang on to the chain with both hands. The view from the top to the bottom is terrifying.

From there on, anything else was tame by comparison. We explored the other structures on the north and south of the plaza. On one side stood what appeared to be royal apartments. The other side seemed made of pyramids built into other pyramids, until one couldn't see where one left off and another began. They were apparently tombs for the royalty that were added onto as the centuries passed. In front of the temples stood stone markers, five feet high or more, carved with symbols and portraits and dates. They are still not totally deciphered and add to the mystery of that awesome ancient Mayan center.

We found a path that led further into the jungle, past mounds that were being excavated and others that may never be. We saw the tree that gives allspice, and another that is the cinnamon tree. We walked from about 9 to 1 P.M., but by 11 A.M. the jungle heat and humidity began to get to us. If you wanted to, you could spend a week going over the ruins, studying the plant and animal life, and watching birds, in Tikal. But we didn't have that kind of time, so when we got hot and tired we returned to the Jungle Lodge.

After lunch, we visited a little museum where we looked at some articles that had been removed from the ruins by archaeologists, and we got an idea of the whole ancient city. It is enormous, and more buildings and tombs are being discovered, or rather, uncovered, all the time. They know they are there, but they have to be careful removing a thousand years of jungle vegetation, including enormous trees with deep roots, from the fragile rock face of each structure. A careless job would destroy what they sought to uncover. It was a wonderful experience, but for those who don't like humid heat, one morning was enough!

The next morning we were supposed to be at the airport by 7 A.M., even though the plane wasn't scheduled to leave until 9:30. We didn't get there until 8 A.M., plenty of time, I thought. When we went to get our boarding passes, the attendant said, "If you want lunch, there's a nice place over there." Lunch? Before boarding a 9:30 plane? What was going on? Well, we soon found out.

When they began calling for passengers to board, they did it by boarding pass *color*. First, the orange people were called. They all boarded the small plane that was waiting with engines revved up, and it took off! We sat there, green passes in our hot hands, and green with envy. The heat was already sweltering. Finally there was an announcement that another flight would leave at 12:30, so we decided to have lunch at that "nice place over there." When we came back, we saw two planes. One was a modern plane; the other was built in 1938! Honest! "We'll surely go on the new plane," I thought. "We've been here since 8 A.M.!" They called the people with blue passes for the new plane. Our passes, and probably our faces, were green. The blue people boarded the new plane and it taxied away and took off. We looked at the old plane. The maintenance crew were putting the seats back in. They had taken them out to deliver cargo and were converting it back to a passenger plane. Finally they began calling passengers to board—but they called those with yellow passes, and our passes were green. After the yellow passes, they called the purple passes, and I wanted to cry out, "Hey, where are all these purple people coming from? Were they here since 8 A.M.?" Finally, when it looked like no one else could fit on the plane, they called those with GREEN passes! I looked around. We two were at the end of the line of passengers. We were the only ones with green passes! And we got the last two seats on that plane, thank God.

Remember the old World War II movies about planes in which stewardesses struggled to close the back door which had mysteriously blown open, the kind of door a spy parachuted out of with a secret message for General Eisenhower? Well, that's the kind of plane we had, and our seats were next to that door. I felt I could not survive the flight without an air sickness pill, but I had no air sickness pill, and neither did the steward, who was also the co-pilot. It was very hot on that sealed-up plane waiting in the jungle heat to take off. The plane had run out of windows by the time it reached us so all I could see was the back of the seat in front of me. The co-pilot did come along with orange juice. That was a help. When we took off the air in the plane was bearable, but when we hit some air pockets I took on the color of my pass again. Lori seemed to be doing fine, and tried to keep up a conversation, but I knew if I opened my eyes and focused on her or on anything else in the plane I'd be a goner. There were no little courtesy bags tucked into the nonexistent pockets in the seatbacks either. So I just closed my eyes, sat very still, and ignored Lori when she grabbed my arm and said, "Hey, look" as we touched down. I was very happy that my stomach was still with me and functioning well. I think I know now why the Pope kneels and kisses the ground whenever he gets off a plane. I felt like doing the same thing! Well, it was an interesting diversion. Now we're back in the real world.

July 18, 1981

Dear Gerry,

We're going at a frenetic pace, trying to get as much done as possible before Lori leaves for vacation back in the States for a month of well-deserved rest and relaxation. If I didn't act as a brake on her, she'd do two years worth of work in a year, and wear herself out in the process. By this time every year, she is *ready* to be renewed. I'm snatching a few minutes to answer your letters before we return to planning the work for the rest of the year.

You wrote that you received the letter officially accepting you into the Maryknoll Sisters' Associate program the very day your Mom died, "the greatest sign that I should stick with my plans and that I had my Mom's blessing." She's definitely with you in this.

Thanks for filling me in on all that happened to you since you got your acceptance. The school kids will really miss you! So will the people in the Bronx neighborhood organizations you were part of, and your friends and Sisters, and especially your own sister. But their love and support are so obvious, that they will send you off as *their* own missioner. The courses you are taking to prepare you for mission work sound very good, especially the one on Basic Christian Communities. I took that one twice, five years apart and in different places. It has been a good grounding for the work I do. I know you will be worked hard in it, though, so rest when you can!

I will now fill you in on the latest of the continuing pressure on the Church from the uncontrolled powers of Evil these days. These are merely highlights, mind you. Many things happen that we who live here talk about daily, but don't regard as unusual any more. It's routine, so to speak. Maybe we're getting used to it. But when a group of us gets together and shares such news in the presence of a visitor from the States, for example, I try to be sensitive to the newcomer. The first time I became aware of the outsiders' reactions was when I saw the look on the face of a visiting friend. Her look said: "How can you speak so nonchalantly about such horror?" I tried to signal the other Sisters by shifting the topic, but they were so involved they didn't catch on. Later I brought it up and they agreed that we should be more sensitive. But when you live in a life-and-death atmosphere, life and death are the most important topics of conversation. Everything else runs a poor second.

So, on the life and death topic, two more priests have disappeared and one more was killed since I last wrote you on the subject. Fr. Luis Pellecer, a young Guatemalan Jesuit, was in his car in front of a church the Jesuits staff in Guatemala City, when he was approached by armed men. They beat him, dragged him from his car, shoved him into an unmarked one, and took him off. He has joined the ranks of the disappeared. Fr. Pellecer was well-liked in the city. He was known for his work with youth and with the poor slum dwellers, and with refugees from the war-torn highlands. He was also active in justice work, and served on a human rights committee. His disappearance occurred in the center of the city, in broad daylight, a block from the National Palace. There were many witnesses. Although his kidnapping provoked a furor, he's still missing.

Then on July 1st, way out in the eastern part of the country where things have seemed relatively peaceful, an Italian Franciscan priest was killed. His name was Tulio Maruzzo; he was fifty-two. It seems the net of church assassinations is spreading across the country. Tulio was killed, along with his sacristan Obdulio Arroyo, as they were driving back from a meeting of Cursillos de Cristiandad.

Two other catechists and sacristans were killed while they accompanied their pastors: Herlindo Cifuentes was with Fr. Conrado de la Cruz and Domingo Batz was with José María Gran. Such men are the unsung heroes and martyrs of the church. They should be included in the modern martyrology of the Church as "companions." When we in the United States think of American Martyrs we think back a few hundred years, to "St. Isaac Jogues and Companions, Martyrs." Now that idea and the list needs updating. There are many modern American martyrs: people who were born in North America, in Central America, and other places, but who were martyred very recently in Central America.

The most recent attack on Church personnel occurred the day

after the murder of Tulio and Obdulio. Another Jesuit, Fr. Carlos Pérez, disappeared. The circumstances of his disappearance are unknown. He is just gone.

And yet, day follows day, and the cycle of seasons goes on, and the sun rises and sets, and the sunsets are beautiful, as you well know, having shared some with me at the shore. And I want to cry out, "How can such beauty and such horror exist on the same planet?"

And you go on, Gerry, preparing to leave your country to become a missioner in Latin America. I'm afraid this news is also part of your preparation, friend.

August 7, 1981

Dear Gerry,

There comes a time when you run out of tears. You catch yourself staring blankly out the window, shaking your head, as if that futile gesture could negate the escalating horror. "They killed Stan." These words were spoken in a broken voice by his friends, passed along to other friends. Francis Stanley Rother, the pastor of Santiago Atitlán. Stan, with the face of St. Francis and a love and a dedication like Christ's. Stan, called "Francisco" by his Tzutuhil Indian parishioners, since that name was easier for them to pronounce than the Spanish "Estanislao." Stan, who spoke the Indian language better than he did Spanish, and who, by working the land with a hoe, earned the respect of the Indian men who love the soil. Stan, who, when asked if he was involved politically, replied: "To shake the hand of an Indian is a political act." Stan, probably the most peaceable of us all, and among the most courageous.

They killed Stan, but it took three of them to do it, fighting with him in his bedroom after midnight. They wanted to kidnap him. He knew they would eventually kill him, so he said: "I'm not going. You'll have to kill me here." Had they wanted to talk he could have, like Jesus, said, "I have done many good works for you to see, works of my Father. For which of these do you wish to kill me?" But his masked executioners had no interest in such questions. They came to do a job and got on with it. And he, aware that there were three terrified young men hiding in an upstairs room, and ten unsuspecting Sisters across the patio, fought silently for his life, well knowing he couldn't win. His assassins finally gave up trying to drag him off to their unmarked jeep in the street, and shot him in the head. Through it all Stan never called for help.

I spoke after the funeral with a man who was a catechist and who had known Stan for years. He said many things, only a few of which I record here.

"Padre Francisco, from the moment he arrived here, worked with the simple people. He worked helping the town, working himself with shovel and tractor. And he did a lot for the church. He worked with couples, counseling them and showing them what God is like.

"The morning they killed him he was going to go to the hospital to give blood for a poor, simple man who needed an operation, but who didn't have enough money to even feed his family. Well, Padre Francisco never got to the hospital, but he gave his blood for all of us, like Jesus did.

"Padre Francisco didn't neglect anyone. He went from house to house when they invited him, especially visiting the sick. He would bless them. And he actually—they told me—worked miracles! He cured a sick man with holy oils.

"And the people of the other churches here in town, we thank them for their support and their visits. He didn't neglect the other churches. He worked directly for God, directly for God! Those who understood what happened cried and grieved with us. The town and people are mourning, but we have great hope that Christ has raised him up. I mean to say that Padre Francisco began a new stage in his life, a stage of tranquility. Yes, the people are mourning, but also have a new hope. We are very grateful that we have been left some of his remains, his heart and some blood. There it is in that box being buried behind the altar. The town wanted Padre Francisco to stay here forever. We offered a place for him, a niche, but his parents requested his body. We are grateful also to the man who donated the wood for the coffin. They tried to find a coffin here in town, but not one was long enough. They had to make a coffin quickly, and we are grateful for the donation of wood.

"Padre Francisco told me himself that he couldn't bear it, the pain he felt when they kidnapped Gaspar Culán [director of the Radio School La Voz de Atitlán]. And when they kidnapped his catechist, Diego Quic, right off the front porch of the rectory, Diego screamed and held tightly to the bannister, but his kidnappers pulled him down to the patio below, railing and all. Padre Francisco never repaired that railing. He left it broken, as a remembrance. Padre Francisco couldn't bear it. What he couldn't bear was this: that some people pull in money by selling their brothers. He said that here, in this church. And that's why they killed him.

"We thank his parents and the Church of Oklahoma for having called Padre Francisco into the life of a Catholic priest. He worked here in our town for fourteen years. We say to them: "Padre Francisco is *alive* here in Santiago Atitlán, and is not dead. He is alive! Every Sunday and every Thursday we will remember him as we pray here in church. And we pray to Padre Francisco now, and we thank him for the gift of his life. He gave his life freely. We are grateful to him for having given his life here in Santiago Atitlán. I thank his parents for having sent Padre Francisco, MARTYR, here, to Santiago."

I attended Stan's funeral. People filled the church, and a long double line of mourners extended from the coffin up near the sanctuary, all the way out the doors and down the steps. Inching forward with the mourners, I watched men and women kiss the coffin as they filed past. Stan was a good-looking man with sandy hair, a neatly trimmed beard, and clear blue eyes. When I came to the coffin, I looked long at that face, now made unfamiliar by the violence that killed him. In farewell, I touched the rough wood of the coffin, still sticky from fresh varnish.

When Mass began, the church was so packed that we could hardly move. All the benches had been removed. Men stood and women sat on their heels, in their accustomed way. I estimated that about 1500 people were jammed into that enormous colonial church, and practically all wore the distinctive costume of the Tzutuhil Indians of Santiago Atitlán.

Stan's own bishop was in Europe, so the Mass was celebrated by another, the bishop of Escuintla, Mario Enrique Rios Mont. He was no stranger to martyrs' funerals. Conrado de la Cruz and Walter Voordeckers, killed earlier this year, had worked in his diocese. This bishop is a fearless and dedicated pastor.

At the offertory, a priest and several parishioners walked into church in solemn procession carrying a large jar of blood—Stan's blood, martyr's blood—and placed it reverently on the altar. There it stayed, near the chalice, throughout the Mass. At the moment of consecration there was a growing wave of murmuring, and a swell of voices drowned out the celebrant. I looked around me and saw tears in every eye. On everyone's lips were the words: "Padre Francisco."

The Church is suffering a persecution the likes of which no one has ever seen here before. It is bringing out the best in some, and making others choose between living their faith or giving it up. Many priests who are threatened leave. It is understandable, when one sees what happens to those who are threatened and stay. But some priests seem to think that as long as they keep their eyes and mouths shut they'll be fine; they have an attitude of "each man for himself." I pray we all take our heads out of the sand and face the fact that we are *one body* that is being persecuted, not bits and pieces. Stan had come back to see how things were at Holy Week. He participated in all the services, spoke with a lot of people, and felt it safe to return. He went back to the States to wrap things up and attend the ordination of his nephew. Then he returned to Santiago Atitlán in time for the parish fiesta. That's when they killed him.

Stan had a tremendous love for the people of Santiago Atitlán. He chose, in the face of death threats, to return to them. I'm sure he was afraid, but he overcame his fear and did what he had to do. That's called courage. I consider it an honor to have known him.

August 21, 1981

Dear Gerry,

It's very late, and I've spent the whole day cleaning house. Tonight at 9 P.M. a man came to ask me to take his wife to the hospital. Since it isn't a case of life or death, we have decided to wait until dawn tomorrow. People don't lightly travel after dark these days. I'm groggy now, and tomorrow won't be any better, but I want to get something off to you.

First, I want to tell you how greatly I appreciate getting three letters from you in a week's time, which is, I believe, a record! If, as you say in one letter, you are a poor correspondent, and have lost friends for lack of frequent writing, what does "poor correspondent" mean? Did they expect letters from you more frequently than three times a week? I *am* fortunate. Of course I realize that three *that* close is unusual. There have been and will be again times when a month or more will pass between letters, but that's O.K. I'm sure another will come eventually.

Unfortunately, I don't have the time to do a proper job of answering, but I want you to know that your assignment is very much on my mind. I'm praying that wherever you go, it will be the *right* place for you.

Something funny just came to mind, because I'm imagining your life as a missioner. Remember when we gave the course in that community tucked back in the hills, and we left after the Celebration of the Word around 9 P.M., in the dark? You were very skittish as I drove over the narrow dirt road with a ditch on either side. I laughingly told you not to worry, because I knew the road. And at that, my left front tire went into the ditch and it was your turn to laugh as I tried to get it out, going forward and back, forward and back, just digging the hole deeper. I realized we'd have to walk a mile back to the last village for help. But just as we began to walk back, several men came over the hill and asked, "Do you need help, Madres?" I was so amazed! How did they know? Of course, it was simple. They heard our car pass, then stop. They came looking for us, to help. Remember how easily they lifted the car out of the ditch and set us on our way? I was properly embarrassed for my boasting, and you had a good mission story to tell your friends in the Bronx. I wonder what stories you will have to tell once you get to your South American mission. I look forward to hearing about your adventures.

At our last catechist session, some of the men told us that strangers in a car that is seen in their area frequently these days asked some women there who the two foreign "Gringas" were who came to their chapel on occasion. They asked what we did there. The women, God bless them, had a good story. They said we were the Madres from town and that we had a devotion to the Virgin in the chapel and when we passed we stopped to pray, and the women gathered to talk to us. It's all true, in a sense, but they were trying to protect us from suspicion.

August 24, 1981

Dear Mom and Dad,

This is just a tiny note, because I feel so guilty about not having written for so long. Actually, things should improve from next week on. Lori is due back from vacation today, and I'll be so glad to see her—I haven't had a day off since she left. It's been a very busy month and I have been barely able to catch my breath! You never know who will come to the door asking to talk, or seeking some kind of help. Day-to-day chores (cleaning, laundry, cooking, etc.) and work I have planned to do take more than all my time. And then there are the unexpected events, like the funeral of Fr. Rother and the aftermath of that. People kept coming to talk about it. Many knew him and can't understand why he was killed, except for the fact that he brought *estudio,* study, to the town, and helped the people learn many things through the parish schools, radio school, leadership, and catechist classes.

I can tell you one bit of good news. Remember Magdalena, the woman with twins who bought her mother a coffin in exchange for her house? She borrowed 30 Quetzales from us to buy it. While we were prepared to forget the loan, we are pleased that she has paid it off, little by little. We didn't charge interest, of course, and she is grateful for that, but is also pleased and proud that she could pay it off, bit by bit. Whenever she came, it was with three or four Quetzales to subtract from the debt. And she always brought the twins for us to see, and some rolls wrapped up in her red woven carrying cloth. We would invite her for coffee and would share the bread together.

A while ago you asked me for something to read to help you better understand why the Church is having so much trouble in Latin America today. I am sending you a book called *Cry of the People* by Penny Lernoux. This book helped me make sense of the craziness going on all around me in Guatemala, and it shows why similar things are happening all over Latin America.

How is everyone at home? I guess all the grandchildren are getting new clothes and materials for school. Exciting!

August 28, 1981

Dear Gerry,

The courses you took sound very stimulating and thought provoking. I would like to have sat in on the one on Non-Violence.

We certainly need more of that in the world. You say that your group is "officially accepted as Associates" since you just signed on the dotted line. Congratulations! The next thing is an assignment, finally. I'm anxious to hear, but not as anxious as you. You must have a hard time sleeping! I'm sure you were terribly disappointed when they told you Guatemala was not being considered because of the latest murders and rumors here. I'd like to know how true the information is that "all priests and Religious will be put out of Guatemala by December." It would help for us to know as we prepare our courses!

In your letter you say that your "inward preparation for mission has been helped by the courses" you took, and that you feel you are getting over your disappointment in not being sent to Guatemala. I like the way you expressed your transformation: "Very shaken last week, but at great peace now. God has brought me this far and I am giving myself to whatever is in store. Once I let go, I felt peace. I hope God accepts my sacrifice of not going to Guatemala and uses it to help the people there." Well, my friend, I hope it does work like that. We can use all the help we can get!

And Gerry, don't be concerned about writing to me in the next few months. You'll be so involved with getting ready to leave: packing, travel arrangements and, the hard part, saying good-bye. Your family and friends will need to have you with them. We might get a phone call in before then, and a note or two, but don't wear yourself out, O.K.?

September 12, 1981

Dear Mom and Dad,

Would you believe it? You're finally getting a letter. Now that Lori is back from vacation, I'm catching up on mail and you are at the top of my list. Mom, you asked when Lori and I will finish our work here. Originally, we had planned to stay here about five years. But after evaluating with folks from town, we decided to stay on for two more years. This way we can further develop what is going well, and reinforce it. What is a bit weak or unfinished we can shore up or complete. We plan to take some courses in the States for about five or six months, leaving the parish groups to function on their own, with all the new work, courses, and ministries that have been developed since our coming. Then we'll return and evaluate with the people. There is still a good deal to be done. We just hope that we can stay to finish it. Rumors are that church people, especially Catholic foreigners, may be expelled before the end of the year. The catechists have been studying the life and message of Jesus. We've been planning our monthly sessions, asking ourselves, "If this will be our last month here, what one idea about Jesus do we want to leave with the people?"

I am sometimes surprised by what they remember from the sessions. For example, on Sunday I was out with some catechists, giving a course in a town far from here. We were returning home through an area where we expected to find hostile soldiers because a bomb had exploded there that morning in a hotel parking lot. It was apparently aimed at keeping tourists away. I suggested that the men get out of the car and hike down the footpath to town to avoid the search and the mistreatment I expected for them, in their Indian garb. Vicente, one of the catechists, looked at me and asked, "And you, Madre? Will you go alone?" "Yes," I replied. He didn't even consult with the others. He just said, "Well, we're going with you." They discussed what they would say to the soldiers if we were stopped, and decided that God would give them the right words. Victor quoted the Gospel text that says "When they drag you before governors and kings, fear not what you will say, because the Spirit of God will speak from within you." Thank God there were no soldiers when we passed!

We have had to find an alternate route to the neighboring towns to avoid a road which is now a haven for highway robbers. They stop any car at any hour of day or night, though almost no one travels after 7 P.M. Our priest, who comes here for Mass, was robbed there last week. He said they took everything he had, including the rag he used to clean his windshield. Another man was shot, as he drove past the men, because he ignored their signal to stop. His car rolled into a ditch. He tried to get out but was too badly hurt, so he could only open the door and fall out. We passed that car about forty minutes after it happened, but didn't know what had caused it. Dad, forget your idea of driving your little pick-up down here and sleeping in the back on a mattress! Anybody who tries that is a prime target for highway robbers, or guerrillas looking for a pick-up truck, or soldiers who are off duty (or even on duty). It's strange that the robbers act with such freedom. There are army posts at each end of the road! I hear they sometimes lob mortar shells across the highway. He (of the pick-up truck) who has ears to hear, let him hear!

September 28, 1981

Dear Mom and Dad,

We were away almost a week, and I thought I'd have time for letters and a week's worth of catching up before we were off again. But, as usual, all the unexpected visits and interruptions have cut into the time. Tomorrow I go to Guatemala City to pick up my friend Gerry at the airport. She has finished her preparation for mission in the States and has been assigned to South America. She will study Spanish in Bolivia and is stopping here for a few days on her way down there. It isn't exactly right on the way. But it's not that big a detour. I'm so delighted that she is coming! We have a lot of catching up to do. So much has happened since I put her on the plane for New York just a year ago, thinking she'd stay in the Bronx the rest of her life!

I was worried I might not be able to pick her up myself because of a big landslide on the road near here. But the road crews worked on it yesterday and today, and it will be passable tomorrow. Gerry will leave on October 4th, a good day to start. It's the feast of St. Francis of Assisi, the gentle but very principled saint. Gerry is a bit like St. Francis. She appreciates nature and the beauties of creation; and she can be very determined when there is an injustice to be confronted.

So, dear ones, you'll have to wait until next week for a good letter from me.

October 9, 1981

Dear Gerry,

Welcome to your new home! This is a quick note just to tell you what you already know: It was wonderful spending those days with you in our old stamping grounds. The memories are warm and happy and engraved forever. Thank you for making that stop on your journey. I look forward to our next face-to-face visit. I should be in the States when you go home three years hence.

And now, it's time to throw yourself into studying Spanish. I know it will be hard, since I went through it myself. But I assure you, one day, when you least expect it, you'll catch yourself *thinking* in *Spanish,* and you'll be so struck by the realization that you'll stand stock still and say: "How long have I been doing that?" Honest!

I look forward to hearing about your companions, your adventures, and your studies. And do make time to use the swimming pool there. I hear it is cold, but enjoyable once you get used to it.

Oh, I almost forgot. Remember the priest I told you about, Fr. Pellecer, a Jesuit who "disappeared" in broad daylight in early June? Well he suddenly reappeared, in the hands of the government, before TV cameras and newspaper people, confessing his sins as a subversive! He said he was not kidnapped, but rather, had "arranged it" to appear he was kidnapped, so he could disappear and become the "guest" of the police for three months without anyone suspecting! I guess he also asked his supposed captors to beat him up so badly that the blood would stain the car's upholstery! There is consternation about this appearance. On the one hand, his family and friends are happy he is alive and seems physically well. On the other hand, no one who knows him can get to talk to him alone. And from his manner of talking, they say he has been brainwashed. He's a different man now.

October 14, 1981

Dear Mom and Dad,

You both must be thinking I'm the "Prodigal Daughter." I have completely lost track of my letter writing. I don't know when I last wrote, because I can't keep track of the days. We've been doing something different each day, and writing letters takes time and quiet, so I haven't been able to get my act together until now. And I want to give you that time, because writing is the next best thing to talking to you on the phone. You know I love you dearly.

Enclosed are two pictures of the mother and baby with the blue sweater set you made, Mom. The baby was born several months after his father disappeared.

Well, my visit with Gerry is a thing of the past, but a happy memory for both of us. We had five days to visit—hardly enough, but days we were grateful for. Who knows when we'll see each other again? It's a miracle that a friendship can grow with so little contact, and mostly from letters. She told me she is not much of a letter writer, which surprised me because she has written to me very frequently, and some were good long letters. If this is the only way to keep our friendship going, we'll keep writing!

We spent a day here in town, visiting her old acquaintances. She was so happy and grateful, because she thought we might not have the time. We even took a boat ride across the beautiful lake to Santiago Atitlán, visited Stan Rother's church, and prayed together at the memorial where his heart was buried behind the altar. There was a simple bouquet of flowers there, stuck in a powdered milk can. We didn't have much to say to each other for a while after praying in that church. There was an understanding between us that didn't need words. We were both now in the same boat with missioners like Stan. But I've been in it a long time, and she just got on board. Funny—a hymn that is frequently sung at funerals for martyrs, "Fisher of People," has a verse that says: "You know well what I have, In my little boat, neither gold nor sword, But this net, and the work of my hands." We missioners can identify with that. We're in the same boat, without power or defenses, with just our work to keep us faithful to the Fisherman who first called us to this sometimes stormy shore.

The last night Gerry was in Guatemala, we were in the capital. She treated me to a birthday dinner at a restaurant with Guatemalan food and atmosphere. I'm not sure if it was to celebrate my past birthday or my coming birthday, since both are far way! We had a lovely dinner and then sat chatting until they closed the dining room at 9 P.M. She was reluctant to leave, and I had to prod her, saying we'd be thrown out if we didn't go quietly. It's hard to close off a visit with a friend you won't see again for years. But I had a surprise for her. I drove her to another restaurant that served flaming brandied coffee. There were practically no other diners in the place, and there were several small dining rooms, since it had been a big old house. So we had our own private performance, with lights dimmed and the flaming liquor pouring back and forth into the cups. After that show it was almost a shame to drink the stuff. We sat talking for about an hour, sipping the brandied coffee, and then went back to the house. I helped her pack and get ready to leave. The next day I took her to the airport myself and prayed her on her way. I hope she finds fulfillment in her mission work. She'll be in Bolivia for three years.

This weekend Lori and I will plan our next two years. All our Sisters in the area say they want us to stay in Guatemala a bit longer, and we also see the need to continue on with our work. As soon as I know what the future holds, at least on paper, I'll let you know.

October 14, 1981

Dear Gerry,

I expect a letter from you soon, telling about your adventures since you left here. When I saw that enormous suitcase your friends bought you, and noticed that its wheels were already beginning to come off, I knew you were in for an exciting trip.

We need another cat. You know where we stored sacks of grain and powdered cornmeal for catechist sessions in the parish kitchen? We never had trouble with mice nibbling on that stuff until Balam abandoned us. I finally noticed a hole gnawed in one of the meal sacks, so I set a trap. And another. And another, and another, and another . . . I've lost count of how many mice I caught. So, we're getting a new kitten.

Fifty men came to our latest annual retreat. These are dangerous times to be traveling the roads and gathering in groups, but they are willing to risk coming together here to learn more of Jesus' message. We built the retreat around three parables that teach us how to treat each other: The Prodigal Son, the Good Samaritan, and the Last Judgement of Mt. 25. After the opening prayer in church, the men divided into small groups to read the parables, discuss them, and pray silently over them. I sit in on their discussion because I learn so much, and get new insights into the Gospel message. It's amazing how they can cut through externals to get right to the heart of the message.

In the discussion of the Prodigal Son, one man said: "How could the father in this story take that wretch of a son back without at least scolding or humiliating him first? What father can be that forgiving? If he were my son I'd try to teach him a lesson, and show him how ungrateful he was! But God is not like me. I have to think about this parable some more. Can I learn to forgive that way? That's God's way, not ours. But Jesus is teaching us that we have to think and act as God would, since we are children of God. Yes, I must think about this story some more."

This was the first retreat where Communion Ministers joined the catechists. Many of these Ministers could not read, because reading is not a requirement for them. Twelve men who couldn't read sat in the church sanctuary listening intently as a catechist read and reread the parable. They wanted to squeeze every bit of meaning they could from each reading, as was clear from their own discussion. Most of these men were elders in their communities who had never been to school. Now they were being schooled as Disciples of Jesus.

Lori sends her love, and wants me to tell you that she gave that little boy Fernando the sweatshirt you left behind for him. You said he always looked so cold. He lit up like a sunbeam when she told him it was yours. He really took a liking to you, Gerry.

Bye for now. I look forward to hearing from you.

October 20, 1981

Dear Mom and Dad,

I just got your letter and want to answer while I have a few minutes. Thanks, Mom, for all the family news. Don't feel bad because you left the keys in the house and had to get the neighbors to help you get in. I have a worse problem: I leave the keys in the car. I can't live down the fact that I did it twice in the same day! I'm getting better, though. Now I actually hold the keys in my hand and look at them before I lock the door. Maybe locking keys in places is passed on genetically, like Mother, like Daughter.

Last weekend, Lori and I packed a picnic lunch and went to a place where we could talk, undisturbed; about our plans for the near future. We decided that we will both go to the States next July to study and to visit our families, then return to Guatemala for another year. While we're gone, the people we have prepared will test themselves and the programs we have developed with them. That is, they will be involved with catechist sessions, presacramental classes, Celebrations of the Word. In the next few months, we will be preparing the communities in our parish for having Communion Ministers so they can have Communion in their Celebrations of the Word. Until now, those services have been mainly scripture readings from the Sunday Mass, a talk on the readings by a catechist, prayers of the faithful, the Lord's Prayer, and a closing prayer, with hymns throughout. But the people really crave Communion. And the way things are going, they may have no priests to travel to their communities for Mass. Those priests who are still in the country are sticking to the parish centers and not going out to the farflung settlements. So the Communion Minister, hand-picked by the community not for his learning but for his life witness, will go to the Mass at the parish church and bring back Communion to the village community. He has to be "wise as a serpent and innocent as a dove" when he passes an army checkpoint, hiding the communion hosts in his market bundle. It is an honor to be chosen Communion Minister but it may be a risk to accept.

October 30, 1981

Dear Mom and Dad,

Happy Day-before-Halloween! As you used to ask me when I was younger, what are *you* going to be this year? I know you enjoyed it when we would get dressed up in whatever we could concoct, and I wish you could get into some costume yourself. It's fun, and you can become a totally different person for an evening.

Here, Halloween has no meaning or celebration, but the feasts of All Saints and All Souls are very important. The mayor gave the order that all the townspeople have to clean their yards and the streets in front of their houses. A group of volunteers, all men, are cleaning around the church grounds right now. The rainy season is supposed to be over, and seemed to be over in mid-October, but it started raining again with a vengeance a few days ago. It's very unusual for it to rain on these November fiesta days, and the all-day celebration in the cemetery may be ruined by a downpour.

The latest bad news is that guerrillas are actively trying to harass the police and army very close to here. They cut down trees at night and use them to block roads to hinder transportation. They also are stopping cars and charging a "war tax" to support themselves. They have dug ditches across highways and dropped boulders on the roads. They have commandeered vehicles and used them to block roads, burning them or removing their wheels. I saw one car in a situation I'd never seen before: The car was on the side of the road. Three of its wheels were off, lying flat on the road like donuts, with the car sitting on top of the wheels! The owner was just putting the other wheel back on when we passed, and he looked very angry. The guerrillas apparently lifted the car up bodily and removed the wheels. Things like this happen often, but you never know when or where, or if you will be in the vicinity at the time. We travel only when necessary and take precautions you would never even think of. We fully expect to be stopped and robbed one of these days. We carry enough money to satisfy the guerrillas, but no more.

October 31, 1981

Dear Gerry,

Well, your long-awaited letter arrived, and filled me in on your saga. When you plan on a trip with three *announced* stops, of course you should expect at least seven other stops along the trip. They are the hidden "perks" of international travel! You must have been exhausted by that trip. I'm glad you were met by friends who got you to a nice soft bed quickly. That bag of yours was so overweight I thought it would cost you much more in excess baggage than it actually did. You must have had St. Christopher along with you on that trip!

You mentioned going to visit a place called Charamoco. Is it far from where your language school is? It's good that you could get away on the weekends and try out the Spanish you've been shoving into your head all this time.

We've been working so hard that Lori and I decided to pack a picnic lunch and get away from the house this afternoon. We invited the new Peace Corps volunteer to join us. We had traditional picnic fare, as much as we could gather, anyway. Hot dogs, hamburgers, potato salad and sauerkraut, plus some nice melon. I even dug up three small Snickers bars which were given to us last year by a passing visitor named Gerry! We went just a little way out of town where there's a grassy plot shaded by a spreading tree. It was private, almost. In this country you always have people coming back and forth from their fields or coming over to greet you. A few visitors passed, calling their greeting from the road. But we had a nice quiet time to eat and just talk.

At one point I picked up some pods that had fallen from the tree, opened one, and found some round, wrinkled seeds inside. I smelled them and to my amazement, found that it was black pepper! That got all of us interested. We noted that there were many of these willowy-branched pepper trees on the grounds. We also saw some very unusual insects that were beautifully colored. We watched a camouflaged inchworm work its way up a tree branch until it looked like a twig on the branch. We almost never take time to admire and wonder over God's creation these days, and it was relaxing to do just that.

Well, I must get back to work, researching for our Bible study course. I love this part of the work as much as the teaching part of it. Do you think you might be doing something similar in a few months?

November 18, 1981

Dear Gerry,

Thank you for sharing the things I gave you about Fr. Stan Rother with your classmates. Having a special prayer service in his honor will help bond you all with the other missioners, living and dead, who have tried to serve the people of God in Latin America.

Are you really working seven hours a day in class? Your brain must be frizzled! You must be exhausted at night. You'll be surprised how quickly the time will pass, though.

It was hard to think of replacing Balam, but we finally broke down and got a new, white kitten. She was cute, but when we got her home she cried incessantly and we threatened to send her back to the manufacturer! But she was saved from that fate by Santos, the little imp who likes to work in our garden. When he came by and saw the kitten one day, his eyes brightened. "Is it a female?" he asked. "Yes, it is," I replied. "Why do you ask?" "When she has kittens, could you sell me one?" he asked. Well, I had the irresistible urge to say, "Why wait? Take her!" but thought I should consult with the other half-owner, Lori. I looked at her, about to ask, when she gave me a knowing nod. She, too, had had it with this whiner!

"Santos," I said, "you can take this kitten, if you wish. But I must tell you that she cries a lot and won't eat tortillas. Do you want her?" "Oh, yes," he answered. "We already have a crying cat, so one more won't matter." I felt a pang of guilt, wondering if his mother would send her right back, but I handed her over to Santos, who clutched her to his heart and ran all the way home.

A few days later, Santos was at the door. "Oh-oh," I thought. But he smiled triumphantly and burst out: "I came to tell you that the kitten is fine. She eats tortillas and she doesn't cry!"—So much for our ability to understand the needs of the Cakchikel kitten. So, we're out one kitten and looking for another, one that doesn't cry.

November 23, 1981

Dear Family and Friends,

Guerrillas have come to some towns around here, entering them, shooting up police stations and municipal buildings, robbing banks and taking off again. They are blocking roads and highways with felled tree trunks and landslides, and are burning cars and buses. Highway robbers are having a field day, stopping ten cars at a time and taking money, cameras, watches, and anything else that may strike their fancy. I know of four priests from this diocese who were robbed that way on four different days. The bishop's chauffeur, out on an errand, was robbed yesterday.

Yet, there is good news in the midst of it all. Our work is beginning to bear fruit, and just in time. This past Sunday, the bishop came officially to install twenty Eucharistic Ministers, or Communion Ministers, for about ten communities of our parish. Most of these small communities have at least one, and our town has four.

It was a long, hard pull to get to this point. After getting the bishop's approval for the program, we visited each community several times, explaining, informing, encouraging, and helping in the selection process. After all that, when we had a good response, we developed and prepared the catechists to teach a four-session course for Communion Ministers. It took us a half-year's work to get to this day.

The day was lovely, as the rains are finally gone. On Saturday, the people of the parish came to clean and decorate the church as if for Christmas. They swept the rough brick tiles, dusted the statues, hung crepe paper streamers, and sprinkled water on the floor to settle the dust. The next morning at 7 A.M., groups were already gathering in front of church. They were delegations from the many communities and their candidates for Communion Minister. By 7:30, we were practicing with the candidates, helping them get a feel for the simple ceremony that was so new to them. I sat in the bishop's chair in front of the altar and Lori guided them through the ceremony we had made up for the occasion. There is a special ritual for this ministry, but it was as new to us as it was to the men, so we adapted where we could to fit their culture.

When the bells began ringing, we joined the people as they streamed down the road to meet the bishop's car, which the lookout had spotted. Everybody went down to meet him and accompany him to the church. Some people carried flowers, and an advance committee went ahead sprinkling fresh pine needles along the path, making a scented carpet for the bishop to walk on. Guitarists and singers led the way back to church, and the leaders of the church communities carried their colorful banners. Finally, everyone was jammed into the church and Mass started.

At one point during Mass, I noticed with horror that the entire center aisle was filled with women. They were kneeling on the floor, holding babies and surrounded by their children. I couldn't imagine how the candidates would be able to come to the altar steps to receive the wooden crosses of their ministry from the bishop's hands. I need not have worried. They did just fine! They seem to be a people who can suspend the law of physics that says two bodies cannot occupy the same space at the same time.

The next day at a diocesan meeting, the bishop praised us and said how well everything had gone. He then read a set of norms, published the previous week by the Guatemalan Episcopal Conference, that gives guidelines for programs of lay ministers. The bishop said we did everything in the norms without ever having seen them! He sees the need for training lay people to take over the running of many aspects of the Church. So, Guatemala's painful moment has produced the fruit of a prepared and dedicated Catholic laity, ready to carry on.

November 23, 1981
Monday

Dear Gerry,

It seems a long time since my last letter. There's been a mountain of work and no time to do it. The garden is going to seed, or rather, to weed. We've been running around trying to do all sorts of things and preparing for several meetings, one after the other.

Now for more bad news, and this is the scariest it's been in several months. Four people who attended a diocesan meeting on a Thursday never got home. They were all in a jeep driven by a young Guatemalan priest. The others were a seminarian and two American Sisters. We knew the women, since we had worked with one of them a short time after the earthquake, helping in a relief effort. The other we met a short time ago when we stopped at their place to visit. It wasn't until Saturday that they were reported missing to the bishop by an American friend of the women. We didn't learn about it until after Mass on Sunday morning, when our priest told us the news. It hit me like a fist in the stomach. And in my mind flashed a picture of a newspaper headline: "Once Again, Four Churchpeople Disappear in Central America." I wanted to shout "NO, No, not again!"

Sunday afternoon, as soon as we could get away, we went to see the bishop to learn what we could from him and to offer our help. He couldn't give us any new information, but he did have a chance to talk about it, which was good for him as well as for us.

Strange, the premonitions we get. Lori, in talking to one of the

Sisters, learned they were finishing their work and leaving for good in mid-December. But she had told Lori that she had a feeling she might not get home! She said she was disappointed in herself for her fear, but she knew God would give the grace needed if anything were to happen to them. But no one had the slightest inkling that something like this might happen. Now we all feel we are reliving a horrible, numbing nightmare. Only we know it's not a nightmare—it's real. It isn't yet a year since the four in El Salvador, and now, these four. In El Salvador they were found—dead, but visible, buriable. Will we ever see these four again? I don't want there to be bodies in this case. I want them to come back and say, "We got through it, with God's help, and we are back to tell about it." I want the Sisters to go home as planned, I want that young priest to go back to work in his parish, and the seminarian to be ordained. But, if they are already with the Lord, yes, I guess I do want bodies, or something to make it final. This helplessness, this waiting for something—anything—to turn up is terrible. You wring your hands and stare into space just so long. I catch myself looking at the poster on our wall of the Salvadoran women martyrs and seeing these two women instead. I have to shut my eyes and turn away. I look at the bare block walls filling up with our beloved martyrs, the first five priests on one poster, a photo of Stan surrounded by his people on the other wall. He was the twelfth, I believe, and now these four are missing. I don't want their pictures on the wall, Gerry. I want them alive and free!

Not long ago, I was quietly hoping there would be a way for you to get to work here. Now I am thrilled that you are in Bolivia! The further away from here the better! Things here are so crazy that you don't know what will happen tomorrow. There is no rhyme or reason to it at all. It is just about two months since the last incident, Fr. Pellecer's brainwashed-self presenting his story before the press, so I guess it's time for the next attack on church people. Things have happened at six-week to two-month intervals, it seems. It gets to the point where, around the two-month time, you begin to wonder what, if anything, will happen, and to whom. Looks like we're running right on schedule.

We are all "guilty by association," and many of us are still cowering in the upper room. I think I know now how it must have felt to be a Jew in Hitler's Europe. You are guilty by birth, religion, work. Your "guilt" is what the enemy says it is, not something you can pinpoint, or that will ever be made clear. And the enemy is everywhere and nowhere, striking with or without any perceivable reason. No one has good reason to think he or she is being sought, and yet no one has any reason to feel safe, either. Maybe not only the Jews of Hitler's time felt this way. It must be the way the martyrs of the early Church felt, and the Christians who didn't get martyred, too. It's a good thing that Christ is with us through it all.

I received your two letters, but since it's almost 11 P.M. and we have to leave early tomorrow morning for a set of meetings in the city (with a Maryknoll Sister psychiatrist to help us Sisters as a group deal with all this crazy violence before we go crazy ourselves) and more run-on meetings till the end of the next week,—I really don't know when I'll be able to write again.

I've tried so hard to write nice, easy, newsy letters, so that you would concentrate on your studies and get your mind off Guatemala and onto Bolivia, but this letter has blown all that! If I didn't write now, I'd have to write later, because what I've told you should be international news. But also, I need to tell *you*.

Gerry, please believe me when I say Bolivia needs you; the Indian people there or anybody you'll work with will need you. God's poor are everywhere. The place for you may be somewhere you least expect. As my Mom used to tell my sister about meeting the "right man": "I know God has something very special in mind for you. Trust." You have become accustomed to taking your life in your own hands, like a football, and running with it. Now you have handed it over to God, who has something special, something good, in mind for you. Sink your roots into Bolivia. It should take all your energies for now.

Am I sermonizing? Forgive me. Keep us in your prayers, as we keep you in ours. Lori and I try to pray together each afternoon before supper, as we did when you and Pat were with us. And there is so much heaviness, and prophetic denunciation, and meaning in the psalms in the praying these days.

NEWS FLASH: THEY'RE FREE, and THEY'RE ALRIGHT! (more or less) Thank God! I just got a telegram from some friends in Guatemala City—the Sisters are flying to the U.S. tomorrow. I'll tell you more when I learn the details.

December 10, 1981

Dear Gerry,

This Christmas card may make you a bit nostalgic. It's from a series done by a Guatemalan artist who chooses familiar Indian places and costumes for the manger scene and Holy Family. They are my favorites, and I've been sending them for years.

I'm surprised that the Bolivian press carried the story of the Sisters who disappeared around Thanksgiving here in Guatemala. You got that story before my letter, of course. Hearing only that they were two American Sisters, no wonder you were concerned about Lori and me! By now you have my letter telling you what I knew at the time. I have just a bit more information now. The Apostolic Nuncio, acting for the Church, and the American ambassador worked fast to prevent another disaster. I have no idea what they did, but whatever it was, it worked. The four were left by their captors on a road and made their way to the nearest parish church. They called the bishop to say they were alright, and arrangements were quickly made to get the Sisters to Guatemala City and out of the country. Their Guatemalan companions stayed, and no one is talking about what happened.

You say your Spanish has reached a plateau. Don't be discouraged. At least you're high and holding. You need time to absorb before more can go into your head. Patience, friend. Also, your first tropical illness will most likely not be your last. I'm glad you had the medicine you needed at hand. Remember when you first came to Guatemala? In Guatemala City you came down with something that gave you chills and made you weak, and gave you a pounding headache. We never did learn what that was, but three blankets were not enough to take away that shivering. I was really worried! Here was this woman, almost a complete stranger, getting sick, and I was no expert on illness. I'm grateful it passed quickly. As you said in your letter, "The life of a missioner is fraught with peril." Let's hope the only peril is illness that pills can take care of!

It's quite understandable that you are teary-eyed at times, missing your friends, Gerry. Writing to them is a big help for both you and them. Please don't feel you have to answer all my letters and write frequently. Take some more time to keep in touch with those friends in the Bronx. The feelings of inadequacy in the language and uselessness right now may be alleviated if you tell your friends all about it. You're telling me, right? And you will start working soon, which will give you real practice with Spanish as well as a feeling of fulfillment. Knowing you, you won't be kept down long. MERRY CHRISTMAS!

January 9, 1982

Dear Mom and Dad,

Happy New Year, and many many more!

As you requested, I used the check you sent to buy sweaters and food for that poor family you wanted to help. After talking to the sick mother, Ana, I went out and bought the basics she requested: rice, beans, sugar, salt, cocoa (special for Christmas), high-protein oatmeal, potatoes, carrots, bananas, oranges, and some other things, like soap and candles. It was a heavy bundle, I tell you. The children got sweaters. The people here are not gushy and don't overwhelm you with thanks. Their custom is to receive with dignity and to thank with dignity. On Christmas Day they all came with their sweaters to take a picture (I took it) to send to you. And last night I got a note from Mario, their father. He asked me to write you a letter of thanks for the gift. He asked a friend to come here and talk to us, to tell us that Mario would like to write you himself, but his Spanish is poor and he speaks no English, so there are no words to thank you. He will sign the letter I write for him today. Actually, he'll thumb-print it, because he never learned to write his name. The note he sent was painstakingly written by his friend.

About the highway robbers—no, they haven't touched us yet, probably because we have no reason to go near the area they control these days. We haven't had courses in that area for a long time and don't plan any for a few months. Maybe they'll be tired of robbing there by then and move on.

We spent Christmas with the same Sisters who always invite us for Christmas dinner. We left here around noon and spent a pleasant afternoon visiting with them and catching up on news. And we promised each other that on Christmas day we would not dwell on the horrors.

January 15, 1982

Dear Gerry,

Your Christmas card was a perfect match for mine: a Bolivian manger scene with Holy Family dressed in typical Bolivian Indian dress. We seem to be on the same wavelength, even in picking Christmas cards. Thank you for the very loving and touching greeting.

How good that you and some classmates traveled during that two-week Christmas vacation. It will probably be the only chance you'll get to see any other part of the country. At least that was my experience. Once I got settled into my work I never went anywhere except for meetings. I'm glad I saw much of Guatemala on weekends while I was in language school.

I am forced to say that, as much as I'd like you to be here, I am very happy you're not. We've had more tragedy hitting the Church. The New Year started off with a terrible series of attacks on Church people. I may as well tell you about them, since you'll read about them in the paper, and may get the wrong details.

The first was the kidnapping of a thirty-four-year-old Belgian priest and a twenty-six-year-old Guatemalan priest, ordained just three months. They were kidnapped directly from their rectory in the area of Esquintla. As you may recall, that's the diocese that Fr. Walter and Fr. Conrado belonged to. Conrado was "disappeared" and Walter was assassinated last May. Well, this time, they killed the sacristan who tried to intervene as they took the priests. Fortunately, strong pressure from the Belgian government and the Vatican got them released. The Belgian was flown home and the Guatemalan stayed behind. As in the case of the four kidnapped in November, no one is saying anything.

We were just about getting over that bit of news when we heard that a forty-five-year-old Guatemalan Sister, Victoria de la Roca, was kidnapped from her convent at 2 A.M.! (Why do we even *try* to figure out ways to escape if they ever come for *us*?) All the Sisters were roused from their sleep by the assailants and were forced to lie down on the kitchen floor. The men piled mattresses on top of them, poured on kerosene, and threw a match on the pile, intending it to be their funeral pyre. Thank God the women were able to get out from under before they were injured. The story made the front page of the papers in Guatemala, and one newspaper had a picture of the fire-gutted kitchen. Had that door been locked, all the women would have been incinerated. As for Victoria, who was already dying of cancer, nothing has been learned of her whereabouts. She is not fortunate enough to have been born in another country and come here as a missioner. Those recent cases of kidnappings show that fast action on the part of the Belgian and U.S. governments resulted in the freeing of the kidnapped missioners. But Victoria was, like her Sisters, a Guatemalan citizen. What government would come to her rescue?

Shortly after her disappearance, the head of the Guatemalan counterinsurgency program of the army accused her of helping the resistance movement. To that, I say: 1) What proof is there? 2) Who else but the military man quoted *knows* she was connected with the resistance? 3)Where is she so she can answer her accusers? 4)If the government and army deny knowledge of her whereabouts, as they do, why do they make a statement that implies she was punished by authorities for her connection with the resistance? 5) Is that the way the law requires the authorities to deal with lawbreakers? I heard a silly rumor being spread by the government that she was hiding dynamite under the tamales or tortillas on the front porch. Really! Even the president came out to say they had positive proof of her subversive activities. Would you believe that a woman dying of cancer, who had had six operations and knew she could endure no more surgery, could have the strength to fight the army?

After these two stories broke, we were having a catechist session, so we added the names of the newest victims to our martyr's board in the parish kitchen, where everyone could see it. We explained their stories. We said that many, many more lay people, catechists like themselves, were also giving their lives.

During the lunch break, several men came over to ask for a word with me. That immediately attracted about ten more men (privacy is not a prized value in the area; what one says may help another). The leader of the group said, "Madre, what you said is very disturbing. We from our little community are very concerned. What will we do if the soldiers come and search our houses and find our Bibles? We have heard that the Catholic Bible is considered a subversive document by the soldiers. Do you think it would be alright, do you think God would be offended, if we buried our Bibles in the floors of our houses?''

You could have knocked me over with a feather! I was expecting the next line to be: ''Do you think it would be alright if we got rid of our Bibles and didn't come to class anymore?'' They certainly had plenty of reason to consider that option. They have families. They don't have to teach. But their faith in the face of adversity continues to grow. We discussed the practicality of burying their Bibles and they came to the conclusion that burying them in the dirt floor of the house was too obvious. Even burying them in the yard outside the house was not wise. They concluded, and all twenty-five or so men gathered around nodded sagely in agreement, that they would wrap the Bibles in several plastic bags to keep them from being ruined, and bury them in their cornfields, where only they knew how to locate them. Then it was time to go back and continue the study of this subversive document, the Catholic Bible.

The Word of God is like a treasure hidden in a field that a man found. Rejoicing, he went and sold all that he had, to purchase it. Gerry, never again will I take that Book lightly.

January 31, 1982

Dear Gerry,

I'm writing a short letter to tell you that everything here is fine. I haven't written in a couple of weeks and I don't want you to worry. There has been no more word on Sister Victoria de la Roca, who was kidnapped. I presume she is dead. I wonder if her death was easier or more painful than the death that awaited her from cancer. She is another martyr. We are also concerned about a Belgian seminarian, Sergio Verten who was captured in Guatemala City on January 20th. I don't know anything else about him—just that he disappeared.

While I am keeping you up to date, I don't tell my parents everything. They would be terribly concerned. You are also, but you have more experience with these issues and can see them from the perspective of your new position in Bolivia as a missioner. By now you should have finished your language study and may even have an assignment of mission work. I am eager to hear the latest developments in your life.

Since I haven't heard from you in a while and have no letter to answer, I'll tell you about the little boy I saw this morning outside our door. You know that the boys here in town make their own tops and string and spin them with skill. Those tops are carved by machete from a piece of pine. When I saw the boy outside today, I thought he was playing with a top and admired his skill. He looked at me, held up his "top" and said: "This isn't a top, Madre, it's a *chichara.*" Then I got my lesson in little boys' toys. A chichara is not carved from wood. It is a hollowed-out nut, like a huge acorn, with a hole on the side. The top of the nut is filled with wax. A pointed stick is inserted through the wax and forced out the bottom of the nut, like a spindle. The chichara is launched by means of a string attached to something like a popsicle stick, made of bamboo, with a hole in it. The string first goes through the hole in the popsicle stick and is then wrapped around the finger. The rest is wrapped around the index finger. (Are you with me? I expect you to make one from these instructions.) If you do it right, you launch the chichara and have it spinning upright very close to you, in the dirt, humming loudly. I tried it. It's not as easy as it looks! My chichara was spinning on its side like a wounded mouse. But the little boy patiently corrected my form and finally I was able to do a decent job of launching the chichara. I was so proud of myself that I bought his from him right there!

Today is the second anniversary of the massacre at the Spanish embassy. Many people today will remember the victims in church or chapel, because they are a symbol of the frustrated efforts of thousands to have their own lives and communities treated justly by the authorities. Like the four women martyred in El Salvador, these dead are considered martyrs in the cause of justice.

February 9, 1982

Dear Gerry,

What are you up to these days? No news is good news? I look for a letter every day, and I know one will come eventually. I hope you haven't come down with another unexpected illness.

Here we are trying to meet the challenge of being available to the people and getting our classes prepared. We just had a visit from Antonio. He asked if we might lend him money to build a house for his old aunt and her widowed daughter, since he heard we had some money from the diocese to help widows. It's certainly a good cause. The house he built for them fifteen years ago, of mud and cane with a thatched roof, is leaning dangerously to one side. He wants to build them a new one around it, then knock down the old one inside and shovel it out the door!

He came with a detailed listing of all the materials and labor costs. He'll make it of cane and mud again, and roof it with thatch. You want to guess how much he estimates it will cost? $60.00! That's right! Of course, that's with a door made of cane lashed together and no window. He felt a real wooden door with a door frame and a wooden window frame with shutters made by a carpenter would be exorbitantly expensive—at least $15 more! We told him to splurge and put on a real door and install a real window. These features would make the house last another fifteen years!

Lori is working hard on improving her Spanish these days. She has the time since we are not going out much because of highway robbers and bus burnings and car robbings and soldier searches. I am doing some much needed catching up on reading and correspondence. Times like this, though difficult, can be golden opportunities for other things. It is not possible to assure ourselves free time, because we want to be available to the folks here. But we do make the effort to spend time together praying each day. These days, I'm finding new meaning in the Psalms. If you had asked me five years ago which was my favorite psalm, I'd have easily told you Psalm 63, because it stayed with me from the first day I ever recited it in common as a young novice. I used to like it because of the first part that begins, "O God, you are my God, you do I earnestly seek . . ." and that ends with, "For your kindness is a greater good than life; my lips shall praise you." Now I seem to identify with the second half that begins, "But they shall be destroyed who seek my life . . ." and that ends with, "the mouths of those who speak falsely shall be stopped." That is where I'm stuck now, Gerry—in the vengeance psalms, in the crying out to God for justice in a time and place bereft of justice, where the just ones "are the prey of jackals," and of the buzzards and the dogs of the field. Only in God can we find refuge, the psalmist says. But another psalm says, "Fight, O Lord, against those who fight me; war against those who make war on me . . . let those be put to shame and disgrace who seek my life . . . for without cause they dug a pit against my life . . . unjust witnesses have risen up . . . Lord save me from the roaring beasts, from the lions save my life, then my tongue shall recount your Justice, your praise, all the day." (Ps. 35) That is a psalm that says what many in Guatemala are crying to heaven. When I was comfortable and fearless, the cries of the psalmist for God's aid and protection against the foe or the evil one left me cold. I had no enemies, and I had no such fears. Way back then I thought those psalms were not written for me and my time. Now I know they were! In the Bible course we have developed for the catechists it is uncanny how the books we had planned to study over the months and years fit right into the reality that is convulsing the country, the people, and, in particular, the Church. The message of the Psalms, the Prophets, the Book of Wisdom, and the Gospels, all make perfect sense now. And in this study we, Sisters and catechists alike, are learning to call on God to save us because we are powerless to save our own lives. The perennial problem, the eternal question of why the good suffer and the evil flourish, comes up again and again in the readings, and we see over and over again God's efforts and commands to right the wrong and restore the balance in the world of human life. And yet, didn't Jesus, the Good One, also die? How does our faith make sense of his death, and of our own?

I guess I'm getting carried away, Gerry. This whole problem of defending the just ones in an indefensible situation is hard to live with, but we encourage each other in prayer, and in interacting with the community of believers in Jesus here in this town. I guess I'm onto the theme because we recently learned of another priest killed. This death was a surprise to everyone. He was shot on the street in Guatemala City by gunmen in a passing car. His body disappeared and yet his superiors didn't even know he was dead until a few days later when they got word from employees of a *mortuary* that they had a body whom the Dominican priests might want to identify. When they arrived, they saw the corpse of thirty-six-year-old Fr. Carlos Morales. He was vocation director for the Dominican priests, and he worked pastorally in a Dominican Parish. He is the fifteenth priest to be killed or to disappear over the last two years here in Guatemala. Will it ever end?

I know and love your favorite Scripture text, Gerry, from the prophet Micah. "This is what Yahweh asks of you: only this, to act justly, to love tenderly, and to walk humbly with your God." Wouldn't it be wonderful if we all tried to live according to what Yahweh asks of us? Then we wouldn't need those vengeance psalms!

February 11, 1982
Feast of Our Lady of Lourdes

Dear Mom and Dad,

The last two letters you sent arrived on the same day. And I was very pleased to get a letter from you, Dad, since it happens so seldom! You usually let Mom speak for both of you, or tell her to write about something. But when you take pen to paper, that's an occasion! Thank you.

This letter will be the last for a while. It will be mailed by a friend going to the States tomorrow. The reason I'm not sending letters from here these days is that the guerrillas are burning buses all around this area, and it's the buses that carry the mail. I don't want to risk sending a letter only to have it be burnt. I can't afford to waste time in that! Maybe they'll leave this area soon. Of course, that's wishful thinking. I guess I should pray that the violence will end soon. It is continually escalating, and both the army and the guerrillas have caused damage and suffering to many people, although the army far outshines the rebels in brutality, and in inflicting suffering on innocent people.

Guatemalan presidential elections will be held on March 7th this year, to put in another president for four more years. The radio is full of catchy political jingles with happy, nursery-rhyme melodies whose words jar against the music. They say things like: "to free us from terrorism" or "to protect us from Communism" in a melody like "Ring around the Rosie." Both the government, headed by an army general, and the army itself say they will guarantee that the elections be free and honest. But as someone recently said to me, "All four candidates are dancing together." No one is really that different from the others. Even the group calling itself "the opposition" doesn't offer anything really different. Politicians who might have offered some alternative, something to the left of extreme right, were killed when they tried to register their parties a few years ago. If that's the case with those who called themselves centrists, you can imagine what would happen if a party of the real Left ever tried to register for elections! Most people believe that the General, the only military man of the four candidates, will win because he is the chosen candidate of the present government. That should be enough to get him elected. But if he *does* win, the runner-up will cry FRAUD!

I spoke about the elections to some Indian men the other day. The gist of the discussion was as follows: It's true that they are obliged to vote, and they will vote, because, "if you don't, and the army stops your bus and soldiers search you and check your voting registration card, and see you didn't vote, they could take you and you'd never be seen again." Beyond knowing the names of the candidates from hearing them on the radio, they say they don't know anything, really, about them, and have no way of finding out. To ask questions about political views of candidates sounds normal to us around election time. But here, to ask a question could mean risking your life! It's not worth it. Many people in this country will vote for a party they have heard of but know nothing about. The only people who may know something are the upper class of Guatemala City who move in the circles of power of the country and run its political life. Many owners of plantations or factories will "advise" their laborers about who they believe to be the best candidate, thus guaranteeing that their candidate gets a lot of votes. All this is common knowledge, so the people will vote cynically. And after the election, our U.S. government will hail Guatemala's "fair, free, democratic elections." It's such a farce.

And the guerrillas know it's a farce and promise to cause trouble. We have cancelled all trips these weeks because nothing short of a mission of mercy to save a life would be worth the risk of a long trip nowadays.

February 18, 1982

Dear Family and Friends,

By now you know about the American Christian Brother, Jim Miller, who was killed February 13 in Huehuetenango, near the cathedral. They say he died instantly from the machine-gun wounds and massive blood loss. The bishop came running from the cathedral, and the Sisters from the hospital, and all got there within a few minutes of the shooting. But he was already gone.

Lori and I heard about it on the U.S. news broadcast which comes over the Armed Forces shortwave station. It was on a Sunday morning, just before our Celebration of the Word (no Mass these months). We usually are rushed on Sunday mornings, but this time there was a bit of time and I turned on the news, and almost immediately we learned that an American Christian Brother had been killed. Lori and I cut short a meeting we had here in town and drove three hours to Guatemala City, arriving just in time for the funeral Mass. I had met Jim once, shortly after his arrival in Guatemala a year ago. He had been assigned to teach in the Christian Brothers' high school in Huehuetenango and lived with the Indian students at a hostel that the Brothers staffed. He was shot off a ladder while he was repairing a hole in the hostel wall.

Filing past the coffin of a martyr is never going to feel like a routine event, but the frequency of my doing it is increasing. Where will it all end? When will it all end? And singing what has become the theme song for Martyrs, "Pescador de Gente," always makes me feel a sense of awe and reverence, as well as deep gratitude for those lives that were given for others, those lives of witness to the living Gospel led in response to Christ's call, and for my own call. As the song so eloquently says:

> You have come to the water's edge,
> Seeking not the wise or rich,
> But only that I follow you.
> You know well what I have,
> In my little boat, neither gold nor sword,
> But this net, and the work of my hands.
> Lord, you have looked in my eyes.
> Smiling, you have spoken my name.
> On the sand I have left my boat
> To seek with you another sea.

We missioners have crossed other seas with the desire to serve, not conquer. If this following of Christ's call is perceived as a threat by those who have gold and swords in their boats, and if they choose to use their gold and swords against our nets, it is a terribly unequal contest. Yet, we will not be pushed to take up their weapons. We continue with our poor little nets, with no defense at all against their superior power, yet encouraging each other that "Our defense is in the name of the Lord, who made heaven and earth."

February 24, 1982
Wednesday

Dear Mom and Dad,

I'm writing this in the hope that I can get it to Guatemala City for mailing. As we get closer to the time of elections, traffic "incidents" like those I mentioned previously have become more frequent. Lori and I are staying put until after elections, and are doing work here at home. I'm researching the next catechist session; Lori is catching up on the bookkeeping. Elections are March 7th. Lots of reporters from the U.S., Canada, and Europe are coming to report on this big event. A young Canadian reporter came to this town and wanted to talk to us, among others. There wasn't really anything we could tell him that he hadn't already heard. He was hoping for a good story, but he found that, apart from the political candidates themselves, it was hard to find people who would talk to him about their thoughts and feelings on the elections. That should have been his first clue that things were not as democratic as they appeared to be!

The murder of Brother Jim Miller was another very devastating piece of news. But each time I hear of a new martyr, I am strengthened in my conviction that I am in the right place, and that this is the right time to be here. Please don't worry, but do continue to pray.

Today, Ash Wednesday, has particular significance in the light of Jim's death. It's not hard to "Remember that you are dust and unto dust you shall return." The fragility of human life is all too obvious all around. But the overwhelming power of faith in the New Life promised us at the end of Lent, the life in the Risen Lord, is also very much around, and is growing within us.

March 13, 1982

Dear Mom and Dad,

In these days of such unpredictable mail delivery, I have received a lot of mail from you! Mom, thank you for the Valentine greeting. You always remember to let me know I'm special on that day. My plans have changed a bit and I'll be home in June. So we'll see more of each other. I plan to do some much needed studying, and get a bit of distance in time and space from what is going on down here. Maybe when I'm on the outside it will begin to make more sense than it does to me now, standing in the middle as it swirls all around me.

I'm enclosing a picture of Stan Rother, taken about five years ago. He looked almost the same when he died, except that he had a bit more white in his beard. The people in his parish have venerated his coffin, and the room where he died has been changed into a chapel of sorts. And there are always flowers at his memorial behind the altar. There still is no priest there to replace him, and the Sisters had to leave shortly after he was killed because they were in a precarious position. But the people are carrying on as he had prepared them to do.

In our catechist sessions we recently read about the way John the Baptist prepared the way for Jesus. Because of all that is happening to Church workers these days, I got a new insight into the connection between the ministries of John and Jesus. We all know that John preached, "The Reign of God is at hand. Repent and believe." In the first chapter of Mark we read that Jesus began to preach the same messge, after John had been arrested. I realized for the first time that John's arrest prompted Jesus to pick up where John had left off, but to go infinitely further. Jesus, in turn, was arrested and killed, and his followers eventually picked up his work. That's the way it has always been, and that is how it continues today.

March 20, 1982

Dear Gerry,

Your long-awaited letter arrived! It took three weeks to get here but it's here. I'm answering it right away.

No wonder you delayed in writing me for so long. Your life has been in transition again! But what a long-awaited transition—to a rural Indian parish in the Bolivian mountains. Wonderful! Perhaps the time you spent with us here in our Guatemalan mountain Indian village will serve you well. I see from your letter that you are already involved in preparing many communities for Lent. You don't waste time! And see, I told you that you would understand the Spanish. Pretty soon you'll be thinking in it. You say, "I really am very happy to be here and I feel a great peace so I'm sure it's what God had in mind for me." That makes me feel at peace with your being there, too. But I *can't* take a side trip to Bolivia on my way to New York, Gerry. Bolivia is as far south of Guatemala as New York is north. It's double the fare or more! I really am grateful that you are willing to save your money to help pay, but we could never do it this time around. Maybe some day. I want to see you and your co-workers in action, and I would love to meet the people of Charamoco. Thank you for the Easter wish of "Happy Resurrection and New Life!"—I need that very much at this time, my friend.

With the dizzying escalation of persecution against the Catholic Church, the implications for us and for the people of this parish community—especially for those who work closely with us—are obvious. If the pastoral leaders such as priests and religious, foreign as well as national, can be killed at such a rate (four in less than two months, and an attempted "disappearance" of two more), what could the catechists, parish councils, Communion Ministers, sacristans and others expect?

Lori and I called a meeting of the five men who were the teachers of the parish's fifty-plus catechists. You know them. We plainly and clearly told them what we thought of the developments. Then I said, "By your connection with us, coming here to study every week and teaching in the catechist sessions every month, you may be in danger. We don't want any one of you to be needlessly endangered. You have no obligation to continue; you are not being paid for your work; and even if you were, we would release you from any obligation to us now. You may choose to retire for awhile. We can cancel the classes until things get better. You are free to go, if you choose."

They sat quietly listening to me, and nothing on their faces betrayed their thoughts. When I finished, there was a pause, and then Vicente spoke.

"Thank you, Madres, for your concern for us and our families. But, for my part, I choose to continue, if you are willing to continue here to help us. Before I joined Acción Católica, my life was in ruins. I drank. My family was always sick. I worked seven days a week and couldn't get out of the hole. I was almost despairing. Then a brother from Acción invited me to study. He taught me what the life of a child of God is. I spoke to my wife, Marcela, and we decided together to study for marriage. That changed our lives. Now, I no longer drink. My family is happy and we enjoy good health. I work only six days a week and can rest and worship and study on Sundays. And I am no longer in debt. I am so grateful to God for this miracle in my life, that I want to share it with others. I want to prepare couples for the Sacrament of Matrimony and want to continue studying and teaching God's Word."

I sat in silent admiration as, one after the other, the five of them spoke. They came at it from different angles and perspectives. Not one repeated the reasons given by the others. I could tell they had been thinking about this issue for a long time. They well knew why they were doing what they did.

Finally, Antonio spoke: "We are doing nothing against the law. We are not doing anything wrong. We are actually following the highest law, God's law, which says love your neighbor as yourself and God above all. We are doing what Jesus commanded us all to do when he said, 'Go into the whole world and preach the good news to everyone, everywhere.' We cannot go throughout the world, like you missioners. But we can go to our own little world, our townspeople, our parish. We can take the word of God's love to them. If we call ourselves followers of Jesus, can we expect to be called on to do less than Jesus did? And he gave his life for us. If they kill me, so be it. I will be in glory. I just hope they do not kill me in front of my children. I worry about my wife and children."

I had come here, years ago, to teach. Yet I have learned more than I could ever have taught. These simple, poor men who struggle daily even to feed their families, who study the Bible at night by candlelight after a hard day in the fields, are willing to give their lives because they love their neighbors, because they believe in the message of Jesus, and because they have hope that one day, God's will may be done here, *on earth* as it is in heaven.

Epilogue

THE TOWN

In what was hardly worthy to be called a house, a small group of Indians gathered at night to pray. Sitting on her heels in a corner, a young mother nursed her baby while two other children fussed sleepily at her side. Her aging parents sat near her on the floor. They waited quietly in the shadows, waiting for Antonio to start the prayer.

Antonio had a definite gift for praying. Everyone in town asked him to their homes to pray, when they thanked God in happy times and begged Divine help in times of trouble. Tonight was one of the latter times. Antonio rose now, and the others rose with him. Carefully, he lit two candles and placed them on a tiny table. In the soft light, his fine Mayan profile emerged from the darkness. Watching him, the family began to feel some of his faith seeping into them.

He began his prayer by presenting to God all those in the house and commending them to God's care. He then explained to God their plight. "Heavenly Father, loving compassionate God, Lord of all things, we come to you tonight with great pain in our hearts. You know all of us here. You know Pedro's family. Help them now, God our Father, because you are their only hope. They are powerless, but you, Lord, you have great power."

Antonio paused, gathering his thoughts. Then he told God what had happened. "A week ago," he said, "Pedro left here for the City. He almost never leaves town because he has to work here each day to be able to feed his family each night. But last week he took some carrots to sell. With the money from their sale and the thirty Quetzales he had saved, he planned to buy fertilizer for his corn, and a new hat."

Accustomed to talking to God as an old friend, Antonio gave a detailed account of Pedro's journey. He told God how the bus was stopped by soldiers, as happens frequently, and how the men had to get off and line up to be searched. But this time, a hooded man went down the line, pointing first to one man, then to another. Those he fingered were pulled out of line by the soldiers. As his horror-stricken townsmen watched, Pedro was yanked out of line and shoved into the small group of accused men. As the silent passengers returned to their seats, Pedro and his new companions were marched off toward the army camp. That was the last his friends ever saw of him. That night, after selling Pedro's carrots, they returned the sack and gave the money to his wife and told her what had happened.

Antonio told God of the wife's anguish, and of her efforts to find her husband. She even offered to pay for his release. But the officer at the army camp told her that Pedro had been sent to the base, far away. She went to the base, then, only to learn that Pedro had never arrived. She had spent some of their precious food money for bus fare, and now she had neither money nor information. All she had now was a growing ache of fear and loss.

"Now, Father," prayed Antonio, "the family turns to you, their only hope. You know the truth. You know Pedro is innocent. We are helpless, but you are all-powerful. Touch the hearts of his captors, loving, powerful Father. Change their hearts and their thoughts to permit Pedro to return to his family, who need him so much. You are a merciful Father, patient and forgiving. We people on earth often mistreat each other. We punish each other for no reason at all. But you, Father in Heaven, Lord of all, you are not like us."

In the corner, the mother shifted her sleeping infant to her back, and began to rock slowly back and forth. Her father nodded gravely at Antonio's words, as the prayer continued.

"We beg you to change the hearts of Pedro's captors with your love, not with your vengeance. Your Son forgave those who falsely accused him. Forgive Pedro's accuser and change his heart. Help him see that to accuse another falsely is a great evil. Help him repent. And we beg you, compassionate Father, to protect and comfort Pedro in his suffering. You alone know what he suffers and where he is. We can't help him now."

"Finally, dear Father, we beg your blessing and help for this woman, María, and her children. They are so poor. Their house is a mud and cane shack, all that Pedro, for all his hard work, could provide for them. Here they cook, eat, and sleep, in the smoke and in the dark. They need Pedro and hope he will soon come back. They don't want the money, the thirty Quetzales the soldiers stole, Heavenly Father. They just want Pedro. We thank you, compassionate Father, for hearing us this night, in this small corner of your great world. Amen.''

LETTERS

San Jerónimo
January 8, 1983

Dear Gerry,

Returning to our little backwater town after a six-month sabbatical in the States was like walking into a time-warp. While in parts of the country the situation has continued to deteriorate, here it seems that the clock has been put back a few years. People go about their daily routine serenely; children play in the dusty streets and attend the elementary school; men go to their fields to harvest the year's corn and come back under their happy burden; women carry water from the town fountain and stop to chat on the way home. The beautiful sunsets add to the feeling of timelessness and peace here. It is a very strange feeling, because this is one of the few spots in the country where there are such sunsets, and such peace.

When I left Guatemala in mid-1982, the country still appeared hopeful of a change for the better under the new president, General Efraín Rios Montt. After his sudden rise to power through the coup of March 23rd, there followed a series of official decrees disbanding and reorganizing the secret police, proclaiming amnesty for rebels who turned themselves in, and launching a campaign for honesty in government officials. Soon after becoming president, Rios Montt promised there would be ''no more bodies strewn along the highway," and he appears to have kept that promise. His predecessor ruled during one of the bloodiest periods in Guatemalan history. It was during the years 1978 to 1982 that thousands of Guatemalans, from highly qualified political leaders to village catechists, were slaughtered. That was also the time of virulent church persecution, in which fifteen priests, an American Brother, a Guatemalan Sister, and hundreds of catechists and village church leaders were either killed or disappeared. With the arrival of Rios Montt on the scene, Guatemala hoped he could turn the murder machine around. But, while death squad terrorism and outright Church persecution have decreased notably, the war against the rural, mainly indigenous population, has grown. Various rebel groups, claiming to represent the people, clash with the army, claiming to represent the people. But the people suffer the consequences.

A few months ago in the next town, soldiers took over the parish property for their own sinister uses, and screams pierced the nights thereafter. Our car was stopped for a routine check by an army patrol, who were dressed in smart camouflage uniforms and maroon berets. Their insignia was "The Cobras," and a sign outside their barracks read "The Devils." An army plane dropped six bombs nearby, destroying fields of ripened corn, a family's food supply for the year. Many vegetable vendors from town say the sellers they meet in the capital are becoming *Evangelicos* (Evangelical Protestants). It seems the safest religion to follow right now, since the president is an Evangelical pastor, as well as an army general. Persecution of the Catholic Church has become much more sophisticated, and much more subtle. So not much has changed for the better in the country, and much has changed for the worse.

And you, my friend, will soon celebrate your first year as a missioner in Bolivia among the Quechua Indian people of Charamoco. I was glad to hear about your work in town with the youth, and the mothers' groups, your first communion classes, and your mule and jeep trips to *thirty-six* other communities scattered over the mountains. You and I do similar work in similar places, for the same reasons. We are very much united. "When will our paths ever cross?" you wonder. I do, too Gerry. Right now we can't plan it, but we can continue to reach across the land and sea in letter, and prayer, and love.

Maryknoll, N.Y.
January 22, 1984

Dear Mom and Dad,

Gerry, my friend, died yesterday.

I read the news on a memo posted on our Motherhouse bulletin board. Bits and pieces jumped off the page at me: "Bolivia; 9 P.M.; flooded river; jeep overturned; Gerry McGinn died." I quickly scanned the page again, checked the names, but nothing had changed. Gerry, two other Sisters, and a little Bolivian boy had died in a flash flood. I wanted to feel something, but I didn't. Or maybe I did: a void that grew within me until I felt I'd burst. I went to my room and stared at the wall, telling myself the news over and over: "My friend is dead." After a while, I washed my face, combed my hair, and went to dinner. Because I returned from Guatemala just three weeks ago, no one here knew that Gerry and I were friends. If the conversation touched on the accident, it wasn't directed to me. I don't remember who was at the table, what was said, or what I ate. I believe the intellectual part of me was working very hard to get the rest of me to realize the meaning of those words, "Gerry died in a jeep in a flooded river."

Gerry's body will be brought back for burial at the Dominican center at Sparkill, New York, so I will at least have a chance to say good-bye.

January 27, 1984

Dear Mom and Dad,

We buried Gerry today, at sunset, on a snow-covered knoll at Sparkill. Gerry loved sunsets; I took a long, hard look at this one, for her, as we left her there on that hill in her wooden Bolivian coffin.

Her life is complete now, and no one could fault her for promises unkept. I'll never collect from her the birthday dinner and ice cream sundae she promised me. But on the back of the program distributed at her funeral Mass was a quote written by Gerry to all her friends in the event of her death: "After it's all over—have a big party and celebrate! I'm home, safe and sound. Love, Gerry." So, though we didn't feel much like celebrating, hundreds of her friends, family, former students, and Sisters shared a meal after the funeral. And as we sat around and talked, sharing our memories of her, the atmosphere turned festive. In spite of ourselves, the supper became a big party, and we celebrated after all.

At her wake, I was asked to lead in the singing of "Pescador de Gente," one of Gerry's favorite Spanish hymns and one that came to have great meaning for me over these last years. I considered it a great privilege, and sang it with all my heart. She deserved it.

Gerry last wrote me in November, while she was recuperating from a bad case of hepatitis. I didn't expect to hear from her again until Christmas. Nothing came then, so I expected a letter from her any day. When I learned that she had died, an irrational conviction grew within me that I would get a last letter from her. It was weird. I'd go to my mailbox saying, "There can't be any more letters from Gerry." Yet I'd still look for the old familiar handwriting. It made no sense, of course, because there is no place to mail a letter in her town of Charamoco. Even if she had written, she would have had the letters with her in the jeep, the night she died in that river.

February 2, 1984

Dear Mom and Dad,

Thank you for your call of concern and sympathy over the death of my friend, Gerry. It's been a hard week, and I didn't sleep well until last night, when I slept without waking once. This morning I woke with the thought that Gerry can live for us, her friends, only if we allow her to die, if we actually allow her to be buried and do not deny that reality. Our faith tells us that resurrection comes after death: "If we die with Christ we shall rise with him." But if we don't let go of the one who dies, there is no handing over to Christ and no resurrection. I woke yesterday with the conviction that I had buried Gerry, and I had let her go.

And now today, as if to strengthen my own faith in the Resurrection and in life after death, I received the letter Gerry owed me. It was dated January 18th, three days before her death. In this last, totally unexpected letter, Gerry sort of smiled on my letting go. She said, in part:

"Now don't faint! Happy New Year, and may all that God intended for our world come true in '84. I hope you get this. . . . It's the rainy season here and that hinders our work in far-out towns, as we can't get through the roads. But the rain is good and necessary for the crops, so we are not complaining! . . . This is a crazy letter, but I just wanted you to know I am still alive . . . ."

I believe her message. Gerry *is* still alive, along with Tarcicius, Sebastian, Agnes, Cecilia, Lucy; Oscar, Maura, Ita, Dorothy, Jean; Guigui, Walter, Carlos, Stan, Jim. . . . All you Martyrs and Saints of God, pray for us.